Conservatism and Collectivism
1886–1914

Conservatism and Collectivism

1886–1914

*'Se vogliamo che tutto rimanga come è,
bisogna che tutto cambi. Mi sono spiegato?'*
(Giuseppe di Lampedusa)

MATTHEW FFORDE

EDINBURGH UNIVERSITY PRESS

© Matthew Fforde 1990
Edinburgh University Press
22 George Square, Edinburgh

Set in Linotron Times Roman
by Koinonia, Bury, and
printed in Great Britain by
Redwood Press Limited,
Trowbridge, Wilts

British Library Cataloguing
  in publication data
Fforde, Matthew
  Conservatism and collectivism,
  1886–1914.
1. Great Britain. Political ideologies
  collectivism. Attitudes of Conservative party. Great Britain. Political
  parties
I. Title
320.530941
ISBN 0 7486 0139 2
      0 7486 0152 x pbk

Contents

Preface

I would like to express my gratitude to Professor F. M. L.Thompson who
has given unfailing support to this project, and has also given his scholarly
advice. I would also like to thank Mrs Delia Lennie, Mrs Susan de
Meynier, the late Professor Miryam Cabiddu, Professor Margherita Gui-
dacci, Professor Lina Unali and Dr Daniela Zizzari. I dedicate this book
to my aunt, Mrs Patricia Cooper, without whom it would never have been
written. I am indebted to Lord Bledisloe, Lord Bridgeman, J.R. Trustram
Eve, G. Lane Fox, Lord Lansdowne and Lord Salisbury for allowing me
access to important historical material in their possession. I am also
grateful to Conservative Central Office for its permission to consult the
party's records, and to Miss June West for her kind help in aiding me in
their consultation. I would like to thank the Royal Institution of Chartered
Surveyors for allowing me access to their records, and to those of the Land
Agents' Society and the Auctioneers' and Estate Agents' Institute. The
Plunkett Foundation permitted me to examine the papers of Sir Horace
Plunkett. I am indebted to many archivists for much kindness in confirm-
ing the accuracy of references and footnotes. I would like to extend my
gratitude to Dr B.S. Benedikz (University of Birmingham), A.E.B. Owen
(Cambridge University Library), I. Hill (Scottish Record Office), K.H.
Rogers (Wiltshire Record Office), Mrs S. Corke (Guildford Muniment
Room), J.S. Creasey (Institute of Agricultural History and Museum of
English Rural Life), R.H. Harcourt Williams (Hatfield House), and D.J.
Butler (Durham County Record office).

For permission to quote and cite archival material I am indebted to the
following: House of Lords Record Office (D. Lloyd George, A. Bonar
Law, L. Renton, C. Morrison-Bell and Willoughby de Broke papers),
British Library (A.J. Balfour and Lord Robert Cecil Papers), the Earl of
Shelburne (Lansdowne Papers), Viscount Bridgeman (Bridgeman pa-
pers), G. Lane Fox (G. Lane Fox papers), Viscount Bledisloe (Bledisloe
papers), J.R. Trustram Eve (H. Trustram Eve papers), the Warden and
scholars, New College, Oxford (Milner papers), Brigadier A.W.A.
Llewellen Palmer (Carrington papers), J.E. Sandars (J. Sandars papers),
T.R. Hartman (R.Sanders papers), the Marquis of Londonderry and

Durham County Record Office (Londonderry papers), Mrs Gay Stafford
(A. Steel-Maitland papers), the University of Birmingham (A. Chamber-
lain papers), the Syndics of Cambridge University Library (S. Hoare
papers), the Wiltshire Record Office (W. Long papers), the Earl of Onslow
(Onslow papers), the Marquis of Salisbury (Salisbury papers), Institute of
Agricultural History and Museum of English Rural Life, University of
Reading (Country Landowners' Association records), Public Record
Office (Cabinet papers, Association of Municipal Corporations records),
Royal Institution of Chartered Surveyors (Royal Institution of Chartered
Surveyors records and Land Agents' Society records), Conservative
Central Office (Conservative Party records), the Plunkett Foundation (H.
Plunkett papers), the India Office Library (Curzon papers), and the Cour-
tauld Institute (A. Lee papers). I have made use of a number of most
informative unpublished theses but I regret that I have not always been
able to trace their authors. My sincere apologies are extended to any owner
of copyright material whom I have been unable to contact or have
unknowingly overlooked.

The terms 'Conservative', 'Tory' and 'Unionist' are often used inter-
changeably in this study. *In general*, and especially after about 1890, no
significant differences of outlook towards social and economic life were
detected between the Liberal Unionists and the Conservatives. This, no
doubt, was one of the reasons why they co-operated, coalesced, and then
fused. Indeed, there is much to suggest that the schism of 1886 was at least
partly animated by anxieties over property also shared by the Tories. It is
most significant that little friction between the Liberal Unionist Party and
the Conservative Party is to be observed between 1886 and 1914. The
focus of this study is on England: Scotland, Wales and Ireland had their
own peculiarities. But light is cast upon all home countries – a national
stage is being examined which was created by Great Britain as a whole;
political policies were usually applied to the entire nation. Both the Liberal
Publication Department and its Conservative equivalents issued sets of
pamphlets and leaflets. These were titled and numbered and are thus
represented in the footnotes. I have converted out of Roman numerals in
recording journal numbers and the volumes of secondary works. All
books cited were published in London unless indicated to the contrary. A
more microscopic examination of Conservative resistance to Edwardian
collectivism is to be found in my Oxford D.Phil. thesis 'The Conservative
Party and Real Property in England, 1900–1914' which is located somewhere on the subterranean shelves of the Bodleian Library. The discipline
of history is a progressive debate: I would be grateful, therefore, for any
correction of fact or interpretation.

Abbreviations

ABP	Arthur Balfour Papers
ACP	Austen Chamberlain Papers
AEAI	Auctioneers' and Estate Agents' Institute
AMP	Alfred Milner Papers
AMC	Association of Municipal Corporations
AOS	Agricultural Organisation Society
ASU	Anti-Socialist Union of Great Britain
BP	First Baron Bayford of Stoke Trister Papers
BLP	Andrew Bonar Law Papers
CAB	Cabinet Papers
CCA	Central Chamber of Agriculture
CCO	Conservative Central Office
CLA	Central Land Association
EOP	Fourth Earl of Onslow Papers
HC	House of Commons
HL	House of Lords
JSP	John Sandars Papers
LAS	Land Agents' Society
LCC	London County Council
LE	Leasehold Enfranchisement
LEA	Leaseholds Enfranchisement Association
LGP	David Lloyd George Papers
LPD	Liberal Publication Department
LPDL	Liberty and Property Defence League
LRC	Labour Representation Committee
LU	Land Union
LVG	Land Values Group
MSP	Fourth Marquess of Salisbury Papers
NFU	National Farmers' Union
NLF	National Liberal Federation
NUCAS	National Union of Conservative Associations for Scotland
NUCCA	National Union of Conservative and Constitutional Associations
NUACLUO	National Unionist Association of Conservative and Liberal Unionist Organisations

PP	Parliamentary Papers
PRO	Public Record Office
SI	Surveyors' Institution
SMP	Arthur Steel-Maitland Papers
SRG	Social Reform Group
SVR	Site Value Rating
TRL	Tariff Reform League
USRC	Unionist Social Reform Committee
WLP	Walter Long Papers

Introduction: Collectivisation of the Nation

In 1894 *The Economist* surveyed the British scene and realised that a development of great historical importance was well underway. The nation was moving towards a large scale expansion in the powers of the state. In an editorial entitled 'The Advance of State Socialism' the journal noticed the increasing role of government in economic and social life, and observed a major shift in political opinion: 'A passion has arisen for asking State aid'.[1] *The Economist* not only grasped that it was living in a period which launched the nation on a collectivist future but also predicted a subsequent reaction:

> We attempt no forecast, but whenever the check comes, and from whatever cause, we shall see a strong and heavy swing of the pendulum back in the old direction. The cry will then be that we are all crushed by officialdom, that the nation has been placed in leading strings, and that individual energy must be emancipated from all this self-sufficient and unnecessary guidance. A Minister will be found who promises 'independence' instead of supervision, and gradually the army of officials who by that time will be employed will melt away.[2]

What was this but to anticipate Mrs Thatcher?

In the 1980s and 1990s this 'strong and heavy swing' is upon us. Great debate is now taking place in Great Britain concerning the role the state should play in people's lives. Conservatives and collectivists (of various hues both) struggle to implement their policies and diffuse their ideas. This conflict has dominated modern politics for nearly a century and its consequences have been of critical importance for our national civilisation. These rival forces appear to represent two distinctive cultures which have their roots deep in British, European and Western history. The outcome of this conflict will have a profound impact on the future course of the nation. It is in order to provide a perspective on modern controversy and to aid in the analysis of contemporary conditions that this book returns to the first great period of struggle between Conservatism and collectivism – the tumultuous three decades that preceded the Great War.

'*L'Etat, c'est moi*'. For a long period in Europe great debate centred

around what the state should be. In the late-eighteenth and nineteenth
centuries the old Continent witnessed profound changes in the nature of
political systems and the character of constitutions. The twentieth century
was more concerned with what the state should do and saw the birth of
totalitarianism. One anti-statist historian has been provoked to write:

> The state was the great gainer of the twentieth century; and the
> central failure. Up to 1914, it was rare for the public sector to
> embrace more than 10 per cent of the economy; by the 1970s, even
> in liberal countries, the state took up to 45 per cent of the GNP. But
> whereas, at the time of the Versailles Treaty, most intelligent people
> believed that an enlarged state could increase the sum total of human
> happiness, by the 1980s the view was held by no one outside a small,
> diminishing and dispirited band of zealots. The experiment had
> been tried in innumerable ways; and it had failed in nearly all of
> them.[3]

Great Britain was a notable participant in this explosion of state activity.
In 1870 government expenditure was 9% of the gross national product.
This figure rose to 26% in 1930 and to 52% in 1972.[4] The outlay of this
expenditure altered out of recognition. In 1890 35.7% of the total sum was
devoted to social, economic and environmental ends. The respective
figures for 1910, 1928, 1950 and 1979 are 52%, 53.3%, 60.8% and
80.7%.[5] The proportion of the working population engaged in public employment reflects the trend: 3.7% in 1891, 6.9% in 1911, 9.7% in 1931 and
22.7% in 1976.[6] All this was accompanied by increased levels of taxation,
public ownership, and executive appointments. Administrative law, that
telling indicator of government size, rose to become a prominent feature
of the British state.[7]

That the low government society of the Victorian period, which so
often aroused the admiration of progressives across the Channel, evolved
into the much governed nation of the last quarter of the twentieth century
is confirmed by Tory behaviour in the 1980s and 1990s. The New Conservatism of Mrs Thatcher and her allies is, to a substantial extent, a direct
response to the rise of the institutions and culture of collectivism. 'The
balance of our society has been increasingly tilted in favour of the state at
the expense of individual freedom', declared the 1979 Conservative
manifesto, 'This election may be the last chance we have to reverse that
process'.[8] Sir Keith Joseph, a leading intellectual light of the recent Right,
observed in 1974 that post-war Conservative governments had failed to
reduce 'the vast bulk of accumulating detritus of Socialism'. 'Socialist
measures and Socialist attitudes', he continued,'have been very persuasive'.[9] 'The great surges of progress and prosperity in this country did not
come directly from government action', Mrs Thatcher told the Conservative party conference of 1983, 'They came from free men, working in a
free society, where they could deploy their talents to their best advantage,

for themselves, for their families and for the future. That is our policy'.[10] Reaction accounts for much of the rage.

Collectivism's origins, progress and consequences demand examination. Where did collectivism come from? How did it advance? What were its results?These simple questions animate an emerging debate. Historiographical concern, once again, reflects political controversy. 'Why, in Britain, has a libertarian, individualist society sustaining a limited conception of government', asks one participant, 'been in so many ways and to such a degree replaced by the positive state pursuing explicit policies of widespread intervention in the name of the public good?'[11] This study seeks to throw light on the collectivisation of the nation by examining the genesis years. In part this is an investigation of the late-Victorian and Edwardian Left. Liberals and Socialists are observed as they try to push society down the collectivist road. In particular, new judgements are presented on the ideas of, and prospects for, British Liberalism. It is hoped that the land question will never again be so severely neglected. In part, also, this is an analysis of the nature of national politics during a key period of transformation. Thus new information is presented on the character of a political system which was undergoing a rapid process of modernisation. But above all else it is a contribution to the history of the British Conservative Party – its beliefs, its composition, and its method. This last peculiarity may be justified with reference to an unfashionable rationale.

Nothing succeeds like success. The old adage that history is the propaganda of the victors is not without validity. There is a great temptation to study the rise of collectivism from the point of view of the collectivists themselves. The Left has not failed to gain historical attention – books with the word 'society' in their title seem never ending. Indeed, one is sometimes drawn towards the conclusion that much of modern British history is an account of collectivists written by collectivists. But much can be achieved by examining a movement from the perspective of its opponents. Antis, from the point of view of utility, are not always antipathetic. A study of opposition to a historical development can throw much light upon its character and progress, and upon its outcomes and consequences. Antagonists themselves can influence the form that a development takes, and even become a part of it. The guiding idea of this work is that an examination of the role the Conservative Party played in the rise of collectivism will not only illuminate the Right and Left but will also provide important clues as to the evolution and nature of British society. The Tory Party is seen as a window into national development. Although this book is first and foremost a study in blue, it seeks to have a wider concern and bearing. History, after all, is the hopeful science.

In addition, there is a strong *a priori* reason for examining the party of Salisbury, Baldwin and Mrs Thatcher. For the Conservative Party, notwithstanding many predictions to the contrary, has proved itself to be the

premier political party of state. The Tories have been the objects of a
remarkable exercise in self-conservation. To a great extent, British
Democracy has turned out to be a Conservative affair. The Tories were in
office in 1890 – in 1990 they still line the ministerial benches. During the
last hundred years the Right has been in government for over two-thirds
of the time. It has obtained consistently high levels of electoral support and
was in 1987, by a large margin, the most popular of the political parties.
An immediate question arises – what has been the secret of this remarkable
success? To this some answers will be given. There is no right-wing body
on the Continent which can remotely rival the Conservative Party in
longevity, influence, or achievement. Long before Italian and German
Christian Democracy, or the Japanese Liberal Democrats, there were the
British Tories. It is a reasonable supposition that much of our national
history has been shaped by this most resilient of political institutions. One
can with confidence make a plea for Conservative studies.

Yet there remains a forceful orientation towards the Left in modern
British political history. A prominent feature of this tendency is a propensity to study the forces of disruption, dissent and change. We know much
more about Liberals, Social Democrats, Socialists, trade unionists and
feminists than we do about the Conservative ascendancy. This is not
unnatural – modern collectivist achievements are regarded as the products
of progress by these historians much as the Whig writers used to praise
previous constitutional reform. The very vocabulary is indicative. The
terms 'progressive' and 'reactionary' symbolise the employment of an
evaluative perspective. Studying the origins of what is now welcomed has
a distinct attraction. But there is another dimension, which relates to the
nature of the British collectivist mind itself. Lying behind much of the
history of the modern period is the assumption that society as it was previously constituted was unjust, and that the forces which challenged the
existing order were a natural outcome of this injustice. Consequently,
there is a desire to illuminate the natural discontent which arose. Description is matched by prescription – the reader is warned against a return to
previous methods and encouraged to look with favour upon continuing
left-wing initiatives. The History Workshop is much more than a workshop.

There is no school of Tory historiography to match its collectivist
counterpart. There are, indeed, Conservatives who write history, but there
are very few who take up the challenge and examine why it was that pre-
collectivist ways could command so much support and consent. 'Social
agreement' receives much less attention than 'social control'. A great and
unnoticed gap has appeared on the shelves of the history faculty libraries
of British universities. Paradoxically, the Tory reverence for history has
failed to produce sustained Tory historiography. A description of the positive reasons for the success and longevity of individualist arrangements

would serve to lend support to those who value them. After all, the past is often seen as a series of experiments to achieve a desirable society. The actual investigation of the forces working for maintenance, integration and cohesion is not only a fit topic for those clearly on the Right. It is a valid subject for any historian seeking to understand the evolution of a nation – such is the principal apologia of this project. There is a further reason for this failure to analyse modern British history from the perspective of Tory individualism. It is rooted in a widespread misconception that pervades much of the view of our recent past: the idea that the Conservative Party has not been an especially individualist force.

Received wisdom holds that the British Conservative Party (or a significant part of it) has always been sympathetic to much of the Left's approach. It is frequently argued that at times the Tories have often and willingly contributed to the construction of the collectivist state. This is part of a wider interpretation which detects an affinity between radicals and conservatives in modern Western history. From Allan Bloom, a cultural observer of a quality to rival de Tocqueville, we have the following reference to

> the fatal old alliance between traditional conservatives and radicals, which has had such far-reaching effects for more than a century. They had nothing in common but their hatred of capitalism, the conservatives looking back to the revival of throne and altar in the various European nations, and to piety, the radicals looking forward to the universal, homogeneous society, and to freedom – reactionaries and progressives united against the present.[12]

From Brian Walden, an ex-Labour MP, commenting on contemporary British politics, there comes the statement that 'Political collectivists, who want to repress unpalatable individual choice wherever it rears its head, frequently make common cause with social reactionaries.'[13]

British Conservatives, when talking about themselves, have done much to promote this view of their own history. 'Social reform has long been the work of the Unionist party', declared Arthur Balfour in 1907, 'as distinguished from the Radical or Socialist Party'.[14] 'Nothing can be more false', pronounced a party publication in 1914, 'than the commonplace of Radical orators that the Tories are the foes of social improvement'.[15] Such opinions receive more recent echoes. 'It pioneered the Factory Acts and much other social legislation in the last century', asserts Francis Pym of his party, 'In this century, it was the co-author of the Welfare State and has instigated many other social reforms'.[16] In 1977 Mrs Thatcher herself introduced a party publication entitled *Conservative Social and Industrial Reform* with the following words: 'Conservative concern for and involvement in what we nowadays call welfare politics has been much more marked, and much more effective, than that of any rival party'.[17]

The idea is echoed widely in the assertions of British historians. 'The party has always been a coalition of left- and right-wing Tories, who have been forced to coexist with one another',[18] writes T. Russel. It has been suggested, perhaps in an attempt to give a historical pedigree to the Alliance of the 1980s, that there is a centrist tradition in modern British politics. It is argued that in the major parties of state there has been a consistent tendency among a sizeable number of politicians to gravitate towards the centre. No doubt the centrists of the Conservative Party would be associated with Russel's left-wing Tories.[19] This overall picture of the Right has been given powerful support by two recent studies which may be taken as symbolic of the approach. One is a political analysis, the other is an investigation of culture. But both are linked in their interpretation of the traditional Tory attitude to state intervention.

W.H. Greenleaf's three volumes on the British political tradition write the nation's political history around the growth of the state. The Conservative dimension is based on the assumption that there have been two strands in Conservatism – the 'libertarian' and the 'paternalistic'. 'There has thus always been an 'inherent collectivism' in British Conservatism.'[20] Greenleaf argues that these 'modes of Conservatism reflect the same twin inheritance of ideas in respect of the tension in our political life between libertarian and collectivist tendencies'.[21] Of one thing this historian is certain: the 'supporters of Conservatism and Liberalism' contributed more to the 'actual development of collectivism' than the Socialists themselves.[22] M. Weiner argues that Tory antipathy to industrialism and an adherence to rural England gave support to a general hostility to capitalist advance. They also encouraged a Tory receptivity to intervention. Left and Right, therefore, had a familiar affinity: 'The world of politics was permeated with the values and sentiments of the gentry counterrevolution against industrial capitalism.'[23] This is a cornerstone of his general thesis that English culture became imbued with attitudes antagonistic to economic growth.

In order to challenge this view of Conservatism (and to achieve its wider goals) this book investigates the first great period of collectivist growth – the strife-torn twenty-eight years which were terminated at Sarajevo. In many respects the years 1886–1914 witnessed the beginnings of modern British politics and initiated party political orientations, alignments and battle-lines which have lasted to the present day. This is a fertile field both for the testing of accepted ideas, and for the establishment of lines of inquiry and the formulation of hypotheses which may serve for a more general understanding of the elusive Right. The period was awash with political modernism. Central government expansion and democratic advance, materialistic perspectives and state growth, welfare legislation and economic regulation, classist thinking and plans for restructuring society, populist politicians and political patronage, trade unionist pressure and parliamentary Labour – all these forces, and others, appeared to an increasing degree on the political stage.These were watershed years and the historian who travels across this terrain encounters a host of signposts as to points of departure, routes taken, and destinations reached. An analysis of the relationship between collectivism and Conservatism in late-Victorian and Edwardian England is a powerful contribution to a wider study of these major forces of the modern British experience.

Of necessity the vision is selective – time and space are harsh taskmasters. Certain areas have not been covered. Local Conservatism cries out for attention. Similarly, much work remains to be done on the organisation of the Tory Party. The peculiar role of the Church of England in supporting the Right and disseminating Tory values merits detailed study. We still know remarkably little about that most elusive of entities – the Conservative intelligentsia. What was its influence in the press, the publishing houses, the schools and the universities? Other institutions that the party supported had their role to play in the promotion of the Conservative cause. The impact of the monarchy has yet to be systematically studied. Did the armed forces act to support Conservative defence policies and promote Conservative attitudes? How did the Tory press shape and influence events? The entire Conservative nation was a large and complicated entity which it would take many a volume to explore. But it is hoped that a study of the Conservative Party itself will throw much light on the response of the forces of the Right to collectivism, if only because that was the institution to which the rightward section of society looked to achieve its ends. The Conservative Party well represented the Conservative nation and was to a substantial extent a cumulative phenomenon.

To perceive the statue within the marble is one thing; to release it is quite another. There arises the question of methodology: how should the national politics of this period be studied? This involves the controversial question of the nature of the political system. The 'high politics' style, conjoining with the peculiar needs of the PH.D student, has made a lot of running in recent years and requires some comment. This style, partly animated by a desire to repudiate the Marxist model of politics as an expression of evolving 'class' interests, has found a number of distinguished practitioners.[24] False ideas, however, often provoke false reactions. At its most extreme this approach to political history tends to play down the role of belief and to play up the jockeyings for power; to raise the profile of administrative preoccupations and to lower that of popular pressure; and to emphasise the distance between the governing elite and the voting masses. Some of this is reflected in M.Bentley's introduction to his *Politics Without Democracy 1815–1914*, the title of which is suggestive enough. The author condemns much collectivist historiography:

> It is though the explanation of political developments should be seen to rest, beneath the skirts of hierarchy, on the discreet power of the masses (untried but insurmountable) against which the behaviour

of politicians must be set in order to be made intelligible. I have chosen to ground this book in a different disposition. For the assumption here will be that the history of Britain's governing classes provides a theme with its own richness and importance; and that political understanding may begin, not only with a knowledge of labour history or a conceptualization of 'class struggle', but also with a view about what politicians believed themselves to be doing and an identification of those perspectives that informed their judgement of objectives and priorities.'[25]

But the imposition of such extreme schemata may be resisted. The point of departure of this study is to be found in a very simple proposition – the Conservative Party was an organism that believed. This was the underlying truth of Tory behaviour. There arose, of course, the question of how Conservative beliefs could be put into practice. This, however, was a matter of the management of the realities of power. On the one hand this involved a balancing of the priorities of government: the claims of revenue and expenditure; the interplay of various interests; the exigencies of legislation; the pressures of policy; the allocation of attention. But on the other hand it necessitated a successful handling of the political system. The chief requisite here, because of the nature of the constitution, was control of parliament. At a time of democratisation the essential feature of this operation was the winning of votes at general elections. The primary art of Tory politics was to balance the implementation of beliefs with the acquisition of electoral sanction. Thus this study has an almost Holmesian passion for detail. A minute examination of the Conservative Party's policy – in the widest sense of that term – when in government and when in opposition serves to show that the major formative influences on that policy were the Tory outlook and the will of the people. To prove many a controversial point it is necessary to wield the microscope – without, however, descending into tunnel vision.

An emphasis on belief and its manifestation in behaviour provokes a consequential conceptualisation. The Oxford dictionary offers as a definition of culture: 'the customs and civilization of a particular people or group'.[26] Yet it may be possible to see culture as a characteristic set of modes of thought and feeling which find expression in patterns of activity. This is in line with R. Williams's 'social' definition of culture – 'a description of a particular way of life, which expresses certain meanings and values not only in art and learning but also in institutions and ordinary behaviour'.[27] The word culture is frequently used in the following pages because a distinct system of causally interconnected forms of behaviour and ways of perceiving is being detected. Indeed, a cultural approach may help to overcome, or to complement, the habitual dividing of life into such categories as the political, the economic, the social, the intellectual, the constitutional, or the religious. After all, if an individual has a mentality derived from a cultural system he brings it with him into all areas of life. There may be value in a quasi-anthropological approach to political behaviour which was far from primitive. The use of the concept 'Tory culture' has proved to be an incisive instrument of comprehension.

Language can reflect cultural development and English has acquired new terms to describe the changes with which this book is concerned. Collectivism may be defined as the creed which advocates increased state ownership or control of property in the interests of a group, groups, or society as a whole, and this to the material benefit of the less advantaged. This particular meaning has become increasingly common in recent years and is used by such historians as Greenleaf or Johnson. Naturally, collectivism involves an associated constellation of beliefs and perspectives. Individualism, collectivism's counterpart, stresses the advantages of allowing individuals to pursue their own material self-interest in a manner untrammelled by government. Interventionism and non-interventionism reflect a divergence in view as to whether the state should or should not actively intervene in the economy. Statism and anti-statism disagree on whether the well-being of a society can be substantially advanced by reliance on the large-scale involvement and intervention of the state. All these terms are connected, and are most useful appellations for political creeds and movements. This is hardly surprising – they have appeared in modern times to describe phenomena of great consequence. These beliefs belong to opposing poles of a spectrum of ideas which has come to dominate British political thinking.

The historian is the victim of his evidence. Before the Great War the telephone was still in its infancy – it has since transformed the evidential bases of political history. Political letter writing had reached its high point. The ideal of statesmanship encouraged the preservation of epistolary exchange. There was a concern for the judgement of posterity. Consequently, much time was spent reading dead men's mail. The immense quantity of political letters and diaries which remain make it possible to go behind the public face of the Conservative Party and to explore the real reasons for public action. Such detailed behind-the-scenes investigation has paid handsome dividends in this study and has acted to illuminate the gap between professed stance and true intention. A mass of party propaganda survives. It served as material for party speakers or as literature for direct electoral consumption. This propaganda provides essential information on the party's policy, and on shifts in that policy, and thus illuminates much of the Right's dialogue with the electorate. This is a much neglected source which also casts light on the Conservative Party's public identity and fundamental beliefs. Cabinet papers, pressure group records, *Hansard*, the national press, parliamentary papers, contemporary publications, Liberal and Labour material, and memoirs, all proved of distinct utility.

The work is divided into two parts - the panoramic and the microscopic. The first chapter describes the general political context and illuminates the war of ideas which animated the political world. The political parties were conditioned both by their environment and by themselves. It is stressed that the Conservative Party was opposed to the 'big state' and had a vision of progress which rejected the idea that collectivism was the answer. There was also a Tory way of understanding society which involved predictions about what kind of a house collectivism would build. Chapters two to five analyse the Right's response to the Left's challenge. The Roman numerals divide the text between collectivism's initiatives and Conservatism's reactions. The Conservative Party's activity is analysed with reference to a taxonomy of Conservative method which is presented in the first chapter. The conclusion returns to a *tour d'horizon*. In addition to an interpretation of the Right's rearguard action, questions are raised as to the true nature of 'Thatcherism', the real character of British culture in the 1980s, the fate of the Tory vision of progress, and the deeper significance of collectivism. Overall, one wonders whether the sound and fury of 1886–1914 was not just another episode in the remorseless advance of Materialism.

One

Beliefs and Power

As Queen Victoria grew older the political life of her subjects was
changing. 'One of the most conspicuous peculiarities of contemporary
political speculation', one of the highest of high Tories told the Industrial
Remuneration Conference of 1885 (which addressed itself to the increasingly topical question of income distribution),

> is the degree to which it concerns itself with the social condition, as
> opposed to the strictly political constitution of the community...in
> the West, where, under whatever variety of external form, the
> supremacy of democracy is thought to be assured, discussions on the
> distributions of power are slowly being replaced by discussions on
> the distributions of wealth... on the Continent it is capital rather than
> land... against which attacks are chiefly directed. In England it has
> been land rather than capital, or as distinguished from capital.[1]

These sentences capture much of the character of late-Victorian and
Edwardian national politics. The philosopher Arthur Balfour had predic-
tive powers: democracy had very serious implications for property. But
the emphasis was specific – Balfour went out of his way to stress the threat
to landed property. He was leaving clues about the subsequent history of
the period which have not received sufficient attention.

After 1885 transformation was the order of the day. Democracy
advanced and popular participation altered the character of the political
system. Orientations changed as economic and social issues grew in importance. Collectivists gained in influence and put the land question at the
centre of their challenge. Conservatives were not happy about these
developments and had to take decisions as to the methods they would
employ to contain the leftist irruption. To understand the battles that took
place over property between 1886 and 1914 it is first necessary to answer
a number of simple questions. What was the nature of this democratisation? What did the Left want? What did the Right want? What was the
composition of the Conservative Party? What options were open to the
Conservative Party as it tried to stem the collectivist advance? Key
contours of the context clearly call for clarification.

I

POLITICS WITH DEMOCRACY

The progress of democracy radically changed the nature of national politics and facilitated the advance of collectivism. Victorian extensions of the franchise altered the social distribution of political power and provided new opportunities for popular attacks upon property. The state could more easily be used as an instrument for the redistribution of wealth. The Reform Act of 1884 greatly augmented the electoral rolls. 'Two millions of voices hitherto silent or unheard will now demand attention', warned the nation's leading Radical in 1885, 'and the claims that they make, and the rights upon which they insist, will be potent factors in our future legislation'.[2] The House of Lords, which had stood out against the tide for many decades, finally lost its veto in 1911. Reforms of town and country government in 1888 and 1894 made the localities more susceptible to public opinion and aided the general process. The emergence of mass political parties, the rise of mass trade unionism, and the growth of mass newspapers were part of a development which declared that politics had to emerge from the narrower confines of a mid-Victorian world which had had the habit of buying time.

How popular was the late-Victorian and Edwardian political system? Much work has been done on the character of the parliamentary franchise between 1886 and 1918. The Franchise Act of 1884 provided for a large increase in the national electorate. But the Registration Act of 1885 maintained many of the previous obstacles to voting. In 1911 there were some 7,904,465 registered voters, who amounted to 29.7% of the adult population or 63.3% of the adult male population. Allowing for a plural vote of about 500,000, it is estimated that about 59% of all adult males were registered voters. It is calculated that 12% of the adult male population were excluded by the terms of the franchise, but about 30% were denied the vote by the requirements of registration. The 1918 Franchise Act was to transform this demi-democracy.[3]

What was the social composition of the effective electorate? A most important and valuable study provides illuminating answers. One historian has demonstrated that registration worked more against the representation of the young rather than against the representation of the less prosperous. It is estimated that if plural voters are excluded the working-classes made up about 73% of the pre-war electorate – a figure not distant from their 80% share of the national population. 'The extent of the anti-working-class bias in the franchise and registration laws', it is concluded, 'and their likely effects on electoral politics, have both been over-emphasised. Working-class voters formed a very substantial part of the electorate'. The Conservatives, then, had to manage an electoral system in which power lay preponderantly with those who were on the lower rungs of the economic ladder.[4] The way in which this power would come to be used was one of the great questions of Victorian statesmanship.

The British body politic pointed to the past and the future at the same time. Democracy advanced but aristocracy remained. The House of Lords was altogether less amenable to popular pressure than the House of Commons but was at times more representative of public opinion. Not for the upper house the periodic perils of the ballot box. In this sphere at least was the nobility peculiarly immune to the democratic danger. The House of Lords, throughout this period, was a bastion of Conservatism. Electoral results did not tamper with its composition. The Liberal Party suffered a major setback in its representation with the departure of the Liberal Unionists over Irish Home Rule, and thereafter it was in a substantial minority. Gladstone's conversion was a renunciation of the dream of an emergent Liberal Lords and a declaration that henceforth the Liberals were to be a single chamber party. The Grand Old Man's plans for Ireland involved constitutional change which had nothing to do with Home Rule (see Table 1).

TABLE 1. Party Representation in the House of Lords 1884-1912

Year	Cons.	Lib.U.	Lib.	I.Nat.	Ind.	Minors	Total
1884	298		198		22	9	527
1890	325	98	84		31	13	551
1894	333	124	64		32	17	570
1899	359	117	66	1	32	15	590
1904	365	114	75	1	25	11	591
1908	356	103	102	1	42	11	615
1912	374	108	117	1	34	13	647

Sources: NUCCA and NUACLUO, *The Constitutional Yearbook,* (1885–1913)

The popularisation of politics was aided by a number of further factors. A panoramic study of the expansion of the membership of the political parties, and of the accompanying concomitants of mass organisation, would surely present a picture of an impulse towards greater political community. The proliferation of pressure groups, like an increase in party membership cards, affirmed that there were greater opportunities for the people to influence their rulers. Trade unions took off in membership during this period and their promotion of the Labour Party was a declaration that labour would be organised to achieve separate representation in politics. Trade unions were potent instruments in the breaking down of old barriers between parliament and the people, and served to involve a major segment of the electorate much more directly in the political process. This sectionalist development came rather late and acted to differentiate Edwardian from Victorian England.

The platform and the press were the principal points of contact between the political parties and the people. They acted as yesteryear's television and provided new bridges between rulers and ruled – the mass media had arrived. In 1885 Joseph Chamberlain replied to Gladstone's remonstrances about his conduct by declaring 'the platform has become one of the most powerful and indispensable instruments of Government'.[5] At outdoor and indoor meetings speakers would propagate and propound party perspectives and policies, and distribute party literature. To achieve success on the platform the political parties had great armies of speakers, lecturers and missionaries, and produced vast quantities of printed propaganda. National politics were littered by a deluge of handbills, leaflets and pamphlets. When parliament went into recess towards the end of the year platform activity increased and these months were termed the 'platform season'.[6] The platform world encouraged the idea of the campaign and both the tariff reform campaign and the land campaign were launched in the season of mists and hectic politicking. The platform, like parliament, also promoted the development of oratorical skills. When anti-democrats lamented a future decline of standards they failed to predict a rise in the quality of public speaking. The platform also encouraged the repetitive use of slogans. 'Three acres and a cow', '9d for 4d' and 'tax land not food' belonged to a world since superseded by different media of mass communication.

A growth in popular literacy and a related increase in the number and circulation of newspapers inaugurated a new era for the British press.[7] It also installed a new nobility – the press barons. Newspaper proprietors became political powers in their own right. Editors themselves did not do so badly. The private papers of the politicians of the time are replete with communications from the fourth estate. One revealing study has thrown much light on this singularly neglected dimension of power politics.[8] The task of investigation, however, is not easy: the manipulation of public opinion has the habit of covering its tracks. National, provincial and local newspapers reported on the national, provincial and local activities of the political parties. The press, indeed, because it often devoted so much space to direct political reporting, constitutes a most important source on the public life of the period. It appears that in this area, as in many others, powerful institutions came to promote the cause of Conservatism. The London and major provincial dailies of 1910 are said to have leaned to the Right in their party allegiance.[9] Newspapers kept people more informed about the activities of their rulers and thereby served to increase popular participation in public life. When a voting Londoner picked up *The Daily Mail* he could remind himself that he too was a player in the Great Game.

Collectivism itself forged new links between politicians and the governed. As the state expanded and penetrated its roots more deeply into society the people were inevitably brought closer to government. One of the most conspicuous features of high Victorian statesmanship was its assault on state patronage. Once again the experience of Great Britain

diverged from that of the Continent. The Northcote–Trevelyan report of
the mid-century was followed by an energetic attempt to professionalise
the Civil Service and reduce the level of political jobbery.[10] Left and Right
co-operated in this joint venture and helped to hasten the virtue of 'merit',
with all its impersonalising consequences, on a long and illustrious career.
Nineteenth century low government acted to erode the more indirect
subsidising of interests: a whole paraphernalia of grants, contracts, tariffs,
concessions, backhanders and percentages were conspicuous by their
absence. The town halls were never a fertile field for money making.
Unlike their Italian or French counterparts, the British political classes
failed to sustain a patronage culture. To adapt Walpole, there was not very
much pasture for a great many actual and potential sheep.

This achievement had major consequences, not least for the essential
character of the political system, which do not often receive comment.
Firstly, it made beliefs even more important. Personal participation in
politics, especially at a mass level, brought few direct material rewards.
Consequently, activity was much more motivated by conviction than by
the prospects of individual gain. This reality confirms the wisdom of
approaching the Conservative Party from the perspective of outlook. It
may also have been a potent factor behind the frequent solidarity and self-
regard of the nation's political elite – and thus a force for stability. Self-
congratulation in the face of Continental corruption built bridges between
unlikely adversaries. It also made organised Labour more attractive to
those working men who aspired to public careers, prestige and power.
Trade union growth, indeed, gained impetus from a cardinal feature of
'The System'. Finally, this achievement must have contributed to the
legitimation of the state and its rulers. This, in turn, could well have created
a receptivity to the idea that the state could be trusted to reform society. Did
not state restriction encourage state expansion?

This relative absence of state patronage, in both the broad and narrow
senses of the term, was partly rooted in the wealth of the top layer.
Financial independence lowered temptation; the possession of interests
generated disinterestedness. Salisburys and Lansdownes could afford to
disdain the porkbarrel. But it also derived from political attitudes. Liberal
anti-aristocratic sentiment had for long found expression in this assault –
Radicals had habitually protested that government often amounted to jobs
for the landed boys. Had not Bright suggested that British foreign policy
was a system of outdoor relief for the domestic aristocracy? Nor were
Tories unsympathetic to the idea that government should be sound
administration and not a font of employment. But of course this assault
went beyond the level of officialdom. Radicals had often perceived in state
intervention a method of aiding powerful interests at the expense of the
community at large. Thus the Corn Laws had been attacked as subsidies
for the landed interest. The Liberal adherence to Free Trade was not only

a question of economic theory – it involved a denial of government protection to special groups. Gladstonianism, especially in its fiscal manifestations, had powerful impulses towards minimalism. Conservatives, for
their part, always feared the confiscatory potential of state expansion. But
this frequently bi-partisan approach, which so helped to make Victorian
England the admired land of small government, low bureaucracy and
decentralisation, was to be swept aside by those developments which form
so much of the subject matter of this inquiry.

'Public corruption, rather than private bribery, is the danger of an
extended franchise.'[11] Sir Michael Hicks Beach MP was expressing a
common right-wing view. Conservatives were often afraid that democratic processes, through the medium of collectivism, would reintroduce
the politics of patronage. 'A matter of favouritism dependent upon the
constitution of the local authority' was how Lord Salisbury described
Radical land policies in 1885, 'a matter dependent upon the way in which
the local authority was elected, and in the end a matter of political
corruption'.[12] In January 1912 Bonar Law charged that the Liberals had
'succeeded in six years in creating a political spoils system which already
rivals that of the United States'.[13] Between 1886 and 1914, and especially
after 1906, more and more groups and sections of society gained direct
material advantage from the state. Thus pensioners received old age
pensions and workers were insured. An increasing number of individuals
secured government employment. Laws were passed which redistributed
property. Thus pressure groups had greater opportunities and 'lobby
politics' emerged as a distinct entity. Was this not the launch pad period
of the greatest lobby of them all – organised labour? The state was well on
its way to becoming a principal source of material enrichment. The
politics of patronage were being installed and the electorate was evolving
into a more clientalist and recipient body. Government was extending its
appeal and citizens became more closely drawn into the intricacies of its
orbit.

One manifestation of this phenomenon was a rise in the importance of
politics. The increasing role of government had to mean that political
decisions became of greater consequence in the lives of the Queen's
subjects. Thus governments acquired the habit of being held responsible
for the material condition of the people. In 1850 Sir Charles Wood could
see a 'black cloud on the horizon'. He explained his fears to Lord John
Russell: 'we are gradually approaching the state of Continental countries,
where the government is responsible for everything, for whatever goes
wrong the government is blamed'.[14] As the next century loomed Lord
Salisbury was already beginning to detect the presence of this black cloud.
'The error of this day', he declared in 1889, 'is a belief that Governments
and Parliaments are much more powerful things than they really are'.[15]
Such a state of affairs, which fed on itself, was an invitation to political

action and activism. Popular orientations moved towards politicians as the latter extended their range of competence.

The professionalisation of politics was a further sign of these times. By this phrase is meant not only the creation of individuals reliant on public life for income and status (in the evolution of which the payment of MPs in 1911 played more than a symbolic part), but the emergence of a class which proffered politics as a means of improving people's lives. Just as doctors, lawyers, architects and academics offered services to their clients, so politicians offered government to the citizenry. This professionalisation of politics, which was intimately linked to state growth, created many of the classical characteristics of a profession – albeit with clear particularities. Ministerial salaries, 'The House', titles, conferences, being kicked upstairs, manifestos and a career ladder were as much a part of a distinct professional life as the emergence of a professional elite exemplified by such types as Joseph Chamberlain and David Lloyd George. A shift from carrying on the King's business to positive government implied such an evolution. The great age of the amateur had many a professional enemy within, not least at its apex. These were early years yet, but politicians of both Left and Right would become vested interests in big government society. Even in the reactive 1980s and 1990s there is no Tory suggestion that the number of executive posts should be reduced; that the prestige of politicians should be diminished; or that those who sit in parliament do not have many of the answers. Before the First World War politicians came to have an increasing professional interest in the involvement of the people in the political process – and not without the desired results.

II

CHANGES ON THE LEFT

'Power in the Hands of the Masses', Palmerston had declared, 'throws the Scum of the Community to the surface'.[16] What would be the consequences of democracy? From the Conservative side of politics there had for long been warnings that extensions of power to the masses would involve a public concern with wealth and a sustained attack on property. Robert Arthur Talbot Gascoyne-Cecil (1830–1903), the third Marquess of Salisbury, was one of the most eloquent of the apprehensive Tories. Salisbury was a landowning aristocrat in the grand style, an intellectual, and Prime Minister from 1886 to 1892 and from 1895 to 1902. He was also a politician of electoral triumphs perturbed by the advance of popular control. Salisbury held to a simple idea – democracy led to attempts by the poor to use state powers to obtain the wealth of the rich. This was one of the cornerstones of his political theory.[17] 'Wherever democracy has prevailed', he once wrote, 'the power of the State has been used in some form or other to plunder the well-to-do classes for the benefit of the poor'.[18]

One of the characteristics of Conservatives, which partly results from their constant apprehensions about the loss of what they consider valuable, is to have a frequent flair for prophecy. The historian will readily find in much Conservative literature unnervingly accurate predictions of future developments. In 1883 Salisbury wrote an article about the way things were going. Like many on the Right he affirmed that democracy would mean much for politics, but he went beyond such a narrow observation to a general account of the future of British society. Democracy, then collectivism, then decadence – that was what was waiting on the horizon. Salisbury entitled his essay 'Disintegration' because he saw on the horizon the fall of the civilisation he loved:

> 'History has not yet furnished us with materials wide enough or minute enough for constructing anything like a science of the diseases and decay of States. But it may at least be said that in popular governments a particular cycle of phenomena has frequently reappeared. Freedom greatly tends to the increase of industry and commerce; and, as they increase, wealth is accumulated, and inequalities of fortune necessarily become more and more marked...After a time the contrast becomes very intense. Vast multitudes have not had the chance of accumulating, or have neglected it; and whenever the stream of prosperity slackens for a time, privation overtakes the huge crowds who have no reserve, and produces widespread suffering... That organizer of decay, the Radical agitator, soon makes his appearance under these conditions. He easily persuades those who are too wretched, and have thought too carelessly to see through his sophistry, that political arrangements are the cause of the differences of wealth, and that by trusting him with political power they will be redressed...Then arises that long conflict between possession and non-possession, which was the fatal disease of free communities in ancient times, and which threatens so many nations at the present day...there is no reason to believe that this malady, when it once fastens on a free State, can have any other than a fatal issue...it slowly kills by disintegration. It eats out the common sentiments and mutual sympathies which combine classes into a patriotic State.'[19]

The decades which followed the Reform Act of 1884 witnessed an increased concern with material issues and an advance of social reform legislation. There emerged a materialisation of political discussion. 'We are all socialists now' Sir William Harcourt could say in the 1890s.[20] Contemporaries were often aware of the great changes taking place about them. 'What is to be the nature of the domestic legislation of the future?', asked Joseph Chamberlain in 1885, 'I cannot help thinking that it will be more directed to what are called social objects than has hitherto been the case.'[21] 'A change has come over the character of political controversy', observed Balfour in 1892, 'properly to be described as a desire for the amelioration of the lot of the great classes of the community.[22] 'We ought to realise that the bulk of the population are alive to their own interests', reflected the chairman of the Conservative Party in 1913, 'and have an exaggerated belief that they can be bettered by legislation to an extent that no one would have dreamed of fifteen years ago'.[23] Reformers passed laws which represented a new departure for British society. National insurance, old age pensions, statutory minimum wages, the increased taxation of personal wealth, the special taxation of land, the separate taxation of unearned and earned income, town planning, central grants for housing – all these measures, and others, reached the statute book.

These developments owed much to changes on the Left of British politics. The Liberal Party underwent a transformation. New attitudes to state intervention led contemporaries to make a distinction between 'Old' and 'New' Liberalism. As the Liberal journal *The Nation* reflected in 1913:

> The theoretical objections of the older Liberalism against the State as an instrument for supplementing self-help and undertaking useful lines of co-operative activity have almost entirely disappeared. Liberalism may be said to have a really open mind towards the various proposals of nationalisation, taxation, State regulation of wages and hours, public housing schemes, and other large projects for strengthening the condition of the workers'.[24]

In 1894 William Gladstone MP (1809–1898), the architect of late-Victorian Liberalism, declared: 'Of one thing I am, and always have been convinced – it is not by the State that man can be regenerated, and the terrible woes of this darkened world effectually dealt with'.[25] But in 1913 David Lloyd George MP (1863–1945), the high prophet of advanced Radicalism, unveiled his government's great land programme with the following words: 'the powerful aid of the State, by legislation, by administration, and by finance, must be invoked to carry these purposes – all of them – into effective operation'.[26] The emergence of the Labour Party buttressed this radicalisation, provided support for the Liberal thrust, but brought with it the promise of more radical measures.[27]

What did the Left want? Liberalism merits most of the attention. Subsequent success should not conceal contemporary weaknesses: the Labour Party, at its peak in 1910, was a 7% force and the years 1911–1914 offered few prospects of immediate improvement.[28] Certainly the Liberal Party came to concern itself with a broad range of reformist politics – such issues as old age pensions, employers' liability, and national insurance were part of the common currency of left-wing dialogue. But its chief preoccupations were of a very special kind. It is time to do justice to the Victorian and Edwardian land question. This work stands or falls on the accuracy of a novel interpretation of the emphases of the reformist politics of the period. A deafening silence surrounds the land question in many of the secondary works on these years.[29] Socialist retrospection, anxious to stress the progressive prerogatives of the Labour pedigree; high political historians reluctant to descend from the glitter of the top ten hundred; and Tories keen to divert attention from highly successful social radicalism, may have all helped to give a misleading impression of the concerns of left-wing politics before the Great War. Contemporaries, of course, knew better.

There was a common realisation that the land question was at the very heart of the challenge to property and a fundamental source of party conflict. 'Before the War our political system was arranged on a two-party basis', reflected Lord Robert Cecil in 1922, 'the parties being divided mainly by their differences on certain great questions such as Ireland, the Franchise, the Church and the Land'.[30] Harold Macmillan remembered Edwardian politics revolving around 'War in South Africa; Home Rule for Ireland; Welsh disestablishment; Dreadnoughts for the Navy; religious or secular education; attacks on landlords and the House of Lords'.[31] The existence of a board game on the land question further attested to prominence.[32] A recognition of the importance of this vital department of national politics throws new light on what is already a much studied historical period; provides a new perspective on the evolution of the British Left; and introduces new interpretations as to the beginnings of collectivism in Great Britain.

What were the origins of the land question? At one level it was the offspring of British Radicalism. 'Radicalism' was the term for the outlook of those on the advanced wing of the Liberal Party, and a 'Radical' was first and foremost a land reformer. Between 1886 and 1914 Radicalism came to gain the ascendancy in Gladstone's old party. To give some idea of figures the land reform activists could secure the adherence of 173 Liberal and Labour MPs to their land tax programme in 1911 – a majority of the Liberal parliamentary party.[33] Thus it was that as the First World War drew nearer the Liberal Party became increasingly preoccupied with the land system. To a substantial extent, Edwardian New Liberalism was merely late-Victorian Radicalism a few years on. Liberal attempts to revive the land question in the 1920s[34] and again in the 1930s[35] were the last flare-ups of a creed eclipsed by more radical developments on the reformist wing of politics. Radicalism and its great cause came to be buried by the First World War and the rise of Labour.

The Radicals had evolved a distinct political culture which placed landownership at its centre. The Radical emphasis on the land question was part of a coherent outlook which combined a reform of the land system with an assault on the political power of the landed interest. Indeed, the Victorian Left's impulse towards democracy was often felt against a background of aristocratic, rather than merely oligarchical, ascendancy. The outlook ranged across domestic and foreign affairs alike and gave inner logic to a broad variety of sympathies and antipathies. Support for East Anglian farm workers and hostility to Tsarist Russia; advocacy of land value taxation and enthusiasm for Liberal Italy; the promotion of tenant rights and the demand for House of Lords reform; commitment to parish councils and the championing of site value rating – all these disparate elements were part of a perspective rooted in preoccupations about landed proprietors.

But the land question was much more than the concern of a militant tendency within national politics. Its controversial character indicated that its prominence was a direct result of the configurations of a society in a state of transition. The subject was perhaps the greatest of the late-Victorian and Edwardian bones of party contention and introduced powerful sources of conflict into the body politic. The problems of rapid urbanisation, the pains of agrarian contraction, the pressure of population, the threat of foreign competition, the expanding fiscal needs of government – all these, by various routes, drew attention to land and buildings. Furthermore, there was the question of social distribution. 'No Continental landed elite in the nineteenth century owned so large a part of the nation's territory as did the English.'[36] Resentment at such inequality found expression in political protest. In addition, the land question was a medium for property relationships – a variety of interests connected with real property settled their differences in the political sphere, not least with regard to the incidence of taxation. Because of the ubiquity of land and buildings these interests were innumerable. Noblemen and shopkeepers, the homeless and the landless, crofters and surveyors, taxpayers and ratepayers, town tenants and rural parsons – these were just a few of the members of a list which helped to raise the land question to dizzy heights. Finally, there was the simple matter of size. The land question was a subject of much complexity, a myriad of issues, and extensive range. There was hardly a political topic which in one way or another it did not touch. Its taxation dimension, for example, impinged on all questions of central and local government revenue and expenditure.

But what was the land question? It was part of a broad but distinctive category of social issues. Victorians and Edwardians tended to place the mass of issues concerned with changes in the material condition of the people under the general heading of 'social reform'. Reform proposals usually fell into two main (and overlapping) categories: those which involved a state provision of funds or services, and those which involved an alteration in property rights. These two categories had their own sub-categories. Funds and services could be provided by (a) central government, (b) local government, or (c) a combination of the two. They could be self-financing, financed from national taxes, or supported by the rates (or a mixture of the three). If they were not self-financing they could be paid for by different classes of ratepayers or taxpayers. Property rights could be altered in a fixed fashion by statute law, or in a more fluid fashion by administrative law. Such alterations generally involved taxation, the character of economic relationships, or the benefits and advantages of ownership. The social question was complicated, controversial and comprehensive. Because of the special character of the British Left before the ascendancy of Labour, material politics were much preoccupied with land and buildings.

In 1913 a leading Tory combatant in the war over property rights offered his definition:

> What is called the 'Land Question' is now very much to the front. But the public mind is in considerable confusion as to what this phrase means. Used in its widest sense it covers a series of problems of the highest importance and of much complexity, such as State and individual ownership, occupying ownership and tenancy, the Housing problem in town and country, the Rating and Taxation of Land and Houses, the Tenure of Agricultural Land, the position of the Agricultural Labourer, the encouragement of higher forms of cultivation, Co-operation in Agriculture and Horticulture, and many minor issues arising out of or kindred to these.[37]

The land question was a complex of issues concerned with the ownership, tenure, taxation, use and provision of land and buildings. The rural land question focused on the labourer's wages, working conditions, housing, and access to land; and upon the tenancy laws, farm rents, the question of game, small holdings, local taxation, and the general status of the agrarian sector. The urban land question was chiefly preoccupied with landlord–tenant relations, the taxation of real property, town planning, housing, and the acquisition of land by public bodies.[38]

The historical function of the land question was to give a powerful impetus to the forward march of collectivist ideas and institutions. A collectivist perspective on property was essential to the Radical approach. The attack on landed ownership relied upon a number of arguments which discredited private claims and substituted collective rights. The people, by virtue of their existence, had a 'natural right' to the land - thus the slogan 'the land belongs to the people'. The land had been stolen from the people by the Norman Conquest, or by the more recent system of enclosures. Many historians thus became involved in the debate about the origins of estates and the dispossession of the labourers.[39] Land values wrongly accrued to landowners and not to the populace. When Manchester expanded into empty fields and created a great increase in land values owners reaped where they had never sown. Hence the endless talk about the 'unearned increment' of land. Finally, it was argued that many landowners lost their moral title to their land when they failed to use it in the best interests of the community.

But the land question played a vital role in the changeover from

Liberalism to Socialism in a wider fashion. The concept of a 'land system' anticipated the concept of the 'capitalist system'. The illegitimacy of rents prepared the ground for the illegitimacy of profits. Attacks on the 'landlord press' and the 'landlords' parliament' predated attacks on the 'capitalist press' and the 'capitalists' parliament'. Both creeds shared the materialist belief that economic reform along statist lines would achieve progress. Both, also, directed antipathy towards individuals not because of their personal behaviour but because of their membership of a socio-economic class. Liberal land reformism constructed some of the foundations for edifices of a size which the Liberals themselves never anticipated. Modern British conditions have unexpected roots in the interests of Victorian and Edwardian Liberals which have been all too often overlooked.

The other great change on the Left was the foundation of the Labour Party. Whereas Liberalism was rather selective in its vision and focused on the land system, Socialism came to subsume this partiality with a condemnation of the economic system as a whole. Yet Labour also had a peculiar antipathy to landlordism – which meant that it was vulnerable to its progressive sister's advanced initiatives – and in this inheritance of Radical culture it came to carry on the Liberal tradition. The Liberal Party certainly concerned itself with social reform beyond land reform, but the Labour Party was much more radical in its aspirations.[40] This more advanced form of collectivism was linked to a new approach to power which had historic consequences. The trade union promotion of the Labour Party was an attempt to organise a specific section of society and to give it special representation in parliament. This initiative employed novel forms of political organisation and by linking the shop floor to the floor of the House of Commons established a new dimension to the nation's political system. The concurrent development of a distinct trade union culture, which put collective action at a premium, gave mental underpinnings to these institutional changes. The Liberals wanted to erode the power of the landed interest, and this was certainly radical. But the trade unionist Labour Party was placing its charges much more deeply in the nation's political structures and was not concerned merely with the role of the nobility and country gentlemen.

III

THE NATURE OF THE RIGHT

The Conservative Party diverged sharply from the attitudes of the parties of the Left. In order to grasp the Tory *telos* it is necessary to understand the Conservative mind. One idea has entered common currency. It is frequently asserted that British Conservatism cannot be identified with a distinctive approach to society. Again and again it has been assumed that no recognisable pattern of beliefs have underlain the party's activities. 'The conscious rejection of ideology by British Conservatives has indeed been one of their most distinctive features', adjudges Dr Ramsden, 'The Conservative Party rarely appealed to the electorate on a matter of belief.'[41] 'Any attempt to provide an explanation of the conduct of the British Conservative Party in terms of a single, coherent ideology', write other historians of the party, 'is doomed to failure'.[42] 'If the main strength of Conservatism is adaptability', writes Mr Pym, 'its main enemy is ideology'.[43] Another view often voiced is that Conservatives have had the habit of not expressing their beliefs. 'Conservatism may rarely announce itself in maxims, formulae or aims', declares Professor Scruton, 'Its essence is inarticulate.'[44] This study seeks to diverge from these views and proposes that a failure to understand the essential beliefs of Conservatism (which were often elaborated at great length) has led not only to a failure to understand the history of the Right but also to an inability to detect fundamental changes within British society. Tory ideas have themselves evolved with the times and have helped to make the party a useful historical weather vane.

What has been the historical function of the British Conservative Party? Conservatism is always contextual and late-Victorian and Edwardian Conservatism reflected many of the peculiar achievements and characteristics of a national civilisation which was shaping the world. There is little dispute over most of the key features of the Right in the period 1886–1914. Stripped to essentials, the party of Salisbury, Balfour and Bonar Law was committed to the maintenance of the monarchy, the House of Lords and the existing national and local franchise; established political, religious and civil liberties; the rule of law and the maintenance of public order; the Union with Ireland, Scotland and Wales; the consolidation and grandeur of the Empire; the rights and advantages of the Anglican Church; and the pre-eminence of British military power. Changes over time in the details of policy did not alter the essential orientation. In all these areas, in fundamental intention, the Conservative Party was conservative. There is much in a name. What is more controversial is the extent to which the Conservative Party of this period (as of others) was committed to the propertied order, the social hierarchy, and the economic system. Put more simply, has Conservatism been an anti-collectivist force?

Tory economic attitudes can not be divorced from the wider Conservative perspective. The right-wing belief in liberty had widespread ramifications. Unlike many members of the Continental Right, the modern British Conservative Party has been a libertarian party. Burke was never a Maistre. The late-Victorian and Edwardian Tories looked back to the Slave Grace and forward to 1940. This libertarianism revolved around freedom from interference – what Berlin has defined as the 'negative' concept of liberty.[45] The Right defended freedom of speech and publication, rights of assembly and association, and a legal system whose commitment to the liberty of the subject was symbolised by juries and *habeas corpus*. Memories of the French Terror, disdain for Continental police methods, a profound respect for Law, a reverence for privacy, a hostility to inspectors, admiration for religious toleration, and 'an Englishman's home is his castle', all belonged to an extensive constellation of ideas which acted to reinforce the Tory belief in liberty. When a party publication declared that 'In the Socialistic State individual freedom would be unknown'[46] it necessarily affirmed that in a Conservative State liberty would be guaranteed. This libertarianism naturally translated itself into the economic sphere and made it very unlikely that the Conservatives would have looked with favour upon state intervention, regulation, or control. A constant hostility to bureaucracy was perhaps the most prominent manifestation of the application of the Tory concept of freedom to the world of wealth. Any proponent of the Conservative collectivism thesis would have to explain a glaring contradiction in the right-wing outlook.

The following exposition of late-Victorian and Edwardian Conservative attitudes towards the economy relies upon an observation of activity and pronouncements. The analysis of activity is presented in subsequent chapters. Right-wing behaviour, because so consistent, was a clear manifestation of right-wing beliefs. Action spoke as loudly as words. There was, it is true, a marked dearth of theoretical publications. Lord Hugh Cecil's *Conservatism* of 1912 broke the rule and thereby illustrated it. Indeed, the relative absence of works of Conservative philosophy after Burke is one of the most salient features of modern British thought. The Right has traditionally suffered from a curiously counter-productive anti-intellectualism. Equally, many parts of the Tory mental world were indeed often unexpressed and only accessible by means of inference. Furthermore, beliefs, by their very nature, do not allow of the same procedures of proof as other phenomena. The model presented here is very much a working model. It is readily conceded that the criteria for its verification are not entirely satisfactory. Yet it is argued that this model well explains the patterns of the Conservative Party's behaviour and even allows of a marked degree of prediction. Although many Conservatives would not have been able to present a coherent statement of their views this did not mean that they lacked a systematic outlook. The description presented here renders explicit what was often implicit.

In 1910 Arthur Balfour's private secretary described the members of the Conservative Party as people 'who naturally prefer the existing order of things'.[47] In general, the Tories regarded the economic system as valuable. 'Nothing has more effective significance in Conservatism than its bearing on questions of property', observed Lord Hugh Cecil, 'the defence of property has been one of its principal purposes'.[48] Orthodox Conservatives believed that private property was inherently just; that the protection of private property (which included the enforcement of eco-

nomic contracts) was a primary purpose of the state; and that such
protection was necessary to economic advance. Generally, they were
opposed to constraints on the individual's free disposal of his property or
labour. Without denying that poverty was undesirable, they held that the
actual system which prevailed in the world of wealth was praiseworthy.

Conventional Conservatives asserted that private property and the
rights that went with ownership were intimately connected with national
prosperity. In the free disposal of property they discerned economic
liberty. Economic liberty was the substance of the free market economy
- the pursuit of private wealth produced the laws of supply and demand.
Such laws allocated resources to the most productive areas of the economy
and regulated wages, prices, profits and rents. General levels of wealth
were thereby raised. Thus private property worked to the benefit of all; the
existing system was progressive. Disagreements existed over the relative
merits of protection and free trade, but this did not imply a lack of
agreement on the basic approach. Conservatives could dispute as to
whether the domestic economy should exist in a protected or open
environment. In economic terms, the taxation of individuals was considered a necessary inconvenience. It was conceded that in some areas, such
as roads, education, communication or sanitation, the state could supple-
ment or even supplant private enterprise, but in general orientation the
Conservatives were non-interventionists. Thus the Conservatives of the
years 1886–1914, in general terms, were opposed to the abolition of
private property, the insecurity of private property, the redistribution of
property, the transgression of property rights, and the erosion of economic
liberty, on both moral and economic grounds. Yet it cannot be denied that
there were differences amongst Conservatives in the level of commitment
they felt towards different parts of the economic order. In their unwilling-
ness to expand government, and thus to give themselves a greater role and
influence, the late-Victorian and Edwardian Conservatives were self-
denying politicians.

In their general non-interventionist approach the Conservatives received substantial support from the writings of successive economists.
The social sciences have tended to be an anti-Conservative force but the
discipline of economics in its early stage gave much credence to the
Right's approach. Notwithstanding variations and deviations, the British
tradition of mainstream economics provided a solid core of free market
teachings. Through Smith, Bentham, Malthus, Ricardo, Nassau Senior,
J.S.Mill and Marshall there runs an emphasis on the benefits of a supply
and demand economy operating within a stable climate of security,
confidence and small government. 'The Classical Economists clearly
considered that a developed economy was a free enterprise one,' writes a
recent authority, 'and that the State's role in such an economy was
primarily to ensure that the private system worked properly and flour-

ished'.[49] From such endorsement the Right must have gained confidence. From the Left came attempts to undermine such theoretical and academic support. Karl Marx and Henry George made their specific contributions to the conflict between Conservatism and collectivism.

Yet unseen in the tradition of classical economy there lurked an anti-Conservative way of thinking. This is not a reference to a disparagement of the economic benefits of existing landownership which found its most vigorous expression in Mill's support for the taxation of the future unearned increment of land and his creation of the Land Tenure Reform Association.[50] It is, rather, a comment on a prevalent aculturalism. There was a marked tendency to define the economy as a detached machine operating independently within society, and to deny the special role of values, attitudes, perceptions, feelings, habits and customs in shaping the economic experience of both individuals and nations. This was part of a more general materialist orientation which put a premium on production and the primacy of market forces. It went against the Tory emphasis on the need for activity within the market, and economic relationships more generally, to be subject to the control of guiding ethics and morals. The Conservative Party was a free market party, but it was much more. A narrow economic libertarianism was not the Tory gospel. There was no desire for Hobbes's civil conflict of 'every man, against every man'.[51]

The Right did not only uphold economic self-interest, it stressed social obligation. The Conservative Party conceived of itself as a Christian force – no account of its beliefs can be complete without an understanding of the influence of the Christian tradition. Tories wanted a society which was bound together by shared values and beliefs, and which practised the ideals of duty, aid, responsibility, and concern. There was also an emphasis on good manners with their function of showing respect and affirming common customs. Courtesy, that most understudied of social phenomena, had a Conservative connotation. These anti-Communists had a communitarian vision. Although they were anti-Socialists they desired a highly socialised society. Thus Tories wanted kindly and generous ties to prevail in the family (which was considered the basic social unit and was upheld as such), between friends, neighbours, and work colleagues, and stressed the importance of dutiful attitudes between employers and employees, and between landlords and tenants. These last were not a matter of 'paternalism', but of a more general ethical approach. Thomas Drummond's dictum that 'Property has its duties as well as its rights'[52] was almost a Tory motto. The focus was upon relationships at an individual level.

In addition there was the world of charity and philanthropy. Once again Christianity was to have a guiding role. Individual public service was the right-wing obverse of left-wing state provision. In this overall attitude the Conservative Party reflected much of Victorian and Edwardian cultural practice. Historians have begun, for example, to stress the important role

of industrialists in benefiting their employees;[53] of leisured women in the
world of charity;[54] and of voluntary bodies in society as a whole.[55] It is
no accident that the organisation which sought to represent charitable societies was powerfully anti-Socialist.[56] The Conservative Party upheld
values which worked for social integration and became a force for such
integration. A belief in political freedom; a stress on economic liberty; and
a firm faith in social duty founded in Christian concepts were thus key
features of the Conservative mentality. As applied to the world of wealth
they produced an approach which could only lead to a conflict with
collectivist tenets. Thus there was a Tory vision of progress – a vision
which had little to do with government direction but much to do with individual action. Because part of it was not overtly political, and because
it was taken for granted by many of its exponents, it was frequently
implicit to the point of invisibility. But its future failure would come to
provoke articulate regret. In the late-twentieth century this vision was
described with the famous phrase 'Victorian values'.

The Conservative leaders themselves, as befitted their position, regularly articulated essential aspects of the Tory creed. Indeed, the late-
Victorian and Edwardian radicalisation of the Left encouraged such
expression by inviting contradiction. The content of the set-piece speeches
to the annual conferences bore witness to the changing concerns of
national politics. Party leaders considered it a part of their task to give
public statements of the party's general outlook. Salisbury, Balfour and
Bonar Law were tribunes of Conservatism. Great platform speeches were
vehicles for the presentation of the true faith; political sermonising was a
regular feature of the Tory experience. Here, rather than in the marginal
writings of peripheral polemical theoreticians, are to be encountered
many of the Right's doctrinal axioms. Those who believe that there was
an absence of distinctive beliefs behind the Conservative Party's actions
should go no further than *The Times*, that invaluable newspaper which so
painstakingly recorded these almost Mosean presentations of principle.

Lord Salisbury combined a Christian social gospel with a faith in
market mechanisms. The Marquess believed that civilisation and prosperity could be advanced by individuals who sought material enrichment un-
hindered by government control and who recognised their social duties
towards others. The primary economic purpose of the state was to ensure
the security of property. Nobody less believed in the left-wing idea of
'changing society'. 'You have heard statements of corruption and you
have heard proposals of legislation by which it was hoped that such
corruption could be stemmed', he declared in 1885, 'There is only one
remedy for such corruption, and that is the true teaching of the principles
of Christianity'.[57] There were few who so stridently condemned the
proponents of interventionist economics. 'All that Parliament can really
do is to free the energies and support the efforts of an intelligent and

industrious people', he observed in 1895, 'It is with them that great efforts must lie.'[58] A few years earlier he had given forceful expression to his view that the Left could ruin everything:

> if I wanted a definition of Conservative policy I should say that it is the policy of the party who preaches confidence. (cheers). On confidence is built the proud structure of our commercial supremacy; on confidence is built the vast fabric of the civilization that we see around us; and if you encourage these peddling philosophers (loud cheers and laughter) with their petty, spiteful acts of confiscation, animated by no philanthropic spirit, but by a mere impulse of class antipathy, if you allow them to have their way, the substratum and foundation of all your civilization and prosperity and happiness will melt away.[59]

Arthur James Balfour (1848–1930) the first Earl Balfour, was Lord Salisbury's nephew, a Scottish landowner and a philosopher of high calibre. He was leader of the Conservative Party from 1902 to 1911 and Prime Minister from 1902 to 1905. Balfour's individualism, unlike his theology, was clear cut and uncomplicated. In 1895 he spoke on social reform to a Manchester audience. The statist road was clearly rejected:

> though Governments and Acts of Parliament may do much, yet, after all, it is the individual, the free individual, using his capabilities to the best advantage, working, co-operating with his fellows in freely organised associations, which, as in the past, so in the future, must do the great share of the work of raising the standard of life, of happiness, of cultivation, and of prosperity.[60]

Balfour, like his uncle, was a champion of the Church of England, and his theology was in part an attempt to defend conventional Christianity against recent trends in scientific thinking.[61] He also had a conventional Tory antipathy to high taxation. 'If you ask from the community at large too great a contribution, even for the best of objects', he pronounced in 1907, 'you defeat your own end by destroying the productive efficiency of the community upon which all your philanthropic efforts must ultimately be based'. Balfour was decisive in his opinions: 'the best productive result can only be obtained by respecting private property and encouraging private enterprise'.[62]

Andrew Bonar Law (1858–1923) is sometimes portrayed as the representative of a new departure in Conservative leadership. Certainly he was a Scottish Presbyterian businessman who lacked a landed estate and had not been to a public school. It is also true that he believed the promotion of businessmen within the party was intellectually a great improvement,[63] and did not see why yet another member of landed society should be made chief whip in 1913.[64] Yet at the level of belief Bonar Law was the true heir of Balfour and Salisbury. As the acclaimed leader of the Conservative Party he could hardly have been otherwise. Keynes wrote that

Bonar Law was 'almost devoid of Conservative principles',[65] but the Bloomsbury economist was in error. Bonar Law stressed social duties like any other good Conservative and paid tribute to the behaviour of landowners. 'I think, and there is nothing on which I feel more strongly, that all property owners have duties as well as rights – (cheers)', he told the National Union in 1913, 'It is my belief that among the property owners of this country there is no class which, to a greater extent than landowners, does recognise their responsibilities, and does try to fulfil the duties of their position. (cheers)'.[66] Bonar Law may not have been able to recognise a pheasant when visting the estate of one of his front bench colleagues[67] but he recognised the Tory respect for the landed. A year earlier, at a party rally at Blenheim Palace, he had stressed how the gospel of class hatred created a lack of confidence in the economy and thus injured the very class on whose behalf the gospel was preached.[68] In May 1912 Bonar Law told a Glasgow audience that too great a state burden on the economy caused poverty.[69]

Unspoken loves are frequently expressed in spoken hates – antipathy indicates sympathy. The emergence of Socialism in the decades before the Great War brought forth detailed Tory denunciations. It is in the Conservative attacks on Socialism that so much of the right-wing approach to life is to be found. This hated enemy, which menaced so much of what the Conservatives valued, served to secure the articulation of certain beliefs which were not often expressed. This is only natural – the Socialist challenge struck at the very foundations of the Tory vision of civilisation. Conservative anti-Socialism was a powerful indicator of the character of Conservatism. A variety of sources could be used for the analysis of this anti-Socialism but here merely one suffices. The party's periodic *Campaign Guide*, an irreplaceable source which instructed party speakers in an exhaustive range of policy and detail, began to publish separate chapters on Socialism as the menace grew greater. The condemnation of 1909, the year of the People's Budget, may be subjected to scrutiny.

The piece began by stressing that although much undesirable poverty remained the existing system had greatly increased general standards of living - 'the progress that has been made during the last century under the present system amply justifies the belief that all further real progress must be based on the present economic, social, and political system'.[70] Socialism was portrayed as alien to British traditions and depicted as a Continental import. Men were not equal and different individuals had different talents. Labour was not the source of all wealth. In a Socialist society the state would be the universal employer and Britons would be told what to do by tyrannical officials. A state directed economy would involve inefficiency and poverty. Socialism would abolish religion and destroy family life. The opinion of Bishop Westcott was warmly cited. '"The popular estimate of the family is an infallible criterion of the state of society...strong battalions are of no avail against homes guarded by faith, reverence, and love.'".[71] The overall assessment was clear: 'Socialism stands for the disruption of society, the elimination of the individual, and the destruction of all private property and profit.'[72] The *Campaign Guide* anticipated that Socialism would bring social disintegration and economic retardation.

Much of the character of the Conservative Party's cultural appeal was represented by the Primrose League. This organisation deliberately avoided the policies and detail of politics to concentrate on essential beliefs and attitudes. It was both an expression of Conservative principles and a deliberate attempt to strengthen and promote Tory values in the general community – in this it attested to the rise of mass politics. Its very activities were a part of the Conservative vision. The Primrose League no longer exists and has long since passed from popular memory, but in its day it occupied an important position on the political landscape. Founded in 1883, it underwent a rapid growth and by 1914 claimed some 800,000 members.[73] The Primrose League is said to have become the 'largest and most widely spread political organization of the time'.[74] It only formally linked itself to the Conservative Party on the eve of the Great War and its previous stance of neutrality was both a device to maximise adherence and an expression of the long standing Tory contention that Conservatism was essentially unpolitical.

The Primrose League dispensed the clear water of essential Conservatism without appearing too partisan. When a member first joined he had to promise to uphold religion, the monarchy, the empire and the estates of the realm.[75] In 1907 the league issued the following pamphlet:

A FEW WORDS TO WORKING MEN AND WOMEN ABOUT THE PRIMROSE LEAGUE...
The Constitution under which England has grown to be what she is – The Greatest Country in the world.
Religion against Atheism.
The Unity of the British Empire.
The Right of every man to his own Property.
A Navy and Army able to protect the vast commercial interests of the British Empire.
Freedom in Religious Instruction for the Education of our children.
The Rights of Labour and the Rights of Property.
Civil and Religious Liberty.
The Prosperity, and Moral and Intellectual Progress of the People.[76]

This was a striking statement of Tory principles. What the Primrose League admired was reflected in what it attacked. The Radicals and Socialists were habitually portrayed as atheistic, unpatriotic, anti-impe-

rial, anti-family, spoliatory, divisive and destructive.[77] The league sought
to 'instruct working men and women how to answer the arguments of the
Radicals and the Socialists and the Atheists in the workshops and in the
public-houses, and at the street corners'.[78] The importance of the Primrose
League in Conservative politics was recognised by the party leaders who
used its annual conferences as platforms for major speeches.

The Primrose League, like Conservatives more generally, envisaged a
Christian patriotic state of classes bound together by common sentiments
and attitudes. Thus did it seek to achieve class harmony, (and thereby
reduce social conflict over wealth), by bringing the classes together in
shared recreational and political activity. The common Victorian and
Conservative idea that women had a special role to play in voluntary,
charitable and social work was reflected in the especial role the organisation gave to women. In 1885 the league distributed a pamphlet with a
preface by Lady Randolph Churchill. Entitled *The Primrose League. How
Ladies Can Help It*, it argued that women had a special advantage in
canvassing because of the 'persuasive gentleness characteristic of their
sex'.[79] Indeed, the Primrose League offered a political outlet for female
activism long before the enactment of female suffrage. Organised along
the lines of local habitations, and combining chivalric images with
somewhat masonic ritual, the league's knights and dames specialised in
fairs, fetes, bazaars, lantern shows, and other forms of entertainment.
'"Vulgar? Of course it is vulgar! But that is why we have got on so
well"',[80] said Lord Salisbury. With its attempts at social integration and its
dissemination of right-wing values the Primrose League was an agent for
the cultural promotion of Conservatism, and was thus a part of the Right's
response to the late-Victorian and Edwardian Left.

☆

The composition of the Conservative Party conditioned the nature of the
Right's attempt to ensure the success of its ideas in two major ways: it
produced an entity which favoured leadership and gave rise to an organism
which was bound up with the landed interest. The Conservative Party was
a hierarchical community. On the whole, to be a Tory was to be ruled from
above. Power was concentrated at the upper levels and the party had a
distinct vertical structure. There were three chief layers – the leadership,
the parliamentary followers, and the mass party membership. The leaders
decided official policy and action, and there was no formal machinery by
which they were controlled or influenced by the rest of the party. The
caucus style was alien to Conservatism. There were, of course, informal
channels and forms of influence – it would be a mistake to assume that MPs
or activists were mere ciphers. Thus in studying the leadership one is
examining those who had great control over the direction taken by the
party – herein lies a justification for observing those in the Conservative
upper branches.

One Tory MP recalled that it was said by right-wingers of the time that the Conservative Party was 'mainly composed of country gentlemen and the British *bourgeoisie*'.[81] Yet such social elevation did not imply a lack of subordination. In the House of Commons the ordinary Conservative MP exercised little control over his party's activity in the chamber and was remote from decision making. Arthur Griffith-Boscawen MP recalled being a 'voting machine'[82] in the 1890s. Earl Winterton MP remembered noting the 'Olympian attitude of my official leaders'[83] in the early 1900s. Samuel Hoare MP recalled that in 1910 'Conservative members were expected to do what they were told' and 'only in question-time had a back bench member any chance of a free run'.[84] In 1911 a group of Tory MPs complained about the 'inadequate means of communication between persons like themselves and their Parliamentary Leaders'.[85] Hoare also remembered that 'there were no party committees such as there are now'[86] to give expression to backbench feeling. In 1909 special committees were set up to combat the Liberal budget. 'Till 1909 & the formation of these committees', wrote J.Arkwright MP, 'I & others felt we were of little use to the Party. We were not an organised force'.[87] The Tory aristocracy was rather more egalitarian. In 1906 a backbench committee of Unionist peers was established which displayed a contrasting measure of independence.[88] The MPs had to wait until 1922 for a similar body. Thus did the nobility lead the commoners in the promotion of democracy in the Conservative parliamentary party. 'If you think our whips 'control' anybody you are mistaken',[89] Lord Lansdowne (1845–1927) told Balfour's private secretary in 1906. 'You know how difficult it is in our House always to get the back benches to follow the lead of the front bench',[90] commented the Earl of Onslow in 1907.

Arthur Balfour, it is reported, said he paid more attention to his valet than to the National Union.[91] The National Union of Conservative and Constitutional Associations (hereafter NUCCA), which became the National Unionist Association of Conservative and Liberal Unionist Organisations (NUACLUO) after its fusion with the Liberal Unionists on the eve of the First World War, was chiefly concerned with the organisation of mass Conservatism. In 1889 its president declared that organisation was the 'primary aim and object of the National Union'.[92] In the same speech it was said that at election times the Union distributed 'millions' of pamphlets.[93] Leafleting was, indeed, one of the organisation's primary purposes. The National Union held annual conferences and passed resolutions on policy, but these were not binding on the leadership. The conferences were much more rallies than forums for decision making. Otherwise the National Union was an institutional expression for the local associations and clubs which flew the Tory flag and had great independence over their choice of candidates. Balfour's reference was not inappropriate. To a substantial extent the National Union was a servant of the general cause. But there is no suggestion that the mass party organisation wanted control. This itself was rooted in Conservative concepts of government and general habits of mind. The Tory ethos had an impulse towards institutional elitism. The natural coherence and discipline of the mass party made it a more potent force in the hands of those who inhabited the Tory peaks.

As the nineteenth century progressed the aristocracy and gentry became increasingly identified with the Conservative Party. In 1911 a member of the Tory front bench could refer to the Conservatives as the 'country gentleman's party'.[94] An analysis of the parliamentary party of the pre-war years, by which time the absorption of the Liberal Unionists was well advanced, gives a statistical demonstration of this very special relationship. The Conservative Party in parliament was largely drawn from the landed, commercial, industrial, financial and legal top drawer. In the House of Lords landownership was the rule. One historian maintains that in 1911, in a house composed of 604 noblemen, some 448 peers (or their fathers) had been listed as owning over 2,000 acres of land in 1883.[95] A detailed analysis of the Edwardian Unionist MPs, which was not without its methodological pitfalls,[96] suggests that in the House of Commons landownership was still the principal presence. The landed interest was essentially a Tory interest (see Table 2).

TABLE 2. An Analysis of the Unionist MPs elected at the general elections of 1900, 1906, January 1910 and December 1910

Category	1900 (401)		1906 (157)	
	Number	Overlap	Number	Overlap
Landowners	130 (32.4%)	29 (22.3%)	53 (33.7%)	9 (16.9%)
Barristers	78 (19.4%)	32 (41.0%)	24 (15.2%)	9 (37.5%)
Manufacturers	66 (16.4%)	11 (16.6%)	24 (15.2%)	5 (20.8%)
Commercial men	54 (13.4%)	15 (27.7%)	19 (12.1%)	4 (21.0%)
Miscellaneous	43 (10.7%)	14 (32.5%)	17 (10.8%)	4 (23.5%)
Military men	27 (6.7%)	—	11 (7.0%)	—
Leisured	19 (4.7%)	—	8 (5.0%)	—
Bankers	18 (4.4%)	8 (44.4%)	7 (4.4%)	5 (71.4%)
Services	12 (2.9%)	6 (50.0%)	5 (3.1%)	2 (40.0%)
Solicitors	10 (2.4%)	1 (10.0%)	8 (5.0%)	—

Category	Jan. 1910 (272)		Dec. 1910 (267)	
	Number	Overlap	Number	Overlap
Landowners	85 (31.2%)	14 (16.2%)	78 (29.2%)	15 (19.2%)
Barristers	62 (22.7%)	19 (30.6%)	59 (22.0%)	17 (28.8%)
Manufacturers	29 (10.6%)	6 (20.6%)	28 (10.4%)	5 (17.8%)
Commercial men	21 (7.7%)	3 (14.2%)	18 (6.7%)	2 (11.1%)
Miscellaneous	17 (6.2%)	7 (41.1%)	30 (11.2%)	8 (26.6%)
Military men	29 (10.6%)	—	32 (11.9%)	
Leisured	16 (5.8%)	—	17 (6.3%)	—
Bankers	9 (3.3%)	4 (44.4%)	9 (3.3%)	3 (33.3%)
Services	6 (2.2%)	2 (33.3%)	9 (3.3%)	3 (33.3%)
Solicitors	16 (5.8%)	1 (6.2%)	16 (5.9%)	1 (6.2%)

This picture provides a variety of at times unexpected discoveries. As the years passed the landed interest did not fall off in representation: 32.4% to 29.2% lacks significance. Indeed, it was the capitalists who were on the way down. W. D. Rubinstein has stressed the relatively low proportion of manufacturers in the modern British elite.[97] The Conservative Party in the Edwardian House of Commons did not dispute such an observation. The manufacturing category, which includes those who produced liquor, fell from 16.4% to 10.4%. 'The Trade', indeed, never made up more than 5% of the MPs of its political champion. Nor was the accession of a Glasgow iron merchant to the leadership of the party in 1911 part of a rising commercial tide. The shippers and merchants dropped from 13.3% at the beginning of the decade to under 7% at its end. From one point of view the Conservative Party was one of the more prestigious inns of court. Except for a dip in 1906 the barristers held their 20%. The special role of landownership among the Tory MPs (this point does not apply to the Liberal Unionist MPs who retained their own whip) was confirmed by a distinct tradition: the chief whip and the other whips were invariably drawn from landed society. Discipline was in the hands of the majority interest.[98]

Other interesting features emerge from this survey. There was a remarkable overlapping of interests, a state of affairs which may have acted to damp down potential internal conflict. Well over a third of the party in the House of Commons held directorships in addition to their main interests. Directorships, therefore, were one of the chief prizes of politics before the payment of MPs and the great expansion in the number of executive salaries. The control and disposal of such directorships is a neglected dimension of modern political life and merits study. How much were they worth? Were they an instrument of party control? Were they a mechanism for the influence of lobbies? Over a quarter of the Unionist MPs had roots in local government. About a half were linked to the regular or irregular armed forces. 'The Conservative benches', recalled one Tory, 'were full of Volunteer and Yeomanry officers'.[99] Thus the Right's MPs were not only connected with important parts of the economy and the professions but had significant links with military and local authority life. Conservative members of the House of Commons were not a removed elite and, at a personal level, could learn much about the condition of the nation. A 'List of Unionist MPs, and Interests Represented' which is to be found in the Robert Cecil papers, seems to relate a member's biography to his political speciality and so captures the point perfectly.[100]

The Conservative Party was proving itself a most successful electoral force in the emerging democracy but there was nothing remotely 'democratic' about its composition in parliament. The Tories themselves would have argued that the views and beliefs they shared with the people submerged any economic differences – theirs was not a narrowly materi-

alist system of social analysis. When the Right received more than a half
of the vote in 1900 it must have been confirmed in such a communitarian
outlook. But the identification of the MPs and peers with property, and
especially with landed property, gave the party a distinct polemical
vulnerability. It was also a major factor behind the intense force of the
Right's opposition to land reform. The link between democracy, Liberal
national policy, and Tory landowners at Westminster was observed by
Winston Churchill when he dwelt upon the rift between Gladstone and
Chamberlain. He remembered a comment made by a landed Conservative
MP. Churchill was first elected at the turn of the century:

> I often used to sit next to Mr. 'Jim' Lowther when I first came into
> the House. He had sat in Cabinet with Disraeli. He was a real
> survival of old times, the perfect specimen of the Tory Diehard, and
> a great gentleman and sportsman to boot. 'We have much to be
> thankful for' he remarked one day. 'If those two had stuck together,
> they'd have had the shirts off our backs before now'.[101]

In addition, any Tory attempts to move leftwards for electoral reasons
would come into conflict with the self-interest of those owners or heirs to
land, or those with property in other areas, who were so well represented
amongst the party's MPs and peers.

☆

What courses of action were open to the Conservative Party in its resistance to late-Victorian and Edwardian collectivism? This provokes a more
general question: how do Conservatives conserve what they regard as
valuable? This, in turn, opens up a fitting subject for study – Conservative
method. The discipline of political science, which has gained from the
expansion of the social sciences, which themselves have gained from state
expansion, seems uninterested. Yet this theoretical subject involves most
interesting analytical perspectives: in a given context what options were
open to Conservatives, which options were chosen and why, and what
happened to the Conservatives in the process? There is no reason why only
revolutionaries should have manuals. Comparative studies could throw
light on the different types of Conservatives and contexts subjected to
study. But it has been a painful feature of modern Conservative studies that
they have been singularly parochial. Wider Western perspectives are not
forthcoming.

The British Conservative Party of these Indian Summer days was
resisting collectivism in a multiplicity of ways. No exhaustive account is
possible but perhaps this book can capture the salient features of the Tory
effort. A list of potential options may serve as an overall framework for the
subsequent analysis. These options were themselves suggested by Conservatives at the time or are within the bounds of practical possibility.
References, however, will be made to more peripheral responses in the
course of this study. These options were not necessarily mutually exclu-

sive and could often be practised at the same time or expressed in the same policy. In analysing the Conservative Party's method it is necessary to grasp that the Right was operating at two interacting levels – the parliamentary and the electoral. It could employ various techniques at Westminster to frustrate the Left and it had to ensure success at the polls so that it would be ascendant in parliament. The electoral level will be considered first. The obvious difficulties in the way of the adoption of certain courses of action will be illuminated. What were the principal options open to the Right in this most important of spheres?

Machiavelli liked to emphasise that the ends often justified the means. What was *The Prince* but an injunction to achievement? Herein lay a possibility for the Conservative Party. Could not the Right make concessions to collectivism in order to frustrate it? The expedient adoption of policies for electoral reasons could attain the power necessary to prevent the enactment of more extreme policies. Opportune behaviour might preserve more of what was valuable than a stance of outright resistance. 'Principled opportunism' or 'pragmatism' are suitable terms for such behaviour and this was an obvious option for the Right. Almost under the heading of principled opportunism, but belonging to a separate category of its own, was the tactic of expressing sympathy for grievances or harsh conditions without proposing any corrective interventionist action. This 'sympathy tactic' involved projecting an image of concern, stressing an affinity with collectivism's intention to raise popular standards of living, and making clear that the Conservatives cared.

But such pragmatism had inherent difficulties for those of a Tory persuasion and these difficulties related to the character of Conservatism itself. Opportunist policies, by their very nature, came up against right-wing beliefs. They involved an unpalatable sacrifice of principle and caused friction with the Tory adherence to the existing order. The sympathy tactic could also offend those who believed that the way things were was valuable. Secondly, there was the question of the rights of the interests which supported the Conservative Party. Left-wing policies, notwithstanding their ultimate Conservative purpose, could cause immediate injury to those institutions, powers and groups which the Right existed to protect. Conservative beliefs and the allied interests were always obstacles in the way of principled opportunism. The practice of expedient reformism had other drawbacks from a Conservative point of view. It could promote a general receptivity and popular taste for collectivist measures and views; accelerate the materialisation of politics; lend legitimacy to the whole leftist approach; and have a ratchet effect on the process of advance towards a collectivist society. Tactical change was not a painless undertaking for Conservatives.

An alternative approach was to concentrate popular attention on issues and subjects distant from the collectivist sphere of concern or of a

character deemed favourable to the Conservative cause. Of necessity this
included the employment of 'diversionary tactics'. Attention could be directed, for example, to Irish, national, military, imperial, religious or
constitutional questions. Related to this was another more intangible
potential course of action. The Conservative Party could have sought to
draw upon, to reinforce and to promote those cultural values within British society which agreed with its outlook and which acted to support what
it regarded as valuable. In short, it could have waged a political *kultur-
kampf.* Lord Willoughby de Broke, who is often dismissed as an ignorant
diehard but in fact was a man of considerable perception, observed in 1912
'to get people to *think* rightly will do much, even more than passing
laws'.[102] A prevention of a further democratisation of the political system
was an obvious step towards further safeguarding the rights of ownership.

'Property owning democracy' is a phrase which belongs to the vocabulary of modern British Conservatism. The Right has well recognised the
value of converting the people into owners and thus producing a general
commitment to the existing order. Could not a wider dispersion of property create Tory bulwarks within society? This 'bulwark strategy' represents an unusual example of Conservative social engineering and could
take many forms. In 1889 Lord Salisbury visited an allotments association
in Nottingham. 'If we look at the history of neighbouring countries', he
reflected, 'we see that the existence of small owners is the strongest
conservative anchor the institutions of the State can have'.[103] British Conservatives were not unaware of Continental tribulations; many a political
observer noted the conservative consequences of a landowning peasantry.
The creation of a sizeable number of owner-occupiers was an obvious
option for bulwark strategists. Profit-sharing was a lesser possibility.

Yet, like principled opportunism, such reformism was bound to come
into conflict with Conservative beliefs and commitments. There was an
inherent structural problem in the bulwark strategy. The acquired property had to come from somewhere and this meant that the existing pattern
of property rights would be disturbed. The Conservatives, however, were
the party of the way things were. Only in the late-twentieth century could
this problem be partly overcome. The question of property was compounded by another: if existing economic arrangements were optimal
would not changes have an adverse effect on prosperity? Thus the actual
implementation of the bulwark strategy would raise a whole host of
objections. Would the existing economic system permit freeholders to be
successful? Would existing property rights be transgressed in the operation? Did the funds exist to bring such owner-occupiers into existence?
These questions, and many others, would inevitably pose themselves to
the Conservative mind. Precisely because of what they were, Tories
entered troubled waters when they considered changing socio-economic
structures.

The French Liberal de Tocqueville has much to tell us about British Toryism. He believed that a major factor in the survival of the nation's aristocracy lay in its readiness to participate in public and social life. 'The English aristocracy has been adroit in more than one respect', he concluded after a visit in the 1830s, 'First of all it has always been involved in public affairs.'[104] In his masterpiece on the origins of the French Revolution he praised the English landowners for fraternising with their tenants.[105] This raised a distinct possibility for the Right in its conflict with the land-reforming Left. Landowners could be made more legitimate in the eyes of the populace by ensuring that they performed their duties and by involving them further in local and national affairs. Yet even this 'legitimation strategy' had its disadvantages. If the landowners were already unpopular or vulnerable could not a raising of their profiles further exacerbate tensions?

There was another approach open to the Conservatives which was altogether more simple – to be unswerving in their Conservatism. The Right could uphold its principles, attack its opponents, and trust to the success of its economic policies. Thus could any opportunism or special strategy be eschewed. The Conservative Party would thus rely on its basic appeal to certain interests and individuals, and seek to gain advantage from the general prosperity and progress which it asserted would result from the existing economic system. In trusting to the purported benevolence of the existing economic system the Conservatives could hope that general growth would take the edge off poverty, reduce social discontent, create greater satisfaction, and spread Conservatism through the populace. Socio-economic inaction could express a very serious Tory strategy. But the Conservatives suffered from an immediate disadavantage when they engaged in the politics of promising prosperity – time. The Left could always promise immediate results. In addition, a multiplicity of lines of attack could be employed against the Left. This 'combative approach' did not create any direct friction with orthodox Tory ideas and attitudes. But the great question was whether it would work in the troubled context of Victorian and Edwardian society. Those who advocated more innovative courses of action would necessarily put up opposition.

What of the parliamentary sphere? The Conservative Party had a permanent majority in the House of Lords. This majority could be used to ward off, modify or reject unwelcome legislation. The upper house was a most powerful weapon. But it was not a weapon which could be wielded with impunity. A too liberal use of its powers might provoke popular and political hostility and lead to attacks upon those powers. When the Conservative Party had a majority in the House of Commons it was in a most favourable position. When it did not have such a majority it could resort to obstructionism – the abandonment of co-operation, attempts at delay, a general attempt to disrupt business. This could hold up the legislative

timetable, tire the government, and raise party morale. In 1902 an
Oxbridge academic, F.Cornford, wrote a small piece on College politics
which involved a perceptive study of conservative method. He emphasised the role of obstructionism in the prevention of change.[106]

Victorian and Edwardian political life was alive with the sound of
pressure groups. They tended to fall into three categories: those which had
a social purpose; those which represented specific interests; and those
which were concerned with political issues. The Tory Party could use such
organisations to promote its cause. These pressure groups could engage in
a whole variety of activities such as the dissemination of Conservative
values; the propagation of Tory ideas; publications and deputations;
campaigns and public meetings; and the submission of advice to the party
managers. The Conservative Party was surrounded with innumerable
such satellites. Their correct use was one of the tasks of Tory politics. They
could be directed against the Left's initiatives.

There was another dimension to Conservative method which bore on
its success. Was the Conservative method of resistance to the Left to be
methodical or haphazard, planned or reactive? This involved the whole direction of the Conservative Party's effort and was thus a question which
concerned leadership. The nature of leadership in the Conservative Party
is a most important subject which would respond well to detailed historical
study. But any analysis of the Conservative Party's handling of its political opponents between 1886 and 1914 must take into account the skill and
efficacy with which the challenge of the Left was managed, and the
requisite needs of the actual organisation of the Conservative Party's
response. The leadership of the party was especially important because
power was concentrated at its apex. When Salisbury, Balfour and Bonar
Law accepted the leadership of the party they assumed much of the
responsibility for the success or failure of Conservatism.

That the options outlined above do not belong to the realm of mere
theory is demonstrated by the activities of Benjamin Disraeli (1804–1881),
the first Earl of Beaconsfield. He anticipated much of the Conservative
Party's subsequent approach during his period of ascendancy in the 1870s.
Disraeli was well aware of the value of a combative approach and
commented that the sentiment of 'that damned Government!'[107] was a
powerful animator of electorates. His social reformism was vague and
imprecise and his social legislation not very substantial, but he passed
moderate interventionist laws and presented himself in a compassionate
light.[108] His early novels and their 'two nations' phrases lent colour to the
picture. Otherwise, Disraelian Conservatism involved a familiar commitment to the constitution, the Empire, the Church, conventional liberties,
the Union with Ireland, national grandeur, property and low government.[109] But the myth had been launched, and Disraeli was for ever after
invoked as an example (or the founder) of an interventionist, collectivist

or 'democratic' strand in Conservatism. But Disraeli, in private, was only too aware of the difficulties of the Tory promotion of reform. He knew, for example, of the dangers of antagonising vested interests. Late in his life he received a visit from a leading British Socialist. 'you think you have some chance of realizing this policy?', Hyndman was asked by Disraeli, 'Not with the Conservative Party, I assure you. The moment you wish to act, you will find yourself beset by a phalanx of great families, men and especially women, who will put you to rout every time'.[110]

IV

TWO CULTURES

Many political ideas have already been analysed. But at times it is necessary to go below the observable first floor to the basement pillars beneath. This is especially true with regard to mentalities. It seems that in this period a distinctive spectrum of political culture began to emerge and to begin its long journey to predominance. It was only natural that the development of a collectivist–individualist divide should have brought with it the establishment of a division of ideas into two camps. Two polarities, although embryonic in form and undeveloped in outline, may be perceived through the dust of party conflict. Each pole was surrounded by a cluster of related ideas which had an internal coherence and were opposed to each other with a remarkable symmetry. Many of their features will be familiar to observers of modern conceptions of civilisation. Indeed, they were differentiated by their views as to how civilisation could be achieved. Berlin's 'two concepts of liberty' here found their home as did many antithetical views of a familiar kind. It appears that the rightward pole was altogether more present and pervasive during these years. Processes on the Left were still working themselves out, but much of the future was already implied. This spectrum is here studied in its nascent form – being present within an actual spectrum bearing certain different features – as well as being presented in cameo shape.

On the Right there was a desire to leave the individual free from government and to stress that national advance could be achieved by correct individual activity within the community at large. 'Negative' liberty and personal duty were the cornerstone concepts of this decided in-dividualism. The cultivation of individual virtue was a necessary goal because only in this way could duties be properly discharged – hence, in part, the ideal of the 'gentleman'. Such voluntaryism looked to the proper exercise of freedom of will in all spheres. 'Nation' was a much more attractive concept than 'society'. The emphasis was upon belonging (and the actual state of belonging was of crucial importance) to an integrated and integrating nation composed of individuals aware of their private and public duties; motivated by a strong sense of citizenship; and bound together by special customs, traditions, and mutual obligations. Thus the

Conservatives favoured an organic evolution of society – a famous idea that went back to Edmund Burke and beyond. This communitarianism (which often led left-wing ideas to be condemned as foreign) admired patriotic cohesion, opposed class sectionalism, and led off into a nationalist promotion of British ways in the world. Underpinning this individualism, voluntaryism and communitarianism were the accompanying beliefs that man had free will, a spiritual dimension, and a social nature.

On the Left there was a tendency to see man as an outcome of societal forces, to conceive of society in terms of conflicting socio-economic groupings, to emphasise the role of material wealth in human fulfilment and motivation, and to stress the need for the individual to aid others by supporting statist action. Such materialism, determinism and classism gave rise to a desire to liberate the individual from economic conditions and to restructure the material bases of society. Citizens would achieve 'positive' liberty through government action. Much was implied in these tenets. The ground was prepared for relativism. Individuals were seen in relation to their class or their society. Egalitarianism was supported by a tendency to evaluate economic status as the outcome of external conditions and not internal ability. DeChristianisation was encouraged – man was to look to the state, not God, for immediate improvement. If there was an affinity between Left and Right it lay in a condemnation of the abuses of economic power. But whereas the Right looked to the influence of moral values the Left advocated a change of system. Different remedies were supplied to situations which aroused similar ire. Self-regulation confronted government-regulation. The habit of recording complaints voiced by both radicals and conservatives, without observing their divergent solutions, has done much to promote the false idea of frequent affinity.

Which of these apparent cultures was to triumph in the long run and what would be the consequences of victory? This was a question which constantly animated Tory minds. A further illumination of the character of Conservative culture can be found in repeated right-wing warnings as to what a left-wing future would involve. Lord Salisbury, in his anticipation of disintegration, did not elaborate upon the cultural details of the processes of decay, although he used the significant phrase 'common sentiments and mutual sympathies which combine classes into a patriotic State'. But the central idea amounted to a Conservative notion which has had a real run for its money: the Left would weaken bonds between individuals by eroding the values and habits which produced social cohesion; a common sense of belonging would be undermined by the destruction of the cultural apparatus of integration. The owner of Hatfield House believed that desocialisation was on the cards. He was neither the first nor the last to make this recurrent Conservative prediction. 'Disintegration', 'eroding the fabric of society', 'destroying the British way of life', 'atomisation' – the notion has given rise to its own vocabulary. The apprehension was powerfully rooted in Tory thinking, which it thereby served to illuminate, and brought out the extent to which the Conservative Party laid great stress on the personal and the face-to-face, rather than on the impersonal and the societal. In the right-wing schema collectivism not only involved disintegrating ideas but diverted attention away from those moral tenets designed to guide the character of individual relationships. In a startling historical symmetry, Tory predictions about desocialisation in the late-nineteenth century have come to be matched by Tory observations in the late-twentieth century.

☆

As Arthur James Balfour predicted in 1885, democratic advance was followed by new challenges to property, and especially to property in land and buildings. A vertically structured and naturally disciplined Conservative Party, which was bound up with the landed interest, stood on the side of the way things were. The great question thus presents itself: how did the Tories seek to achieve their aims? In the 1950s an obscure Italian nobleman published a novel about a Sicilian aristocratic family which underwent the tribulations of the Italian Risorgimento. Artists are often able to achieve perceptions not available to academic theoreticians. Amidst the author's exemplary prose one can detect the presentation of a distinct model of Conservative method. Prince Lampedusa discerned how Conservatives make concessions in order to achieve the maximum degree of conservation and for this he employs the image of swallowing toads. But in this process Conservatives not only offend their more conservative associates but end up by changing themselves. 'If we want things to stay as they are, things will have to change' – such is the motif of *Il Gatto-pardo*.[111] Did the Tory Party make concessions in the face of pressure and in so doing change both itself and the civilisation it was defending? Was its communitarian, voluntaryist and individualist culture subjected to potentially fatal compromises? To what extent did the Conservative Party come to be a component part of profound historical changes of which it had only an imperfect cognisance? The analysis begins at the beginning – the twenty years of increasing political extremism which followed the Third Reform Act of 1884.

Two

Irruption and Reaction

'I confess to much doubt', Salisbury was told by a worried Hicks Beach in 1886, 'whether the country *can* be governed nowadays, by persons holding opinions which you and I should call even moderately conservative'.[1] Beach recognised that the dynamics of politics threatened the Tory cause. The Liberal Party radicalised in the late-Victorian period and came to lay increasing emphasis on material issues in politics. The land question was central to this process and Liberalism's proposals in this department of national politics made up the substance of its collectivist initiative. Linked to this land reformism was an attempt to further weaken the power of the landed interest at the level of both national and local government. At the same time British Radicalism sought to render the aristocracy and gentry less legitimate in the eyes of the people. Anti-landlordism was increasingly the order of the day. Profound cultural and institutional reform was being projected. The radical events of the early 1880s set the trend for this pattern and gave it impetus. Notwithstanding a moderate Gladstonian leadership, the essential dynamic was clear. The governmental proposals of 1906–1914 were a natural outcome of the *fin de siècle* Liberal Party. Organised Labour came to underpin the Liberal effort but broadened the province of intended reform. Urban local authorities made their own contribution to the threat. What were the chief features of the left-wing challenge?

I

British Radicalism (at least in its domestic preoccupations) presented its essential characteristics in the great 'Unauthorised Campaign' of 1885. This initiative combined a conspicuous use of modern political methods with a strong stress on economic issues. To many observers it expressed the menace of Democracy. It was launched by a group of Radicals on the Left of the Liberal Party led by Joseph Chamberlain.[2] Chamberlain (1836–1914) became one of the great figures of late-Victorian and Edwardian politics, and in his public advocacy of the state as a means to advance civilisation he was a true precursor of the twentieth century. In his promotion of mass organisation and advanced techniques of electoral communication he also led where others were to follow. To a certain extent he resembled his contemporary Karl Lueger, the reforming Mayor of Vienna. Chamberlain always had strong nationalist and imperialist leanings, and in these early days he expressed a kind of National Radicalism.

Chamberlain made a fortune as a screw manufacturer in Birmingham and then proceeded to acquire a national reputation as the city's reforming mayor. He rose quickly in Liberal politics and became President of the Local Government Board in Gladstone's second ministry. Chamberlain was a Unitarian who had three wives, two famous sons, vaulting ambition, and a formidable bent for conspiracy. He always wore a lily in his buttonhole, and at one time possessed thirty-seven greenhouses to grow the flower. Tenderness towards plants was not matched by tenderness towards fellow politicians. Chamberlain was known for his ferocity (especially towards former colleagues), and his motto was 'never explain and never complain'. The storm of dust which surrounded his progress does not, however, make him unfathomable. He switched allegiance from Left to Right during his career but throughout his political life he emphasised material issues. Slogans such as 'three acres and a cow' and 'tariff reform means work for all' symbolised the link which connected the early Radical Joe with the later colleague of the Hotel Cecil. They were also expressions of his consistent tactical conservatism. The importance of Joseph Chamberlain is reflected in a growing number of biographies.[3] Part of his significance lies in his sustained attempt to reconcile the material demands of an evolving democracy with the defensive reflexes of an entrenched social order. Whether it is recognised or not, Chamberlain occupies an important position in the anti-collectivist pantheon.

The Radical Campaign of 1885 combined an attack on aristocratic power with a social programme dominated by land reform. Was not the man from Birmingham the 'Radical Agitator' of Salisbury's prophecy? Chamberlain condemned the political predominance of the landed interest and pointedly praised the recent Franchise Act: 'for the first time the toilers and spinners will have a majority of votes, and the control, if they desire it, of the Government of the country'.[4] The demand for a reform of county government amounted to an attack on the local powers of the squirearchy. Anti-landlord sentiments were ever present. Overshadowing the calls for free elementary education, graduated taxation, and a free breakfast table (the absence of indirect taxes on principal items of food), were the policies relating to real property.

'Well, what is the Radical programme?', asked Chamberlain in one of his great platform speeches, 'The most important of these proposals refer to the question of the land.'[5] At Ipswich he declared that 'The question of land reform is really urgent at the present time.'[6] 'The evils of the present land system are apparent to everybody',[7] he observed at Hull. A collection of subsequently familiar policies were inscribed on the Radical banner. The taxation of land values, the rating of vacant property, levies on mineral

royalties, changes in the death duties on realty, expanded tenant rights, the
local provision of small holdings, allotments and artisans' dwellings by
means of compulsory purchase, alterations in the laws relating to transfer,
settlement and primogeniture – all these, and others, made up the Radical
Programme.[8] It is often suggested that Victorian Radicalism failed to
evolve and was eclipsed by the emergence of Socialism and its Edwardian
Liberal imitator. One historian suggests that the programme's ideas and
policies ran into the historical sands.[9] But Lloyd George's land campaign
of 1913–1914 brought much of Chamberlain's radical campaign of 1885
to telling fruition.

The Chamberlainite Radicals were drawing on a long left-wing tradition of anti-landlord reform most recently represented by O'Connor's land
company, the Anti-Corn Law League, and the demand for 'Free Trade in
Land'. Chamberlain maintained that he was 'completing the land programme of Cobden and Bright'.[10] But these advanced Liberals were also
building upon more recent developments on the radical wing of national
politics. The publication of *The Bitter Cry of Outcast London* in 1883
served to stimulate interest in urban housing reform. Written by a London
Congregationalist minister, the pamphlet received extensive publicity and
drew attention to the housing conditions of the poor in the great cities.[11]
Reformers, in turn, used it to advance their cause.[12] One year later the
Leaseholds Enfranchisement Association was formed. The LEA drew upon
the resentments of town tenants, and especially retailers, to promote the
policy of giving occupiers the compulsory right to purchase their free-
holds. Henry Broadhurst MP was the association's parliamentary champion, and leasehold enfranchisement (LE) was its watchword.[13] Yet these
agitations were eclipsed by events of far greater importance to the history
of the Liberal Party – the establishment of pressure groups committed to
the taxation or nationalisation of land.

Henry George (1839–1897), the American political economist who
had previously been a gold prospector, sailor, cowboy and campaigner for
the Democratic Party, was a leading figure in the Liberal land question. He
owed this to his book *Progress and Poverty* which was published in
America in 1879 and in England two years later. It was followed up by
speaking tours in Britain and strife-torn Ireland and by the establishment
of the Land Reform Union in London in 1883.[14] George played an
important part in the growth of collectivism because he provided a
theoretical underpinning for Radical anti-landlordism. In 1897 another
left-wing economist, J.A.Hobson, recorded that George had 'exercised a
more directly powerful formative and educative influence over English
radicalism of the last fifteen years than any other man'.[15] This was a tribute
indeed, and calls for some explanation.

In many respects Henry George paralleled Marx and rendered similar
services to the British Radicals that his counterpart rendered to the British

Socialists. Without sharing the same intelligence, the two thinkers never-thless had a certain set of perspectives in common. Like Marx, George detected an economic system at the centre of society and proffered a materialist method of advance. Just as the scholar of the British Museum undermined the capitalist's claim to his property so the sage of San Francisco challenged the right of the landowner to his land. Both alike stressed that existing economic procedures were retrogressive, and fo-cused attention on conflicts between classes over wealth. Both Marx and George form a part of Great Britain's inheritance of collectivist thought. The message of *Progress and Poverty* was simple: the private owners of land drew off wealth from the community as an economy expanded and increased the value of land. George argued that landowners appropriated land values created not by actual improvements but by the presence of the population. He proposed a 'Single Tax' on this 'unearned increment' of land to pay for all government expenditure, and launched the slogan 'The Taxation of Land Values'. George thus appealed to the Radical precept that the land system was unjust and inefficient, and gave theoretical exposition to the assumption that reform was both morally right and economically productive. A simple, and simplistic, cure was being offer-ed for the nation's ills. Here was an early example of an unsophisticated collectivism well tailored to the needs and desires of the dominant Victorian brand of that creed:

> It is seen that private property in land, instead of being necessary to its improvement and use, stands in the way of improvement and use, and entails an enormous waste of productive forces; that the recog-nition of the common right to land involves no shock or dispossess-ion, but is to be reached by the simple and easy method of abolishing all taxation save that upon land-values...A consideration of the effect of the change proposed then shows that it would enormously increase production; would secure justice in distribu-tion; would benefit all classes; and would make possible an advance to a higher and nobler civilisation.[16]

George's influence was most obviously manifested in the English, Scottish and Welsh Land Restoration Leagues which followed on from the Land Reform Union. Their very names were provocative and to Tory minds resonant with menace – property was to be restored to its proper popular owners. The Land Restoration Leagues propagated George's ideas, policies and perspectives, and came to achieve prominent positions in the Liberal world. These organisations were noted for their energy and drive, and were motivated by a mixture of idealism, faith and hatred.[17] In the 1890s these Georgeites toured the countryside in coloured vans spreading the true gospel.[18] 'For some years an extreme socialistic section of the Radicals have been carrying on a sort of anti-landlord campaign in the villages', reported a Conservative publication in 1896, 'by means of peripatetic orators, who live in vans, circulate literature, and deliver lectures and speeches as they travel about the country'.[19] Here one is dealing with far more than marginal faddists. The English league is said to have become by 1905 'one of the strongest pressure groups in the country'.[20] By 1911 these societies could claim the allegiance of over 170 Liberal and Labour MPS.[21] Yet Liberalism more generally seems to have come under George's influence, a fact most indicative of the true nature of the late-Victorian and Edwardian Liberal Party.

Altogether less important was Alfred Russel Wallace (1823–1913). Wallace was a distinguished naturalist and explorer who had presented a joint paper with Darwin in 1858 which anticipated much of *The Origin of Species*. Wallace was also interested in the evolution of societies. In 1881 he founded the Land Nationalisation Society (LNS) and in 1882 he published its bible – *Land Nationalisation*. The LNS, under Wallace's direction, was far weaker than its Georgeite counterparts, and advocated a complicated plan of part state, part individual, ownership.[22] There was further radical activity out on the margins of national politics. In 1881 the Democratic Federation came into being; in 1883 it transmuted into the Social Democratic Federation.[23] In 1884 the Fabian Society began its long career as the flagship of the Socialist intelligentsia.[24] These early Socialist organisations were much concerned with land reform and overlapped with the Radical societies. Thus was anticipated the single greatest bond which linked New Liberalism to new Labour.

The history of the National Liberal Federation (NLF), the mass party organisation, exemplified the increasing collectivist tendencies of late-Victorian Liberalism. It also brought out the major concerns of those tendencies. The secession of the Liberal Unionists over Home Rule in 1886 aided the leftward drift of the Liberal Party. The existence of the Liberal Unionist Party was a powerful instrument in the polarisation of politics. From the 1880s to the 1900s the NLF's programme of social reform centred around land reform. The guiding idea was that state intervention in the economic process would be conducive to national progress. Accompanying this programme were sustained anti-landord polemic and a series of measures designed to weaken the power of the landed interest in the political system. Essential preoccupations were apparent from the outset. In 1881 the NLF called for increased rights for tenants, improved access to land, and measures to facilitate the sale and transfer of land.[25] In 1885 the federation's social platform consisted of free elementary education, leasehold enfranchisement, and similar policies to those of 1881.[26] Chamberlain had had a major hand in the promotion of the NLF and it was reciprocating by supporting his policies.

The late 1880s witnessed a further radicalisation. In 1884 Salisbury gave his portrait of the Liberal Party: 'An inclined plane leads us from the position of Lord Hartington to the position of Mr. Chamberlain (hisses),

and on...to the depths over which Mr. Henry George rules supreme.'[27] As
the years progressed the depths came increasingly to the surface. At the
annual conference of 1888 a number of measures were added to the
previous demands: the division of rates between owners and occupiers, the
equalisation of the death duties on real and personal property, the taxation
of land values, ground rents, and mineral royalties, housing reform, and
alterations in the Factory Acts.[28] Temperance reform had already been
proposed;[29] further education reform was requested in 1889.[30] In 1891 the
NLF adopted the famous 'Newcastle Programme'. It was much promoted
by Liberal candidates during the 1892 general election.[31] The conference
endorsed Irish home rule, Welsh disestablishment, free elementary education, various constitutional changes, and a reform of the powers of local
authorities in relation to small holdings, allotments, dwellings, village
halls, and other such provisions. It then passed an omnibus resolution
amidst general acclamation. This may be reproduced here because it well
illustrates the interests and emphases of the mass party. Land was the
dominant concern:

'Omnibus' Resolution...
'A thorough Reform of the Land Laws, such as will secure –
'(a) The repeal of the Laws of Primogeniture and Entail;
'(b) Freedom of Sale and Transfer;
'(c) The just taxation of Land Values and ground rents;
'(d) Compensation, to town and country tenants, for both disturbance and improvement, together with a simplified process for
obtaining such compensation;
'(e) The Enfranchisement of Leaseholds;
'The direct popular veto on the Liquor traffic;
'The Disestablishment and Disendowment of the Established Church
in Scotland;
'The Equalisation of the Death Duties upon real and personal
property;
'The just division of rates between owner and occupier;
'The Taxation of Mining Royalties;
'A "Free Breakfast Table";
'The extension of the Factory Acts; and
'The "mending or ending" of the House of Lords'.[32]

Orientations did not change between 1892 and 1906. Land reform
resolutions were joined by demands for employers' liability and alterations in the legislation relating to factories, workshops and mines 'as the
growing social needs of the community demand'.[33] The collectivist spirit
was ever present, but once again was chiefly to be found in a familiar
province: 'That this Council, holding that the land should be utilised for
the benefit of the community as a whole...'.[34] In 1904 the Liberal Party was
on the threshold of office and the following resolution was passed: 'That

this Council again calls attention to the urgent necessity of Social Reform, particularly in connection with the Housing Question, the reform of the Land Laws, the Equality of Rating, and kindred matters.'[35] By late 1905 the long period of Unionist ascendancy was over and the leader of the Liberal Party was installed in Downing Street. A general election loomed: 'this Council regards a right settlement of the questions of ownership, transfer, tenure, and taxation of land as the indispensable condition of any satisfactory scheme of social reform...'.[36]

But the party activists were aiming at far more than the pockets and property of the landed aristocracy and gentry. They were seeking to reduce their political power. There was nothing new about this dual attack. Had not Cobden and Bright linked the repeal of the corn laws to constitutional reform? The Newcastle Programme was a good example of the approach. The House of Lords, which was the most conspicuous institution of the landed interest and served to defend its rights, was to be reformed or extinguished. Registration reform was a call to further democratise the House of Commons. This would involve further pressure on the landed classes by the masses, or so it could be supposed. Longstanding calls for reform of rural local government had been met by the Tory legislation of 1888. But continued attacks on the country landowner were expressed in the calls for parish and district councils. The recently created London County Council was proving a repository of advanced Radicalism, and the demands for extending its powers constituted a further assault on the metropolitan ground landlords.[37]

Running through the pressure groups and the mass party was a sustained measure of anti-landlord propaganda. The publications of the Liberal Publication Department in the 1890s may be taken as representative. The behaviour of the Tories towards the 1894 budget provoked the charge that landlords had been until recently the owners of the House of Commons and were still striving to assert their control.[38] The treatment of the Employers' Liability Bill and other measures by the House of Lords produced a leaflet menacingly entitled *The Peers & the People*.[39] The 1896 Agricultural Rates Act provoked especial anti-landlord fury and even the House of Lords' amendments to the Light Railways' Bill brought forth the blazoned *The Landlords' Government*.[40] In 1899 George Whiteley crossed the floor. A leaflet entitled *How I Became a Liberal* reported his judgement that the Conservative Party was 'dominated by landlord ideas'.[41] In 1900 the department produced its summarising and critical *Five Years of Tory Government 1895–1900*. Major items of legislation were denigrated as mere doles to landlords.[42]

By 1905 the Liberal Party had arrived at a destination far removed from the old Liberalism of 1885. In December 1905 Campbell-Bannerman (1836–1908), the new Liberal Prime Minister, unveiled the intentions of the government in a great election speech at the Albert Hall. The domestic programme consisted of 'retrenchment', 'self-government', and 'constructive social reform'. Of what did the last consist? Far above trade union reform and Chinese labour in importance was the land question. Land reform was now at the heart of the official programme and constituted the core of Liberal reformism. The Prime Minister, himself a Scottish landowner, pleased the party faithful with his attacks on those in possession of the countryside. Campbell-Bannerman was drawn towards the 'efficiency and waste' line of attack:

> There may be, and I believe there are, fresh sources of taxation to be tapped. We may derive something from the land (cheers)...We desire to develop our undeveloped estates in this country (cheers) – to colonize our own country (cheers) – to give the farmer greater freedom and greater security in the exercise of his business; to secure a home and a career for the labourer who is now in many cases cut off from the soil. We wish to make the land less of a pleasure-ground for the rich (loud cheers) and more of a treasure-house for the nation. (Renewed cheers)...We can strengthen the hand of the municipalities by reforming the land system and the rating system, in which I include the imposition of a rate on ground values. (Prolonged cheers). We can make it easier for them to relieve the congestion of the centre and to promote orderly and healthy development on the outskirts'.[43]

One sample of election addresses shows that 68% of Liberal candidates in England mentioned land reform, 52% referred to land value taxation, and 36% advocated housing reform.[44] Another member of the Liberal hierarchy, Lord Crewe, wrote in November 1905: 'More than ever before the Liberal Party is on its trial as an engine for securing social reforms – taxation, land, housing etc.'[45] His Liberal lordship was not to be disappointed.

Labour also provoked Conservative fears for the future. As the twentieth century approached, trade union activity and membership increased. The more militant 'New Unionism' which emerged in the late 1880s gave radical impetus to organisation and assertion. In 1893 and 1894 the Trades Union Congress resolved to support only parliamentary candidates who were in favour of the 'collective ownership and control of the means of production, distribution, and exchange'.[46] The Independent Labour Party came into being in 1893 and campaigned in similar vein.[47] The Social Democratic Federation and the Fabians, although 'pitifully weak',[48] continued their activities out on the fringes of politics. In 1900 the TUC combined with the left-wing societies and created the Labour Representation Comittee (LRC) to give separate parliamentary representation to Labour.[49] The manifestos of the LRC were not welcome to the right-wing mind. That of 1900 made clear that 'Democratic State' control of the economy 'in the interests of the entire Community' was the ultimate

Labour goal.[50] The 1906 manifesto was a powerful expression of materialist collectivism.[51] Land reform was a prominent plank in both platforms. New Labour was lining up behind New Liberalism to pose a real challenge to the forces of Conservatism.

Statism is usually associated with central action, but during this period it found local expression. 'Municipal Socialism' was one of the political catchphrases of these decades. Reformers had a powerful local government orientation. Chamberlain's reforming mayoralty of Birmingham had done much to associate left-wing ideas with town council activity. The nation's municipal authorities made up the other great force for interventionism. The Association of Municipal Corporations (AMC) had been established in 1872 and by the Edwardian period it claimed the allegiance of nearly every urban council in the land. From 1890 to 1906 the president of the AMC was Sir A.K.Rollit MP (1842–1922). He proved himself a most articulate champion of the municipal campaign to expand the role and duties of urban local authorities. From one point of view this campaign anticipated the collectivist future; but from another it was the final flowering of the Victorian belief in civic initiative. The municipal effort, which gathered strength in the 1890s, fell uneasily between past and future conceptions of government. This   fundamental ambivalence was one factor behind the municipal campaign's failure in the face of Edwardian Liberal centralism.

'The sphere of municipal work has been extended, is extending, and will vastly extend, in my opinion, in the near future', Rollit told the AMC's general meeting of 1895. During the same speech he staked the localist claim to the future: 'There are some of us who thus look through the widest local government, through decentralisation and devolution, to the solution of grave imperial questions.'[52] Hence town councils were active in the field of water, gas, electricity, telephone and tramway supply. They also sought new sources of funding for their expanding services, as well as legislation to permit the performance of new duties. One potential source of funds was central government grants. In 1897, for example, Rollit emphasised the 'need of a further government contribution in aid of local taxation'.[53] Another such source was local property. Thus did the AMC come to demand the right to levy a special rate on the value of sites. In 1898 it called for some means 'by which the owners of land (whether occupied or vacant) shall contribute directly to the local revenue'.[54] This linked up with Liberal developments and the Radical land reformers formed strong connections with the municipal campaign. London and Glasgow were especial centres of town hall radicalism.[55] Yet another source of funding was borrowing. The Conservative Party's *The Unionist Record* reported that local debt in England and Wales rose from about £181.5 million in 1886 to around £243 million in 1896 and reached some £438 million in the United Kingdom in 1903.[56] 'The indebtedness of local authorities is rapidly increasing', lamented the chairman of the Industrial Freedom League, a pressure group set up to combat the AMC's aspirations, 'and they tend more and more to launch out into commercial undertakings'.[57]

Gladstonian leadership exercised a brake on the advance of Radicalism. William Gladstone's hostility to what he called 'construction',[58] and his warning in 1893 as to the 'perilous course' of 'socialistic legislation',[59] were linked to a marked opposition to the cause of land reform. In 1885, at the height of the Unauthorised Campaign, he wrote that it was a 'very high duty to labour for the conservation of estates, and the permanence of the families in possession of them'.[60] The Grand Old Man was himself a country landowner and much devoted to the rural social order. With his devotion to traditional courtesy, Gladstone in his personal life often had the Tory touch. Balfour remembered visiting him at Hawarden and shocking the People's William by arriving from the station on a bicycle. Balfour adjudged that Gladstone was 'in everything except essentials, a tremendous old Tory', noting a particular sensitivy 'in the matter of dignities'.[61] But Balfour missed the point – Gladstone's courtesy was a natural part of a conspicuous wider conservatism.

The leader of the Liberal Party lacked sympathy for the Newcastle Programme,[62] and roundly condemned the doctrines of Henry George in a parliamentary debate of 1891.[63] Yet Gladstone's habitual championing of the masses against the classes, and his oft-repeated idea that the people were, in the words of one historian, 'the repository of true political virtue',[64] appealed to Radicalism's hostility to the landed interest. By this route, indeed, could a partisan Radical voter, as J. Vincent puts it, find 'great vicarious excitement in identifying himself with an attack upon authority'.[65] Gladstone's moral populism was a powerful bridge between himself and his land reforming followers. His emphasis on the manly individual conscience agreed very well with the Radical opposition to personal subordination to landed proprietors. 'Which will you be', a party leaflet asked in 1910, 'Peers' Men or Free Men'.[66] The ideas of the Hawarden landowner, by roundabout lines of connection, had a striking concordance with the anti-landlordism of his more extreme supporters. In this, as in so many other respects, Gladstonian Liberalism was a harmonious amalgam of seeming opposites.

Lord Rosebery (1847–1929), who succeeded the People's William as Prime Minister, was both a landowner and the owner of a successful stable. He also was out of sympathy with collectivist developments and shared Gladstone's hostility to the Newcastle Programme.[67] It is significant that he too had a pronounced belief in the value of good manners.[68] Rosebery was opposed to the most Radical measure of his administration – Harcourt's plan to equalise the death duties on realty and personalty. The Chancellor of the Exchequer was 'much amused at the high Tory line taken by R'.[69] '"The horizontal division of parties" was certain to come as a consequence of household suffrage', Harcourt wrote in reply to his chief's remonstrances, 'The thin end of the wedge was inserted, and the cleavage is expanding more and more every day.'[70] Rosebery's drift away from the party he had previously led was powerfully animated by his opposition to some of the central intentions of New Liberalism. In 1909, in a much publicised speech, he roundly criticised the social programme of the Liberal government and singled out Lloyd George's land taxes for especial opprobrium: 'I think my friends are moving on the path that leads to Socialism.'[71] Lord Rosebery became a neglected relic of the pre-collectivist Victorian Left – an unhappy monument to a creed eclipsed by telling transformations.

The underlying developments on the Left of national politics were clear. Conservative commentary did its duty by reflecting this radicalisation. Was this not a direct outcome of extending democracy? W. H. Smith MP (1825–1891), the Leader of the House of Commons in Salisbury's first great ministry, certainly thought so. 'The extension of the suffrage has brought us face to face with the most grave possibilities', he told the Prime Minister in 1889,

> It has made the extreme Radicals masters of the Liberal party, and men support a policy now from which they would have shrunk with horror ten years ago...Men who are strictly honest in their transactions with their neighbours have come to regard Parliament as an instrument by which a transfer of rights and property may equitably be made from the few to the many.[72]

Thus did one leading Tory believe that collectivism was already changing attitudes within the community. The owner of Hatfield House was in pessimistic agreement. After all, was this not what he had predicted in his famous essay on disintegration? 'I agree in all you say as to the gravity of our present condition', replied Salisbury,

> We are in a state of bloodless civil war. No common principles, no respect for common institutions or traditions, unite the various groups of politicians who are struggling for power. To loot somebody or something is the common object under a thick varnish of pious phrases.[73]

How did the forces of the Right try to win this war?

II

The Conservatives did little to advance the collectivist locomotive and thereby illuminated their purpose in politics. By 1905 national insurance, old age pensions, land value taxation, central grants for housing, and statutory minimum wages were still absent from the statute book. Conservative non-interventionism was powerfully expressed in the Right's attitude towards   budgets. Collectivism and finance were bound up; taxation and expenditure were indissolubly linked with state growth. The party's fiscal policy was a direct outcome of the Conserative vision of society and an integral feature of the Right's approach to government. The fiscal question was at the heart of the struggle between the Left and the Right because it bore upon the whole question of the social distribution of wealth. The Conservative Party sought to prevent intrusion into property rights by means of taxation and to hold back the proportion of the national product appropriated by the state. 'This question of the incidence of taxation is in truth the vital question of modern politics. It is the field upon which the contending classes of this generation will do battle', Lord Salisbury had predicted in the 1860s, 'the taxation of the State is an engine which may be used almost without limit for the transfer of property from one class to another.'[74] 'One of the greatest dangers of the future', echoed Bonar Law in 1912, 'is Socialism carried into operation by means of Budgets'.[75] Yet the Tory task was not easy and involved a multitude of dilemmas.

The years 1886–1892 were a period of relative plain sailing for the Conservatives in their administration of central finance. In 1895 the party claimed that under Salisbury national expenditure per head, the national debt, and the income tax had all been reduced.[76] The Tory aim was to keep funds in the economy, to engender a sense of confidence and security, and to contain expenditure. There was no move to embrace the Radical proposals to tax land, to graduate the income tax, or to reform the death duties. From 1895 to 1905 the Tories ran into heavy weather. National expenditure rose rapidly, pushed up by defence costs and the expanding population. The Boer war was an especial burden. Both the national debt and the level of income taxation climbed significantly.[77] This was not welcomed by the Conservative mind. 'I grieve that so much of the resources of this country', said Salisbury in 1895, 'must be spent on what is essentially an unprofitable expenditure'.[78] There was room for a little expediency – the government overruled many of its backbenchers and refused to repeal Harcourt's raised death duties.[79] They were proving a productive source of revenue at a time of swiftly mounting costs.[80]

Internal documents reveal a Unionist leadership striving to halt the upward trend. Sir Michael Hicks Beach (1837–1916), a Gloucestershire landowner, was at the Exchequer from 1895 to 1902. In 1901 he circulated a memorandum to his Cabinet colleagues which stressed that a 'real check'[81] had to be placed upon the growth in expenditure. Salisbury, shortly before his death, declared: 'some very drastic reforms will be necesary in order to bring back our finance into a healthy state'.[82] The 1900 Queen's Speech declared that the time was 'not propitious for any domestic reforms which involve a large expenditure'.[83] Charles Ritchie (1836–1906) succeeded Hicks Beach and pleaded for retrenchment in a detailed Cabinet memorandum.[84] 'The situation for the Chancellor of the Exchequer is undoubtedly most difficult', Hamilton advised the ministry in 1904, 'Indeed, I do not remember a more difficult one.'[85] Austen

Chamberlain (1863–1937) became Balfour's third Chancellor in the same year. 'A *good* Budget I believe to be out of the question', he wrote in November, 'All my efforts are required to avoid fresh taxation.'[86] But the Right would not adopt Radical or Socialist solutions.

The Conservative Party's approach to local finance was similarly conservative, but here also there were unwelcome factors at work. British government was still very much local government. Town and country councils outstripped Whitehall in levels of spending.[87] Party policy towards the localities, therefore, plays a large part in the whole story of state growth. The background requires illumination. In late-Victorian and Edwardian England there was a multiplicity of local authorities. Legislation in 1888 and 1894 had created county councils, county boroughs, urban district councils, rural district councils and parish councils. These were on top of the boards of guardians and school boards. These last were abolished in 1902. London had its own peculiarities. Education, police, relief of the poor, roads and a mass of services usually placed under the heading of 'public health' were variously performed by these bodies.[88] This Joseph's coat system required money. Where did it come from?

Local government in England and Wales derived its funds from two chief sources: from Whitehall in the form of grants and from the local population in the form of rates. The grants system had a chequered history between 1870 and 1914. The Local Government Act of 1888 established the 'assigned revenues system' by which certain central revenues were allocated to the local authorities through a 'local taxation account'. From 1888 to 1906 certain additional revenues were made available to the account and separate grants were given to relieve the local taxation burden on agricultural land and tithe receipts. The assigned revenues system was modified by the Liberals after 1906 and the Exchequer came to pay fixed grants into the local taxation account in lieu of many of the assigned revenues. The local taxation base was a curious historical inheritance. Rates were levied on the rateable value of occupied real property. Local assessment committees established an 'annual value', the property's hypothetical yearly market rent, to estimate the rateable value. In the case of many low value tenanted properties the rates were paid by the landlord, a practice known as 'compounding', but on the whole it was the occupier who was the ratepayer. As the Great War drew nearer local government approached crisis – rate demands rose steeply and central grants failed to keep pace with increasing local costs and responsibilities.[89]

In this neglected area of Victorian and Edwardian concern the Conservative Party was the professed party of reform. In order to do justice to Tory attitudes to property and to state expansion, and to give a background to the shifts and turns of party policy, it is necessary to digress at length into the Conservative approach to local taxation. The Right declared that the local taxation system was unjust to real property. Conservatives constantly expressed their desire to see the system changed. The 1885 *Campaign Notes* declared: 'the existing local taxation is anomolous and unfair in its incidence'.[90] In the Tory scheme of things the actual incidence of the local taxes diverged from their formal incidence. By means of the rent mechanism it was said that both landlords and tenants came to pay the rate, though their respective portions varied according to the character of the property. The Right had no distinctive local taxation doctrine, although it had a collection of arguments and remedies which made up a discernable approach. Attitudes towards the local taxation question made up one of the chief lines of demarcation between Liberals and Conservatives. Rates must be rated highly on the contemporary scale of political priorities. What was the Tory perspective?

Four arguments were used to sustain the charge that the rating system was an inequitable burden upon land and buildings. The first argument was simple and straightforward. Conservatives argued that it was an unfair act of discrimination between two classes of property to place local taxes upon real property (land, buildings, and structures) but not upon personal property (income, stock-in-trade, securities and business capital). The second rested upon the Conservative fiscal principle of 'ability to pay'. This principle laid down that a tax should be levied in proportion to an individual's material means – the greater the capacity the greater the appropriate burden. Rateable value was deemed to be an inadequate indicator of ability to pay. A poor shopkeeper, for example, could occupy business premises of equal rateable value to the residence of a very rich man. The third argument maintained that certain locally provided services – education, relief of the poor, main roads, and police – were of benefit to the whole nation and were therefore the fiscal responsibility of the national government. These services were said to be 'national' in character and the cost of their provision was alleged to be an 'onerous' burden upon the ratepayers. The fourth was the most complicated. It began with the assertion that local property ought to be taxed to provide for those services from which it benefited but not for those from which it did not benefit. Real property, therefore, was said to suffer from a double injustice: it had to pay for those services which were beneficial to local personal property, and it had to pay for those 'national' services (relief of the poor, police, education and main roads) which benefited neither forms of property.

Four main remedies, sometimes suggested in conjunction, emerged from these four arguments: a local income tax to pay for locally provided services; a national income tax to pay for the locally provided 'national' services; the subjection of local personal property, in addition to local real property, to local taxation; and the provision of central grants to pay for the locally provided 'national' services. Most Conservatives probably agreed on what constituted the ideal solution: the subjection of local personal property, in addition to local real property, to local taxation for the local 'beneficial' services; and the transfer of the cost of the locally administered 'national' services from the local authorities to the national Exchequer. But such a comprehensive scheme was not possible in the imperfect Victorian and Edwardian world. The Conservatives fell back on a compromise – a readjustment of the burdens between real and personal property and between local rates and national taxes. Thus emerged the official local taxation policy of the Conservative Party: national subventions to the local authorities in aid of the locally provided 'national' services. The attractions from a Tory perspective were simple. Central government thus assumed more of its proper fiscal obligations; the incidence of national taxes meant that personal property was making a fairer contribution; real property was not paying so much for services from which it did not benefit; and because national taxes were levied more in accordance with the principle of ability to pay the whole system of local finance was being made more equitable.[91]

This policy of central grants in aid of national services had obvious electoral possibilities. It could appeal to ratepayers in general and a number of special interests in particular – farmers, shopkeepers, landlords, landowners, manufacturers, merchants and professional men. But it was not so easy to put into practice. It required national funds and this bore on the entire fiscal question. Furthermore, if only a partial scheme of relief was possible another difficulty arose: political decisions had to be made as to the allocation of the grants. Finally, there was the question of the control of expenditure. National grants were advocated by many left-wingers as instruments of social reform. Central subventions were to become a conspicuous feature of the collectivist vision. But the Right saw these grants as instruments of rate relief. The distinction is most vital – the observer must not confuse the separate aims which lay behind the same policy. Yet the question arose as to how the grants could be made to be used by the local authorities to relieve the rates and not to increase or expand local services. The Conservatives were the champions of local autonomy and they drew back from proposing that the expenditure of their national grants should be controlled by Whitehall. As such, they gave extensive latitude to local government. Conservatism and localism agreed very well and shared common roots in individualist concepts of civic duty.

The Conservative Party's local taxation policy between 1886 and 1906 suggested a gap between professed aims and private intentions. National subventions increased but they did nothing to remove the perceived injustice to real property which remained. They eased the pressures on local finance without effecting any fundamental reform. Hicks Beach was Chancellor of the Exchequer in 1885 and in December he presented an unsuccessful plan to 'bring into contribution to the expenditure of these local authorities the profits derived from capital invested in personal property as well as real property'.[92] G.J.Goschen (1831–1907), the banker whom Randolph Churchill forgot, was at the Treasury from 1897 to 1892. His *Laissez-Faire and Government Interference* of 1883 contained many warnings about left-wing developments. In 1888 Goschen established the assigned revenues system.[93] In his report on local taxation in 1893 the Liberal President of the Local Government Board pointed to recent increases in central subventions and observed that the provison of free elementary education in 1891 had put further burdens on the Exchequer.[94] Party propaganda called attention to the increase in national grants and claimed that the Conservatives were the ratepayers' party.[95]

In 1896 the Unionist government appointed a Royal Commission on Local Taxation. Its terms of reference were typically Tory. The commissioners had to inquire into the system by which taxation was raised for local purposes, to find out whether 'all kinds of real and personal property contribute equitably to such taxation', and, if they did not, to discover a method by which such an end could be achieved.[96] A report on valuation was presented in 1899; a special report on valuation and rating in respect of tithes appeared the same year; the final report was issued in 1901. The report on valuation brought out the chaotic character of much of local government. Three systems of valuation existed outside the Metropolis: the assessment committees of the boards of guardians; the county rate committees of the county councils; and the committees of the borough councils. The commissioners saw duplication and duplicity, inefficiency and inaccuracy, and they called for a single county-based valuation authority which would insure a uniform, correct, economical and up-to-date valuation for all rating purposes.[97] It is a sign of the lack of the Conservatives' commitment to rating reform that by 1906 they had failed to achieve an overhaul of the valuation procedures.

The final report followed Conservative thinking in arguing that the local 'national' services were an 'onerous' burden on real property. The commissioners wanted the national government to assume responsibility for these services but realised that this was not practicable. Thus they suggested increased national grants towards the cost of such services.[98] In the House of Commons Balfour rose to declare that the government felt 'bound to take steps to legislate further at no very distant date'.[99] No comprehensive scheme was attempted between 1895 and 1905, although partial measures of relief were effected. In 1896 agricultural land was relieved of one half of its rates and the local authorities were given a fixed central sum in compensation.[100] Chaplin,who was in charge of the bill, later recalled how it provoked opposition from urban members.[101] Notwithstanding many misgivings as to expediency,[102] the government proceeded to reduce the levels of local taxation paid by parsons.[103] By successive Education Acts the Exchequer increased its funding of the 'national' service of education.[104]

But increased financial pressure on local authorities and longstanding

Tory aspirations did not combine to achieve a reform of the local taxation system. The overall view was that the cupboard was bare. In his comprehensive memorandum of October 1901 Hicks Beach wrote 'we are not now in a position to hold out hopes of additional grants from the Exchequer, either in aid of rates or for old-age pensions'.[105] In February 1903 Ritchie acknowledged that the local taxation question required solution but he proffered no plan.[106] In December 1904 the President of the Local Government Board presented a memorandum on local taxation to the Cabinet. Long acknowledged that the funds required to put the Royal Commission's recommendations into effect were not available at the 'present time'.[107] But of course taxation and expenditure were matters of preference and principle - the means to reform were only ruled out by the axioms of Tory thinking. The Right was not prepared to extend the taxation of property to achieve substantial relief of the rates; the national economy was not to be subjected to a further extraction of resources. It was always unlikely that the party of low government was going to provide the means for an expansion in state activity. Notwithstanding its stance as the proponent of Whitehall subventions, the Right inhibited the historic movement towards a large-scale system of Treasury grants-in-aid.

At the same time the Conservatives opposed all attempts to alter the incidence of local taxation. Both Radicals and municipalists argued that site value rating (SVR) would increase revenue and aid urban development. The Right put up a barrage of hostile arguments and feared that the separate local taxation of the value of sites, as opposed to the composite taxation of sites and structures, would lead to even more radical measures.[108] There was a latent receptivity to the idea of rating unoccupied property in the Conservative approach to local taxation. After all, such property received benefits from services towards which it did not contribute. But even here there was no Tory concession. The Royal Commission on the Housing of the Working Classes of 1884 advocated the rating of vacant or underdeveloped land in urban districts at its real annual value. The proponents of the plan voiced the common view that landowners were deliberately withholding their property from the market in order to raise its price. Such taxation would release such land for building and secure additional revenue.[109] Lord Salisbury, who was a member of the commission, dissented from the proposal.[110] The Select Committee on Town Holdings, in its report of 1892, came out against SVR or the rating of vacant or building land, but did propose the division of rates between owners and occupiers.[111] The Conservative government was unmoved.

The increasing importance of the land tax movement in national politics was acknowledged by the publication of a separate chapter on 'The Taxation of Land Values' in the *Campaign Guide* of 1900. 'The most popular, and in some respects the most practicable, of the proposals', it asserted, 'is the proposal to tax vacant building land within the municipal area at its real annual value, as distinct from the rent which it at present returns'.[112] Rapid urbanisation was putting pressure on housing space and giving landowners great windfall profits. Such conditions lay behind popular support for much of the land tax movement. The Royal Commission on Local Taxation of 1901 rejected SVR,[113] but a minority report proposed an additional rate on urban sites.[114] In 1904 the President of the Local Government Board received a municipal deputation which gave voice to a whole host of complaints and demands. Walter Long conceded that with regard to the rating of unoccupied property there was 'no doubt a good deal to be said' but the government would not 'undertake the taxation of ground values at any time'.[115] Between 1900 and 1906 several SVR bills were introduced into the House of Commons. They were applauded by the Liberals and the AMC but received little support from the Unionist side of the House.[116]

The Conservative door was also closed on the expansionist demands of the municipal authorities. Rollit recognised that the parliamentary Tories were not on his side. 'I see it markedly in the House of Commons', he complained in 1895, 'that there is some spirit both of ill-founded distrust of corporate action and of opposition to any material extension of such powers'.[117] The 1906 *Campaign Guide* condemned the increase in municipal debt.[118] Successive Unionist governments opposed the separate rating of sites and refused to subsidise local activism. A Select Committee on Municipal Trading was appointed but this seemed a matter of shelving. The committee produced a report on auditing.[119] Not only did the Right frustrate the municipal campaign but it launched a counter-attack. The London County Council (LCC) had been a centre of advanced Radicalism and constituted the vanguard of 'Municipal Socialism'. The statist Webbs were especially attracted.[120] 'It is the place where Collectivist and Socialist experiments are tried', declared Lord Salisbury in 1894, 'where a revolutionary spirit finds its instruments and collects its arms'.[121] The Conservative Party replied by curtailing the LCC's powers. The London Government Act of 1899 established a system of metropolitan boroughs. County Hall thereby suffered a substantial devolution of its duties.[122] The Right also overhauled and reinvigorated its organisation in municipal politics.[123] A victory in the LCC elections of 1907 marked an increasing Tory grip on Edwardian town government.[124]

Accompanying Conservative non-interventionism and fiscal minimalism was a sustained attempt to dissuade the electorate from following the Liberal or Labour paths. The Tory critique of left-wing policies often changed over time as the Right came to concede certain of its opponents' measures. A key feature of the Conservative polemical attack was that the projected policies would injure the entire community and cause especial damage to those on the lower rungs of the social ladder. Thus the defence of property was in the interests of all. Linked to this argument was another

– that the Left was constantly causing injury to the economy by undermining the confidence considered essential to its smooth operation. These attacks brought out the nature of the party's beliefs. Tory denunciations were expressed in parliament, in the press, on the platform, by pressure groups and in printed propaganda. A cursory reading of the party's *Campaign Notes* of 1885 or its *Campaign Guides* of 1892, 1894, 1895, 1900 and 1906 well confirms the point.

The Conservative Party responded to the Left's challenge by pointing to the fruits of its own economic policies. Between 1886 and 1914 the Tories hoped that prosperity would produce a more Conservative nation – a constant element in the party's method. During Salisbury's ascendancy the Right did not seek to conceal that it was generally opposed to intervention. The party praised its free market methods. Salisbury set the tone in his major speeches: in 1889 he declared that Conservatism meant confidence;[125] in 1895 he proclaimed that good government was low government.[126] The British economy grew markedly in the late-Victorian period.[127] Progress did not mean impoverishment. The Conservatives claimed much of the credit for this continuing economic success. Their propaganda repeatedly expressed the idea. *The Unionist Record* of 1900 presented the claim in a classic statement of Tory orthodoxy.

BETTER GOVERNMENT MEANS BETTER WAGES

From the time the Government came into office up to the present time there has been a steady expansion of national trade, and an equally steady increase in the wages of the working classes. This result is not so much due to legislation as to the feeling of confidence inspired by the Government.When a nation has a Government which is known to be wise, strong, and patriotic, trade flourishes, capital is invested, new enterprises are undertaken, wages rise, employment increases, while pauperism, crime, and misery decrease. That is the secret of good government. And that is the explanation why trade during the past generation has always been better under Conservative than under Radical Administrations.The Radical policy of wanting to pull down everything that exists, of springing proposals which involve great constitutional changes upon the country at the most unexpected moment and in the most sensational manner, destroys confidence, prevents the investment of capital and paralyses trade. These are facts that can be proved by the statistics regarding the growth of trade and the increase of wages which have taken place since 1895.[128]

Non-interventionism also constituted a powerful appeal to the established economic interests with which the party was linked – the loyalty and support of such interests was intensified by inaction.

Conservatism held that the economy should operate naturally in an atmosphere of security, confidence and low taxation. The great point about the Conservative Party was that it did not seek to halt or check organic economic change. The Right was not in favour of conserving elements which were being overtaken by evolving forces. This was powerfully manifested in the Conservative Party's treatment of agriculture and the country areas between 1886 and 1906. During these years there was marked agricultural depopulation and apparent agricultural depression. Contemporary comment and statistical analysis bore witness to a major change in the nation's internal structure.[129] The country was continuing to move away from the countryside and its cultivation, towards the world of the towns and cities, industry, trade, and commerce. The Conservative Party found that society was changing under its very feet. In many Continental countries right-wingers attempted to check the contraction of the agrarian sector. In Great Britain the Right was characterised by a tendency towards practical indifference. Thomas Hardy's implicit pleas for rural cultural conservation failed to be reflected in official Tory policy.

The Conservative benches in the House of Commons and the House of Lords were full of landowners. But immediate material self-interest was not reflected in direct political activity. The landed interest in parliament constantly refrained from a championing of agriculture. This was one of the great refusals of the late-Victorian and Edwardian Conservative Party. An agricultural committee existed on the Tory side of the House. Earl Winterton remembered that it was the only such backbench committee in the Conservative ranks when he entered the House of Commons at the turn of the century.[130] Far from being a powerful expression of the landed interest, the committee was weak and uninfluential,[131] and seems to have been subjected to schism after 1912.[132] When the Earl of Onslow became President of the Board of Agriculture in 1903 he was struck by how few MPs were concerned with agricultural issues.[133] Agricultural activists never ceased to complain about this refusal.[134] The governing tradition of the aristocracy and gentry probably helped to create this state of affairs. Landowners may have become accustomed to think in terms of the national interest rather than a sectional interest, and to have had public horizons rather than pastoral orientations. Whatever its origins, one of the results of this lack of interest was that there was no powerful lobby of Conservative MPs and peers constantly pressing for measures to benefit agriculture.

British politics is full of lost causes: Republicanism and Centre Parties; anti-democracy and teetotalism. Free trade had a long run for its money until it fell foul of the protectionist EEC. The agriculturalist tendency in Conservative and British politics was one of the obvious failures of Victorian and Edwardian England, yet its past existence has been scarcely registered. But it had its institutions, its leaders and its creed. In 1906 it probably had more MPs than Labour. Agriculturalism deserves its historiographical niche. The agriculturalists were active in the Central and

Associated Chambers of Agriculture and the Central Land Association. The leading lights were Albert Pell, Henry Chaplin and the Earl of Onslow. Charles Bathurst (1867–1958), the future Lord Bledisloe, represented agriculturalism in its purest strain. He was a Gloucestershire landowner who had won the gold medal at the Royal Agricultural College at Cirencester. After entering the House of Commons in 1910 he established himself as the 'most promising ally of the agricultural interest that we have had in Parliament now for some time'.[135] Bathurst was perpetually active in agricultural politics. One friend recalled that even when watching cricket Bathurst's conversation constantly turned to agriculture.[136] Agriculturalists like this Gloucestershire squire believed that agriculture encouraged superior virtues in those connected with it, aided racial development, bred strong soldiers and sailors, supplied vital food supplies in time of war, and provided an invaluable base for the national economy. In 1915 Bathurst wrote a preface to the official history of the Central Chamber of Agriculture, of which he was the chairman. He described how the organisation's previous leaders had believed that 'upon the well-being of Great Britain's oldest industry depend the ultimate economic welfare of her people, their physical and mental virility, and that healthy outlook upon national problems which alone can maintain her pre-eminent position'.[137] Bathurst and his kind were rare birds, of a species on its way to extinction.

The agriculturalists, therefore, were the most conservative of the Conservatives. By inclination they wanted to preserve a section of society, even a way of life, which was in decline. The agriculturalists' small numbers, and the failure of their cause, throws doubt on the intense adherence to rural life and agrarian values which some historians profess to detect in late-Victorian and Edwardian Conservatism. The ineffectiveness of Tory agriculturalism indicates the extent to which the Conservative Party moved with the times and accepted the social configurations produced by the economic mechanisms it sought to protect. It also gave some credence to the Right's claim to be a party of the national interest – on the whole the agricultural interest was neglected. The experience of the Tory agriculturalists, which involved one of the major lost causes of the period, was in part a product of the Conservative view that the free market economy, when permeated by suitable social ethics, was progressive. If the Right had attempted to turn back the agrarian clock, or at least sought to halt its hands, it would have been untrue to itself. Agriculturalism illuminated the character of Conservatism.

Organised agriculture was also characterised by debility. The Central Chamber of Agriculture (CCA) had been established in 1865, and sought to link up the nation's owners and farmers who belonged to local chambers of agriculture and farmers' clubs with the representatives of agriculture in parliament.[138] The very existence of the CCA proclaimed its weakness. The industrial revolution had made it necessary - a pressure group was needed where established positions of power would previously suffice. That the agricultural interest required organisation meant that it lacked influence within the political system. The historical emergence of the CCA was a concomitant of urbanisation and attested to changing patterns of power within the nation. The CCA's lack of success resulted in demands for the formation of an Independent Agricultural Party in 1907[139] and to the creation of new agricultural pressure groups in the Edwardian period. The Central Chamber of Agriculture claimed party political independence and achieved the adherence of a number of moderate Liberals, but with its emphasis on class co-operation and its commitment to the existing rural order this pressure group was always within the Conservative orbit.

As the nineteenth century progressed the agrarian sector found itself increasingly subordinated. Rural malaise failed to provoke government remedies. The difficulties of the agricultural interest were revealed by the formation of the National Agricultural Union in 1892. Earl Winchelsea was its leader and it was essentially a Conservative (though agriculturalist) affair: the three agricultural classes were to be united behind a programme of protection, rate relief, bimetallism and extended tenant rights. This last was probably an attempt to secure the loyalty of the farmers.[140] The organisation was an implicit protest against the CCA's lack of success and a response to a sustained period of agrarian failure. Salisbury reflected on the programme and opined that only rate relief was within the realm of practical politics.[141] The 1896 Agricultural Rating Act was the Conservative Party's sole substantial response to the rural crisis of the late nineteenth century. But subsequent events called into question the degree of Tory commitment. By 1904 the President of the Board of Agriculture was complaining that increased levels of local taxation had often negated the benefits to agriculture of the 1896 subsidy.[142]

The obstacles in the way of producing beneficial policies for agriculture, the non-agriculturalism of the Tory mainstream, and the Conservative reluctance to interfere in the natural workings of the economy, combined to produce a degree of immobilism towards England's oldest industry. This was exemplified by Balfour's only government of 1902–1905. William Hilliers Onslow (1853–1911), the fourth Earl of Onslow, was a Surrey landowner whose career had had a painfully horizontal quality before he became President of the Board of Agriculture in 1903. Onslow was a figure of some importance in the politics of this period and merits serious consideration. He was well versed in the land question, having been chairman of the Conservative group on the LCC and a moving spirit in the 'vestry movement' to curtail the Council's powers. But Onslow was also a prominent agriculturalist leader and it was only natural that he brought enthusiasm and commitment to his new appointment. Onslow set up a number of departmental committees, established a

national network of correspondents to inform his department on local
conditions, and toured the countryside meeting those engaged in the
beloved industry.[143] But more than this, as befitted an agriculturalist, he
dreamed of bringing people back to the land.

Onslow produced a plan to give central loans to landowners so that they
could create small holdings on their estates. 'I addressed a letter to the
Prime Minister', he recalled, 'urging the Government to take some steps
to facilitate the creation of Small Holdings, in order to stem the tide of
depopulation into the towns from the country'.[144] The faddist Jesse
Collings rejected the idea in favour of his own;[145] Balfour rejected the idea
in favour of nothing. Salisbury's nephew was typically Tory. For him the
economy was naturally progressive. The potentialities of industry, he told
Collings, were almost unlimited – the country had to look to areas other
than agriculture for its future.[146] In addition, the nation was commited to
the way it was going. 'The Prime Minster was not sympathetic', lamented
Onslow, 'he held the view that for good or for evil, the country had at the
time of the repeal of the Corn Laws determined to be an industrial and
urban community and not a rural and agricultural nation'.[147] The proposal
failed to bear fruit.

Balfour's government was more generally neglectful of the agricultural interest and failed to pass even minor bills. In addition the rate burden
on agriculture continued to rise. This was especially galling because local
taxation was the great issue of agricultural politics. It was said to have
interested the Chambers of Agriculture more than all other subjects put
together.[148] 'The Cabinet of which a clear majority of members are directly
interested in agriculture', wrote the editor of an agriculturalist newspaper
in 1905, 'is not regarded as likely to move a finger to help what may be
specifically described as agricultural interests!'.[149] After his resignation
Onslow wrote an open letter to the newly formed North Eastern Agricultural Federation. In it he condemned this neglect in unequivocal terms.[150]
The Conservative chief whip was furious.[151] Onslow's letter may be taken
as a more general expression of the frustration of Tory agriculturalism in
the face of official Conservative indifference – it was the protesting cry of
a failed tendency within British Conservatism.

A reluctance to halt urbanisation must have been underpinned by an
awareness of one of its benefits. The countryside may have been contracting but suburbia was expanding.[152] The Victorian period witnessed the
beginnings of one of the more important and understudied of modern
political forces – suburban Conservatism. Suburbia has often provoked
amused contempt. Lord Randolph Churchill talked mockingly of the
'lords of vineries and pineries';[153] the Grossmiths produced Mr Pooter and
The Diary of a Nobody. But Lord Salisbury, with his usual perception,
took the whole development very seriously and sensed that political
conditions would never be the same again. For once, it appeared, history

was going the unhappy Marquess's way. As early as 1882 he had told Northcote that Villa Toryism needed organisation.[154] In 1900 he mused on the results of that year's general election to the National Union and drew attention to the force of suburban Conservatism in London.[155] Liberals were similarly impressed and a young Liberal intellectual, Charles Masterman MP, devoted a separate chapter of his *The Condition of England* of 1909 to 'The Suburbans'. He could not help noticing that suburbia was a hotbed of Conservatism and couched his observation in prescient terms – 'Here the individualism of the national character exercises its full influence.'[156] The 1910 general elections showed that suburban England tended to colour the electoral map blue.[157] Why should the Tories have striven to halt fundamental socio-economic changes when they brought such benefits as this?

Another economic process which resulted from natural developments, and which may have aided the Right, was emigration. 'British emigration rates', writes one scholar of the period 1851–1913, 'were among the highest in Europe'.[158] In 1892 annual emigration rates in England and Wales were running at about 0.6%; by 1912 they had risen to 0.87%.[159] Perhaps potential anti-Conservatives were removing themselves. Certainly the Conservatives encouraged the process; many of the imperial pressure groups saw emigration as a means of developing the Empire.[160] Emigration was perceived as a way of maintaining living standards at home. It was almost an anti-collectivist policy, a natural market response to domestic difficulty. Salisbury gave the official stamp of approval in a number of speeches. At Nottingham in November 1889 he praised 'all those measures which have for their object the giving of facilities to emigrate – to emigrate especially to other parts of our own Empire'. Emigration would give labourers opportunities abroad and ease the pressure on wage rates at home.[161] From 1886 to 1914 the Tories gave their moral support to a process which appeared to aid popular welfare. By an indirect route emigration was anti-collectivism. It was part of the Right's response to the Left. An unnoticed thread ran from Henry George to Rhodesia.

There is another point to be made about Conservatism, emigration and Empire. Sizeable numbers of voters were directly linked by family ties to settlers, administrators, soldiers, missionaries and businessmen who lived and worked in those parts of the atlas coloured red. This constituted a dimension of electoral sociology which has yet to be explored but whose figures invite new paths of speculation. An analysis of the electorate from the point of view of 'kith and kin' ties with the overseas territories may further reduce the importance attributed to domestic socio-economic structures. It is estimated by one historian that between 1900 and 1910 alone over two million inhabitants of the British Isles migrated to the overseas Empire.[162] The right-wing expansion of British rule after 1870 necessarily made the domestic electorate more imperial and established a vested interest which crossed many a class boundary. One thing is certain – the Conservative defence and promotion of the Empire was a direct appeal to a home constituency with very personal imperial connections.

It is clear, therefore, without arguing the case too much, that the Conservative Party was altogether more *laissez-faire* in its attitude than has generally been assumed. What, then, of those Rightists of the years 1886–1906 traditionally identified with an alleged interventionist tendency within Conservatism? Greenleaf sees Lord Randolph Churchill and Joseph Chamberlain as examples of the Right's inherent collectivism.[163] Was not Winston Churchill's father the champion of 'Tory Democracy' and the man from Birmingham the previous intervening Radical? From one historian we have the statement that Churchill was 'Conservative only in name; he was in reality a rebel against his class and the structure of society'.[164] In 1906 Lord Rosebery gave his account of the Salisbury years. The Conservative Party of the period defended Anglicanism and property but was prepared to bow to pressure if absolutely necessary. The pressure, Rosebery continued, came first from Churchill and then from Chamberlain.[165] Sir A.K.Rollit, the Conservative MP who led the campaign to expand the role of urban local government, might also be taken to represent the supposed statist strand. Among this trio should be found the famed Tory Left. In fact, all these individuals turn out to be proponents of pragmatism. They differed from their right-wing colleagues not in ends but in means. Contrary to expectations, Churchill, Chamberlain and Rollit serve to exemplify the essential antagonism of late-nineteenth century Conservatism to emergent collectivism.

Lord Randolph Churchill (1849–1895) was the son of the Duke of Marlborough and thus integrally linked to the landed interest. His career was epitomised by an erraticism and impulsiveness which renders difficult any evaluation of his Conservatism. He rose to prominence in the first part of the 1880s and only those meteoric years will be considered here. Churchill responded to democratisation by becoming a brilliant and famed platform speaker. He had great oratorical panache and flair, and one Tory later described him as the 'darling of the Conservative Clubs and the Music Halls'.[166] He specialised in vituperative attacks on the Liberal leadership and gained such appellations as 'cheeky Randy' or 'the music hall cad'. Churchill also called for advances in party organisation and became the chairman of the National Union. In the House of Commons he associated with a group of MPs known for their illumination of the weakness of the official leadership. From this 'Fourth Party' Churchill became Secretary for India in 1885 and Chancellor of the Exchequer in 1886. He resigned late that year and never held office again. Lord Randolph later died of syphilis, a disease which may have manifested itself in the wildness of these years of prominence. Salisbury likened Churchill to the Mad Mahdi. Gladstone noted his inconsistencies and described him as a flea.[167]

During these years Churchill became the self-styled champion of Tory Democracy. It is a phrase which belongs to party mythology and with which Churchill has always been connected. To what did it amount? The question, because of Churchill himself, does not allow of an easy answer. Yet it seems that the man from Blenheim was responding to developments on the Left of national politics. The precise nature of his proposed policies confirms this interpretation. In Cabinet, in 1885, Churchill sent a detailed memorandum to Lord Salisbury. He argued that the Tory task was to keep the boroughs and win the counties: 'this can only be done by an active progressive – I risk the word, a democratic – policy'.[168] He was quite prepared to take up the materialist challenge and he proposed, *inter alia,* a number of land reform policies. The subject matter betokened the purpose. Here was a direct response to the Radical concerns of the early 1880s. Only by grasping the importance of the land question is it possible to bring out the true character of Lord Randolph Churchill's Tory Democracy. Churchill advocated a reform of county government, the creation of small holdings and allotments, the enfranchisement of future leaseholds, copyholders, and lands held in mortmain, the abolition of primogeniture in cases of intestacy, and the compulsory registration of title.[169] His famous Bradford and Dartford speeches of October 1886 promoted policies of the same character.[170] Late in 1886 he admonished Salisbury for his lack of support for a Conservative allotments bill and subsequently declared 'I am afraid it is an idle schoolboy's dream to suppose the Tories can legislate'.[171] In this he acknowledged the orientations of Conservatism. Churchill's social reformism, however, was itself powerfully conditioned by Tory beliefs. It did not extend to the world of fiscal redistribution and central grants – he repeatedly called for a 'genuine and considerable reduction of public expenditure and consequent reduction of taxation'.[172]

Beyond the level of concrete policies Churchill was much engaged in image projection. The appearance of interventionism was being manufactured. Churchill had a flair for talk and attitudinising. The sympathy tactic was being employed. 'Trust the People' was one of his famous phrases.[173] In 1884 he declared in parliament that unless the Tory Party showed a readiness to deal with great social questions it would not return to office for a long time.[174] 'All this outcry against the supporters of Mr. Broadhurst's bill – this gabble about Socialism, Communism, and Mr. George', Churchill told a public correspondent in the same year, 'betrays a prevalance of very deplorable and shocking ignorance as to the extent to which the rights of property can be tolerated, and the relation of the State thereto'.[175] In all this he carried on from Disraeli, and his son came to promote the myth in a famous biography. Perhaps the filial biographer even believed it. 'A strong Conservative Party with an overwhelming majority and a moderate and even progressive leadership is a combination which has never been tested before', Winston Churchill wrote to his wife in 1925, correctly expressing a historical truth, 'It might well be the fulfillment of all that Dizzy and my father aimed at in their political work', he added, expressing the myth.[176]

What was the purpose of Churchill's policies and posture? Power, no doubt, but to what end? One historian has recently written 'Churchill's tory democracy consisted of new means rather than new ends. He simply wished the new electorate to dance to the old tory tune: defending the established constitution.'[177] To this should be added the existing propertied order. For nowhere in the heyday of Tory Democracy was there a sustained attempt at major social reform. Indeed, Churchill was often vigorous in his attack upon the more extreme Radical proposals. It was the brilliance of his combative approach which so often delighted his partisan audiences. In his October 1885 address to the electors of Birmingham he warned of the plunder of both small and large property owners in the names of 'ransom' and 'graduated taxation'.[178] The reformist stance must be adjudged an exercise in expediency. Churchill himself admitted this. 'To tell the truth I don't know myself what Tory democracy is', he said in 1885, 'But I believe it is principally opportunism.'[179] William Gladstone had mused on the character of Churchill's creation earlier that year. For this veteran of politics it was an example of Conservative 'demogogism' which was 'in secret as obstinately attached as ever to the evil principle of class interests'.[180]

After the secession of the Liberal Unionists Joseph Chamberlain rose to dizzy heights in the Conservative world. In 1895 he entered the Cabinet as colonial secretary, thus indicating his imperial commitment. His secretaryship was noted for an innovative attempt to make the Empire pay; interventionist methods were employed in Africa to reap material rewards from imperial rule.[181] By 1906 Chamberlain led the majority tariff reform faction within the Conservative Party; a subsequent stroke prevented further progress. But there was nothing surprising about this rapid rise. Chamberlain's attitude towards the Empire and Ireland was distinctly Conservative. He himself felt at home among the Conservatives and fully participated in Tory high society. Chamberlain told one aristocratic hostess that 'no-one had more profound veneration for the historic importance of the ancient families of England and their homes' than himself.[182] More than this the Birmingham screw manufacturer shared the general Conservative approach to the social order. Where he deviated from the bulk of his colleagues was in the means he proposed for its maintenance.

Chamberlain's principled opportunism was well apparent in the apparently Radical days of the 1880s. The Unauthorised Programme must be understood within the context of the time. Chamberlain was reacting to extreme political developments which he believed heralded a most unwel-

come future. Of this he made no secret. In 1883 he wrote an article for the
Fortnightly Review. Land was his great apprehension:

> The wide circulation of such books as the *Progress and Poverty*, of
> Mr. Henry George, and the acceptance which his proposals have
> found among the working classes, are facts full of significance and
> warning. If something be not done quickly...we may live to see
> theories as wild and unjust as those suggested by the American
> economist adopted as the creed of no inconsiderable portion of the
> electorate. The enjoyment of wealth and leisure is not a crime, but
> neither is existence under these conditions altogether without re-
> sponsibility. By accepting this responsibility the rich may still
> protect themselves against the dangers which threaten them, but the
> time for apathy and indifference is passing away. 'Some day,' writes
> a great dignitary of the Church whose organization gives it exceptional
> knowledge of the inmost thoughts of the very poorest of
> our population, 'this crater will overwhelmn London: theWest End
> can now insure itself against fire; soon it will be too late'.[183]

During the 1885 campaign Chamberlain made clear that his reform
proposals had a defensive purpose. 'What insurance will wealth find it to
its advantage to provide', he asked. 'I am putting the rights of property on
the only firm and defensible basis', he declared, 'I believe that the danger
to property lies in its abuse'.[184] Timely reform was necessary to avert
future extremism. 'I am sorry to see that your friends are so angry with
what I say', he wrote to one aristocratic correspondent in 1883, 'Some day
they will discover what a good friend I have been to them, and how I have
saved them from the "wrath to come".'[185] Chamberlain correctly perceived the future importance of the land question. The whole tactical
character of the Unauthorised Programme is revealed by Chamberlain's
subsequent comment to Balfour – 'There were only two things I cared for
in that; Free Education and Small Holdings'.[186] And how great was his real
commitment to the latter?

Chamberlain's initiatives of the early 1890s closely paralleled those of
the early 1880s, although their character changed to take account of
changing circumstances. In both instances he was moved to promote
collectivist policies as a counter to left-wing radicalism. In the 1880s the
land reformers led him to take up land reform; in the 1890s Labour
encouraged him to adopt Labour issues. The concerns of these policies
indicated their reactive origins; they were a response to a threat not the
product of inner conviction. In a sense, the timing was everything.
Nothing could be more suggestive than that nearly all of the land reform
of the 1880s had been dropped by the 1890s. Radical Joe, the scourge of
the landed classes, if ever he had existed, was dead. But in his emphasis
on Labour issues in the last decade of the century Chamberlain may have
been making a mistake. Thus did he reveal one of the chief pitfalls of

expedient reformism – prediction. Land reform was to continue to be a great left-wing cause for two decades.

Chamberlain had been alarmed by the flare-up of Labour and trade union radicalism in the late 1880s and early 1890s. Once again he wrote an essay for a review. 'The Labour Question' of 1892 addressed itself to recent events in the Labour world. Apprehension was its keynote. Recent developments on the Labour Left meant that 'more ambitious schemes of social reconstruction are brought into view'. Once again Chamberlain produced a reform programme in response. He advocated old age pensions, industrial arbitration, increased employers' liability for accidents, control of pauper immigration, extension of the Factory Acts, local authority loans for working-class home ownership, and changes in the legislation relating to town planning and housing. Although Chamberlain had been the famous reforming mayor of Birmingham, he was distinctly lukewarm to municipal enterprise. This was a further sign of his opportunism.[187] In the same year Chamberlain urged the Tory leaders to introduce such a programme into the Queen's Speech.[188] His very language was suggestive. 'The movement for "social" legislation is in the air', he told Balfour, 'it is our business to guide it'. In the same conversation he complained about the general political strategy of his fellow Liberal Unionist leader, Lord Hartington, and condemned his Whiggism.[189] Thus was Joseph Chamberlain the advocate of timely and not last ditch reform.

In 1894 Chamberlain submitted a social reform programme to the Conservative leaders. It contained very similar proposals to those of his review article. He wanted to give the House of Lords a progressive image, and thus make it less vulnerable to the Left's attacks, by introducing the projected legislation through this eminently aristocratic assembly.[190] Chamberlain's arguments in favour of his programme shared the approach to be found behind its Radical equivalent. The future colonial secretary was in no doubt as to the importance of material issues in politics. 'The electors are much more interested at the present time in social questions and the problems connected with the agitations of the Labour Party than they are with either the House of Lords or any other constitutional subject', he wrote in his memorandum,

> The men who have anything to lose are getting uneasy now that they see that Gladstonianism is not likely to be confined to an attack upon Irish landlords or British millionaires, but will probably result in an onslaught on capital generally...The resolutions of the Trades Union Congress...amount to universal confiscation in order to create a Collectivist State.[191]

Chamberlain's reform Conservatism was further expressed to Balfour:

> The intermediates – the men who hold the balance of elections – are disgusted and frightened...at the projects of confiscation which are in the air and found expression at the Trade Union Congress the other day,

he argued,

> they want to be assured that the Unionists will take up the question
> of Social Reform in a Conservative spirit and meet the unreason-
> able and dangerous proposals of the extremists with practical pro-
> posals of their own.[192]

Such reasoning passed through many a Tory mind during these menacing
decades of leftist pressure. No doubt it was also intended to give the
Unionists the image of being the Caring Party.

Sir A.K.Rollit could not compare with Churchill or Chamberlain in
importance, but he was a second rank politician of the first grade. Rollit
was a shipowner and solicitor from Hull, the Conservative member for
South Islington, the chairman of the National Union in 1889, and the
president of the Association of Municipal Corporations for more than
fifteen years. He was an accomplished speaker, a talented organiser, and
in his activism he anticipated the trend of politics. Like Churchill and
Chamberlain, Rollit was a keen advocate of modern political methods, and
in his presidential speech to the National Union he told the party faithful
to 'make wise, organise, revise'. 'Organisation', he asserted, was 'all-im-
portant'.[193] Rollit was also a dedicated exponent of principled opportunism and he succeeded in converting it into a coherent and articulate creed.

In 1889 Rollit told the National Union that the country was 'face to face
with social problems which will not wait for solution and which may
sweep away those who persistently resist them. The statesman's duty is to
effect peacefully what may otherwise become a social revolution.' 'True
Conservatism', he contested, 'is progressive'.[194] That, indeed, was what
his municipal activity was all about. For Rollit tramways and social
stability were connected. In 1895 he gave an address to the British Institute
of Public Health on the subject of 'Municipalism'. The central idea was
simple: 'the ready acknowledgement and performance of duties and
obligations is the best protection of both rights and property'.[195] In 1898
he informed the AMC that the presence of extremes of wealth and poverty
in a society were socially and politically dangerous. They needed to be
'modified by a wise and enterprising appreciation and application of the
municipal spirit'.[196] Rollit's Conservative municipalism was a bold attempt to halt the Left's advance by means of localist action.

The great point about Churchill, Chamberlain and Rollit was that they
largely acted as independent agents. They were individual stars rather than
tribunes of an interventionist Toryism. There was no Churchill group of
MPs; no Tory Democracy Committee existed. The 'Fourth Party' was most
emphatically not a forerunner of the Unionist Social Reform Committee
or Tory Reform Group. One of its members recalled 'it possessed no distinctive creed; its very name was an accident of debate'.[197] There was no
cluster of left-wing Unionist MPs around Joseph Chamberlain. Henchmen
such as Jesse Collings did not count. Rollit was associated with a number

of Tory municipalists, but they were never an organised or active force. All this was not surprising because there were no such interventionist MPs. Internal representation or expression could not be given to something that did not exist. The agricultural committee was significant in its uniqueness. Throughout this period there was an occasional *rara avis* in the Gorst–G.Whiteley–Henry Bentinck manner, but they were the exceptions which illustrated the rule. Churchill, Chamberlain and Rollit could not be rallying points because there was no one to rally. It is rather difficult to mobilise vacuums.

These prominent proponents of tactical reform were distinguished from their colleagues by the methods they advocated not the goals they sought. The same may be said for their diehard counterparts on the other side of the party. Edwardian divisions in the Conservative Party over tactics and strategy were anticipated in the late-Victorian period. The cause of no concession was most consistently promoted by the Tories of the Liberty and Property Defence League. The LPDL was established in 1882, and the original idea, suggestively enough, was to call it the 'State Resistance Union'.[198] The association's president and guiding light was Earl Wemyss, a Scottish and Gloucestershire landowner. In 1866 he had warned that the 'eventual question' of franchise reform was 'property'.[199] Wemyss's organisation attempted to create a militant front of economic interests, and the league waged a constant campaign against collectivist legislation. Its cause was simple: 'The League opposes all attempts to introduce the State as competitor or regulator into the various departments of social activity and industry, which would otherwise be spontaneously and adequately conducted by private enterprise'.[200] But the LPDL never made much headway within the Conservative Party and at the turn of the century it could command the adherence of less than ten MPs.[201]

But though lacking in impact the LPDL had great significance. Much can be read in the dusty volumes of its forgotten meetings. It was a reflection of, and a response to, changes on the Left of British politics. Established in 1882 and moribund by 1914, the society was a direct product of collectivism in its first important phase. As a phenomenon the LPDL was an important indicator of historical evolution. 'The old Radical was all for liberty and freeing men from State restrictions', declared Wemyss in 1888, 'But the neo-Radical is for putting restrictions upon men and abolishing liberty'.[202] 'Robbery in Parliament in the shape of bills brought in is more or less rampant', he asserted a year later, 'No doubt the first great interest that has been marked out for attack is land.'[203] The municipal campaign received full-scale opposition. Wemyss and his colleagues set out to combat 'outbursts of the restless and meddlesome spirit beginning to animate modern local government in town and country'.[204] The New Unionism was met by the systematic organisation of blackleg labour and interference in industrial disputes.[205] The very idea of mobilising the great interests indicated that the political system now posed a threat to their welfare. The landed interest was the most vulnerable, and appropriately enough Wemyss had originally intended to create an organisation to defend those with property in land and houses.[206] The LPDL was another creation of franchise reform.

The Liberty and Property Defence League represented an approach to the New Left which was not adopted by the Conservative Party. There was nothing uncongenial about the essential beliefs and principles of this pressure group, all of which were welcome to the Tory mind. Indeed, the LPDL espoused the pure milk of Conservative orthodoxy and thereby illuminated its character. But where the LPDL diverged from its parent institution was in its consistent opposition to interventionist legislation, even where such legislation was considered by the party mainstream to be politically necessary. These were Lampedusa's conservative associates *par excellence*. By 1899 this most unbending of Tory societies had seen enough Conservative concessions. Its officials were calling for a 'free, independent, unofficial, *bona fide* Conservative Party in the House of Commons'.[207] Disagreement over methods was provoking a division within the Unionist coalition. The league would not countenance opportunism, and it lamented the electoral origins of its Tory promotion:

> Until experience has had time to produce its chastening effects the democratic vote will continue to be recorded for such legislative aids towards the millenium as the Radical-Socialist finds it suits both his instincts and political self-interest to originate, but which the Tory-Democrat copies from political self-interest alone. The latter forces himself, with a conscious effort, into the competition of the political market.[208]

Weymss knew all about the pragmatic wing of his party.

How, then, is it possible to explain the interventionist statutes of the years of Unionist ascendancy? This legislation has been frequently cited as evidence to support the Tory collectivism thesis. It certainly seems to sit unevenly with the Conservative Party's taxation policy and Tory praise of the achievements of the free market approach. Yet as with Churchill, Chamberlain and Rollit, a close inspection reveals an anti-collectivist intent behind the promotion of leftist measures. Internal correspondence and a chronological perspective serve to illuminate the opportunism; the very nature of the legislation bore the marks of the Tory beliefs from which it originated. Moderate left-wing policies constituted one of the chief devices by which the Conservative Party sought to meet the challenge of the radicalising Left.

Tory allotments and small holdings policy between the Radical Campaign and the Tariff Reform Campaign was both politic and principled. The 1885 general election indicated that there was much electoral danger to the Right in the Liberal land question. One historian asserts that the Left's promise of 'three acres and a cow' damaged the Conservatives in the counties.[209] Walter Long recalled that together with 'dear bread' it had dominated the Wiltshire hustings.[210] One form of Tory response was that embodied in the Land and Glebe Owners' Association for the Voluntary Extension of the Allotments System. Led by the Earl of Onslow and Long, it sought to secure the provision of allotments by voluntary means. This, of course, agreed with Conservative voluntaryism and had the obvious aim of countering the Radicals with a more moderate policy. The organisation was small and led by right-wing landowners.[211] In 1886, one year after the association's foundation, Onslow wrote what amounted to its manifesto. One of the declared objects was to explain to the labourers that voluntary action by the landowners would achieve better results for them than 'the operation of local bodies bound to respect the interests of the ratepayers, and exercising their powers compulsorily and in antagonism to the owners of land'.[212] This was probably the thinking behind the bill promoted by Long and Onslow in 1886.[213] Pragmatic legislation was another possibility.

In December 1886 Lord Salisbury submitted a memorandum to the Cabinet on the measure being proposed by his government. 'The only argument in favour of the proposal that I have heard', he wrote in revealing fashion, 'is that a certain number of Conservative members, pressed by election pledges, will vote for it, and it will be carried in the House of Commons'.[214] Certainly recent events on the Left had changed the party's position. Conservative Central Office issued its *Campaign Notes* in 1885 and this publication offered no promise of allotments legislation.[215] Party propaganda in 1886 was unsympathetic and at times hostile.[216] Salisbury himself was opposed to change and argued that natural forces would supply all the allotments that were needed. The Marquess did not favour compulsory purchase and stressed that subsequent democratic pressure would lead to further such infringements of property. He did not want his party to endure the ignominy of adopting for electoral purposes an anti-property measure which it had been vehemently denouncing some twelve months previously.[217] But the legislation went through. The Allotments Acts of 1887 and 1890 permitted local authorities to buy land, by voluntary or compulsory means, and to let it out to suitable tenants. The Allotments Compensation Act of 1887 gave the allotment holder favourable compensation for unexhausted improvements; the Allotments Rating Act of 1891 provided him with advantageous local taxation terms. The Glebe Lands Act of 1888 aimed at a parallel conversion of ecclesiastial property into local government allotments. Once these statutes were enacted the Conservative Party could pose as the sincere author of concrete social reform.[218] Their genesis permits of a rather different interpretation.

Conservative pragmatism drew back from the extremes of an active small holdings policy. Despite the pressure the Tories would not concede. Arguments relating to economics and property exercised a determining influence. The party's *Campaign Notes* of 1885 began its chapter on 'Peasant Proprietorship and Land Nationalisation' with the following condemnatory summary:

> The miserable results of Peasant Proprietorship–wretched condi-
> tion and poor food of Peasant Proprietors in France–Peasant Pro-
> prietors artificially created in Russia, and in twenty years reduced to
> starvation – Peasant Proprietors in England encumbered with mort-
> gages and in a worse condition than Tenant Farmers – Peasant Pro-
> prietors in Italy; their miserable condition.[219]

In the same year, in his paper to the Industrial Remuneration Conference, Arthur Balfour declared that the introduction of small freeholding into Britain would be a 'disastrous failure'.[220] In 1888 Joseph Chamberlain and Jesse Collings set up the Rural Labourers' League.[221] Collings (1831–1920) had achieved fame and fortune in Birmingham, where he had also been one of Chamberlain's closest associates. But his heart was always with his village origins and his entire political life was devoted to the recreation of old England's peasant proprietors and yeomen.[222] The ideas of the league were broadcast in its journal *Rural World* and in its propaganda.[223] Concrete proposals were expressed in a House of Commons bill which enabled the Board of Agricuture to convert labourers into proprietors, and farmers into owners, by means of Exchequer loans and voluntary pur-chase.[224] Collings was a rather bucolic figure who lacked gravity. Both he and his organisation were of little influence within the Conservative Party.

A Select Committee on Small Holdings reported in 1890 in favour of a highly moderate scheme.[225] The Cabinet drew up a bill. 'I shall resist compulsion', Salisbury wrote of the measure, 'I have a strong conviction that I can get better terms for property out of office, than I can in office.'[226] The Small Holdings Act of 1892 was a classic example of a common nineteenth century dead letter – local government administered social reform. Between 1892 and 1907 less than 1,000 acres were acquired under its provisions.[227] The Act had no compulsory powers and allowed for no central aid. It merely permitted county councils to purchase land by voluntary agreement and to sell it or rent it to applicants of their choice.[228] Other small holdings initiatives came to nought. Collings attempted to make the 1892 Act more effective, but his ideas were not adopted.[229] When the Agricultural Holdings Bill of 1900 was being drawn up certain Cabinet members sought to make it more palatable to the landed interest. They proposed central loans so that landowners could create and equip small holdings on their estates. The suggested clause, however, was dropped.[230] Onslow supported his 1905 initiative with the following opportunist argument: 'Our opponents will inevitably advance some such policy, in all probability including powers of expropriation.' Long and Austen Chamberlain gave backing to the proposal but to no avail.[231] The 1892 Act must be interpreted as windowdressing. All in all the Conservative Party's allotment and small holding legislation amounted to little. In 1900 the Liberal Party charged: 'The Government has done nothing to facilitate the acquisition of either small holdings or allotments.'[232] The ineffectiveness of the Tory measures bore witness to their expedient origins. Right-wing hearts were not in this kind of land reform.

The Conservative Party's handling of the question of employers' liability between 1890 and 1900 was most illustrative of its pragmatism. From 1886 to 1892 the Conservatives did nothing. In 1892 Salisbury made it clear that his party had no social legislation in the pipeline.[233] The Liberals then took action against a background of rising trade union militancy. In 1893 Gladstone's last ministry promoted a parliamentary bill which greatly extended the provisions of the previous legislation of 1881. Many more workers were to receive compensation from their employers for accidents they suffered at work, and the rates of compensation were to be more advantageous. Tory voluntaryism reared its head. The House of Lords insisted on a contracting out clause. Much insurance was already obtained by workers and employers through such instruments as mutual aid societies. Lord Salisbury told Balfour 'we cannot stop all the evil the bill would do – but we can stop that which is urgent & most threatening – the destruction of the existing societies'.[234] These societies appealed powerfully to Conservative communitarian instincts and voluntary methods. Thus did the Employers' Liability Bill reveal aspects of Conservatism. 'This voluntary system of insurance', asserted a party publication, 'has been the means of bringing together the employers and the workmen on the most friendly footing'. Class co-operation was adjured: 'It stands to reason that what is done in a voluntary spirit is done in a more gracious way, and that if legislation is avoided, the future relations of master and men must be of a much more friendly nature.'[235] The Unionist House of Lords insisted on its amendment and the Liberal bill was lost.[236]

When the Conservative Party returned to office in 1895 it had a political opportunity which it was quick to take. The Right could now pass legislation which was bound to come and thus gain for itself any electoral popularity which was in the offing. But it could also frame that legislation in accordance with Tory principles. Salisbury's government enacted an Employers' Liability Bill of its own in 1897. For one Tory MP of the period it was perhaps the most notable achievement of the 1895–1905 Unionist administration.[237] The Act provided for compensation to workers for accidents incurred during the course of employment (though by no means all workers were covered by the legislation), and permitted contracting out provided the terms of independent arrangements were deemed by the Registrar of Friendly Societies to be as favourable as those in the Act.

Subsequently the Conservatives pointed to their creation as evidence of their social reforming credentials.[238] The Royal Commission on Labour, in its fifth and final report of 1894, proposed a system of voluntary conciliation and arbitration in industrial disputes. It would have no truck with statutory minimum wages.[239] This approach was congenial to the Conservative mind, and in 1896 the Conciliation Act was passed. The state was involved in the organisation of arbitration, but there was no thought of compulsion. Economic liberty was not disturbed.[240]

Cyclical unemployment was one of the more painful features of the Victorian and Edwardian economy. Walter Long, the President of the Local Government Board, was alarmed at its prominent appearance in the early 1900s. Long (1854–1924) occupied an important position in right-wing politics between 1886 and 1920. He was a Wiltshire country gentleman who became a permanent part of the Tory leadership. Long constantly cultivated support within the party,[241] and if there had been an election among the MPS in 1911 he would have become the leader of the opposition.[242] Long was totally Tory in his attitudes, but he exemplified how Conservatives could be more wedded to certain parts of the propertied order than others. When it came to landed society and rural property Long approached the diehards; but he had a receptivity to opportunism when it was applied to the urban sector. In 1905 Long informed the Cabinet that he had recently established a system of voluntary committees in London whereby the metropolitan boroughs could help those without work. In a rather opaque memorandum it appears that Long wanted to make this system statutory in London, to extend it to the urban areas of the rest of the country, and to secure funding from the rates.[243]

The President of the Local Government Board was in no doubt as to the expediency required by the circumstances. He told the Cabinet that support from the rates was imperative. There was a 'strong feeling amongst a certain section in favour of the State providing employment, and if my scheme broke down for lack of funds', he argued, 'the demand for such State intervention would be greatly strengthened. It seems to me to be most desirable to avoid any contingency of this kind.'[244] Long's opportunism flew in the face of Tory beliefs. 'Among my own friends it was regarded as being too much akin to Socialism',[245] he recalled of his suggestion. In Cabinet the new Lord Salisbury was vociferous in his opposition. He argued that the poor would come to use the state as an instrument of reward: 'Those who are relieved are to retain their votes, which they will, no doubt, use at the next election to raise the rate of wages given to the unemployed.'[246] Some months earlier Balfour had already ruled out central aid for metropolitan relief. The Prime Minister argued that it was not wise to yield to sentiment and to pass measures which would ultimately damage those they were intended to help. He also told Long that a dangerous precedent would be set which would be capable of dangerous extension.[247] But Long's proposal went through and in 1905 the Unemployed Workmen's Act was passed. Yet this was not without the most serious Conservative misgivings. In July 1905 one of the whips confided to his diary: 'I imagine the unemployed bill is the most unpopular measure among our men which has been introduced during the last ten years.'[248]

Conservative housing legislation also bore all the marks of reluctance. In 1890 Salisbury's ministry put the Housing of the Working Classes Act on the statute book. The measure was both innovative and consolidatory. It had three principal parts. The first two dealt with the replacement and repair of existing houses. The third section represented a new departure. It enabled local authorities to borrow money from the Public Works Loans Commissioners to buy land (by compulsory purchase if necessary), to build houses, to let the houses thus built to working-class tenants, and to lay out land and to lease sites for the erection of dwellings. Conservative adherence to market mechanisms left its imprint – local authorities were to charge market rents for these houses. Subsidised housing was not envisaged.[249] The AMC campaigned for more central aid. In 1901 its president declared that housing was 'the municipal problem of the day'.[250] But in the same year Long told a deputation that his government was not sympathetic to such a policy.[251] The Royal Commission on Labour suggested central loans to landowners to ease the difficulties of rural housing.[252] Such a moderate suggestion was not adopted. There was no significant Tory departure from market forces.

Despite a great deal of pressure and much aired expediency nothing came of the idea to introduce old age pensions. Left-wing pressure had been building up on the subject. In the middle and late 1890s many leading Conservatives expressed sympathy for the idea.[253] In 1898 a hundred Unionists petitioned the government to pass appropriate legislation.[254] Blue-books were discussing the subject. A royal commission came out against old age pensions in 1895;[255] a departmental committee did the same in 1898.[256] A select committee argued in favour in 1899[257] and a departmental committee costed its proposals in 1900.[258] By 1899 the Cabinet was subjecting pensions to serious examination.[259] Long made clear much of the nature of the inside story in initiating the debate. Once again he leaned towards action. Opportunism was a most influential force:

> In regard to the question of Old Age Pensions, it seems to me desirable, both from the point of view of policy and expediency, to deal with the question, if we can do so, in a reasonable and satisfactory manner. Many Members of Parliament on our side have pledged themselves to a policy of this kind. No doubt, in so doing they have gone far beyond any statement made by their leaders, but the difficulties of their position are obvious, especially in the case of Members representing purely rural constituencies, where such a subject is especially attractive, and where it is not always easy to

find topics which are at the time interesting to the audience, and which come within the range of practical politics.[260]

But there were many Conservative arguments against old age pensions. Hicks Beach, for one, wrote that pensions could offend powerful interests and lead to undesirable consequences. 'We should not accept the new and dangerous idea of relieving those who, though no doubt poor, are able to support themselves'; 'the Opposition', he argued, 'can easily outbid, in the view of the agricultural labourer, anything we could propose; and we should lose far more friends than we should gain'.[261] But Tory backbenchers pressed ahead. In 1902 Long presented all sorts of manoeuvres by which the Cabinet could secure the failure of a private members' bill.[262] The Liberal Party did not hesitate to spell out the gap between right-wing promises and right-wing performance.[263] In subsequent years Conservatives liked to claim that it was the Boer War which had prevented the enactment of old age pensions during their tenure of office.[264] But this was akin to special pleading – the Conservatives did not want to levy the taxation, or rearrange expenditure, to allow such a policy. This may have been a most impolitic decision, a political false economy on a grand scale.

The Aliens Act of 1905 was a measure of social legislation which illuminated Tory inclinations. Its acceptability emphasised the unacceptability of other measures; its presence on the statute book highlighted noticeable absences. Previous decades had witnessed increasing pauper immigration, especially from Russia and Eastern Europe.[265] In 1901 Gerald Balfour told the Cabinet that this influx had not had an effect on wages, which were continuing to rise, but had had such pernicious consequences as overcrowding, poor sanitation, a loss of trade to shopkeepers, and social tensions.[266] The Act put restrictions on this immigration. It agreed with the Conservative Party's nationalist stance and offered to improve social conditions without cost to the Exchequer or the transgression of property rights.[267] Other legislation, such as a number of Factory Acts,[268] or the Agricultural Holdings Act of 1900,[269] were extreme in their moderation. Their minimal degree of intervention served to highlight Tory non-interventionism.

The Conservative Party's social legislation was integrated into a distinct image projected by the Right. The Conservatives constantly expressed concern and sympathy for the condition of the poor. There is no reason to suppose that this was insincere. After all, social duty was axiomatic to the Tory vision of the world. Lord Salisbury's speeches towards the end of the century regularly contained regret at the extent of poverty. In October 1895, for example, he said 'We have got, as far as we can, to make this country more pleasant to live in for the vast majority of those who live in it.'[270] Tory legislation was cited by party propaganda as evidence of this concern. The perennial line was that the Conservatives were real and practical friends to the the working man. The Liberals were portrayed as insincere and theoretical. In 1889 the NUCAS began a series of pamphlets entitled *Real Conservative Reform* which exemplified the approach.[271] Successive *Campaign Guides* emphasised the way in which Conservative legislation had sought to help the working classes and devoted special chapters to the subject.[272] The degree of emphasis on this legislation, and not on the benefits of non-intervention, suggests a deliberate response to the collectivist challenge.

What of the bulwark strategy? One of the themes of this study will be that the greater the threat to property the greater the Tory movement towards the creation of owner-occupiers. Yet the impulse was constrained by the practicalities; Conservatism both produced the vision and hindered it. Operating in a society of low government, which they favoured, the Conservatives lacked the fiscal or state resources to achieve a sizeable creation of small freeholders. Paradoxically, it was precisely the advance of collectivism which would later come to lay the pre-conditions for the surmounting of these obstacles by the Right. A belief in the economic efficiency of the existing system produced doubts as to the economic wisdom of artificial interference. Thus, for example, it was asked whether peasant proprietors could survive in the harsh world of the agrarian economy; or whether urban artisan freeholders would not become burdened with debt. In addition, there was the Conservative adherence to property rights. The bulwark strategy could involve their transgression, and this provoked a certain antipathy. The bulwark strategy, then, revealed much about Conservatism. Support for the ends attested to a desire to maintain the existing order; anxiety over the means arose out of the beliefs which produced such a desire. Between 1886 and 1914 the Conservative vision of an expanded class of owner-occupiers was a dream produced by fear; a will o' the wisp pursued by a party frequently lost as to the proper direction to take.

During these years of Unionist ascendancy the bulwark strategy merely began to stir as a response to the radicalisation of the Left. On the agrarian front almost nothing was achieved. There were some appropriate sentiments about the 1892 Small Holdings Act. 'I believe that a small proprietary constitutes the strongest bulwark against revolutionary change', Salisbury declared, 'and affords the soundest support for the Conservative feeling and institutions of the country'.[273] But words were not matched by deeds. Ireland, of course, was another country. The Unionist Land Purchase Acts, which created owner-occupation on a large scale, were a peculiar product of the Irish context.[274] They were not extended to the mainland. With regard to tenant farmers the bulwark strategy had little purpose. Conservatives and contemporaries habitually regarded the nation's farmers as a Tory class. The Farmers' Alliance, a pressure group with Liberal inclinations, had sprung up in the 1880s, only to fade in the face of the Conservative character of its intended constituency.[275]

The urban sector was similarly untouched by a substantial policy. Lord Randolph Churchill supported leasehold enfranchisement (LE)with frequent bulwarkian arguments, which further indicates his essential Conservative purpose. In 1884 he asked the House of Commons 'Who was the more likely to be a contented and patriotic citizen – the man who was a freeholder, and who was safe in his property, or the man who was at the mercy of a colossal landowner?'.[276] In its official publications the Conservative Party adopted a stance of studied neutrality towards LE.[277] But this was without conviction. The Right would not countenance such a compromise of the privileges of property. The Select Committee on Town Holdings in its report of 1889 advocated a limited scheme of working-class leasehold enfranchisement, [278] but such moderation could not move the Right. In the same way the Conservative Party made no effort to change the urban tenancy laws.

The Conservative idea of a freeholding urban working-class has its origins in these early anti-collectivist days. In 1885 Salisbury had wondered whether it would not be a good idea to increase house ownership by permitting local authority loans for purchasers or giving the owner-occupiers of new buildings rate and house tax exemptions for five years.[279] The Small Dwellings Acquisition Act of 1899 enabled local authorities to obtain central loans so that they could lend money to workers to buy their own homes.[280] The Earl of Selborne introduced the government bill into the House of Lords. 'The diffusion of real property among the people is, perhaps, less advanced in this country than in any other country in Europe', he said, 'and I believe it will greatly add to the permanence and stability of our institutions if there is a large addition to the body of our freeholders'.[281] But once again the means were not to hand. Parallels with the 1892 Small Holdings Act are precise. Between 1899 and 1907 a mere £50,000 was spent under the Act's provisions.[282]

Conservative beliefs acted as a powerful brake both upon the practice of opportunism and the enactment of the bulwark strategy. Conjoined with these beliefs was another potent factor, which arose from the Conservative Party's social foundations – the influence of affected interests. Lord Salisbury constantly referred to this dimension to Conservative politics. After all, he himself was a prominent member of that most conspicuous of Tory interests, the landed interest. In 1886 he responded to Churchill's promptings with the following most prescient sentences:

> The Tory party is composed of very varying elements, and there is merely trouble and vexation of spirit in trying to make them work together. I think the 'classes and the dependents of class' are the strongest ingredients in our composition, but we have so to conduct our legislation that we shall give some satisfaction to both classes and masses. This is specially difficult with the classes - because all legislation is rather unwelcome to them, as tending to disturb a state

of things with which they are satisfied.[283]

Some years later he deemed a leasehold enfranchisement policy to belong to that 'class of measures known from a celebrated instance as aiming at the result of "dishing the Whigs"'. The danger of adopting such a policy, he argued, 'is the risk of alienating old friends without conciliating any new adherents'.[284] In 1894 Salisbury gave a considered evaluation of Chamberlain's social reform programme. He stressed that some of its provisions would antagonise traditional sources of Tory support. 'The question then follows – would these measures gain for us an adequate compensation among those who otherwise would vote for us.' Salisbury was sceptical.[285] The existence of these interests, and the influence they wielded, makes the 'Tory collectivism' thesis even more unlikely.

An intrinsic feature of the Conservative response to the challenge of Liberalism and Socialism was an emphasis on issues beyond the narrowly economic. An investigation of the Conservative Party's handling of material politics requires an examination of activity beyond the confines of social issues. Patriotism was axiomatic to the whole Tory stance. The Conservative Party was the party of national pre-eminence, the Union with Ireland, the Empire, military strength and the monarchy. The Union Jack was as much a party symbol as a national symbol. It was constantly used in party propaganda and to adorn Tory platforms. The Conservative Party's nationalism did not only consist of a collection of policies and stances with an electoral appeal. It constituted a distinct right-wing form of self-definition and political perspective. In this Tory scheme of things the individual was to see himself as part of a unified people with a European, imperial and global mission. He was to be a promoter of British ways. The Tory vision was at work. Of necessity, this rivalled the left-wing individual who was often to see himself as the victim of unjust economic arrangements. Conservative nationalism and imperialism offered a self-conception and consciousness to counter the collectivism and materialism of the emergent radical Left. Indeed, the decades before the Great War witnessed a constant struggle between the political parties to direct political attention towards different areas and visions of life. The Right tended to lean towards national grandeur; the Left had inclinations towards economic hardship. A great deal of Conservative England lay overseas.

Throughout this period the Right identified itself with, and promoted, the Empire. Was this one of its greatest strengths? Recent research has tended to stress the popularity of imperialism.[286] During the Boer War the Conservative Party was able to present itself in all its imperial colours and the 1900 triumph was the greatest of its election victories.[287] A whole clutch of imperial pressure groups operated within the Tory orbit – the Victoria League, British Empire League, Imperial Federation League, Imperial South African Association, Navy League, National Service

League and League of the Empire.[288] The 'scramble for Africa' and the planting of the flag in whole tracts of the dark continent could only serve to bring the Empire into greater public focus. Bound up with the party's imperialism was its Unionism. The Conservative Party never ceased to stress its commitment to the union with Ireland. Opposition to Home Rule was a permanent and dominant feature of its propaganda. Unionist was often synonymous with Conservative. Ireland was one of the chief determinants of political allegiance during this imperial age and the Right's Unionism was perhaps the most conspicuous feature of its political identity.[289] This patriotic party was also the party of strong national defence, and this became increasingly emphasised with the rise of the German menace.[290] The Conservatives were also the monarchist party. The Crown was the symbol of imperial and national greatness and cohesion. The Golden and Diamond jubilees of 1887 and 1897 agreed very well with the Tory emphasis on the nation's role in the world.

Tory cultural politics extended beyond the Primrose League. An attempt to promote Conservative ways of thinking and feeling may be detected in the party's policy towards the Church of England. Much research remains to be done into the impact of Anglicanism on popular attitudes in general, and the relationship of Conservatism to Christianity in particular. It seems possible to suggest that the Church of England played a significant role in supporting the communitarian and voluntaryist vision of society held by the Right. Liberal and Labour hostility to Anglicanism may have reflected a realisation that the Church was an antagonistic force. Was not the Church of England mocked as 'The Tory Party at prayer'? The Church of England, by its charitable activities alone, aligned with Conservative anti-statism. One Anglican organisation, the Girls' Friendly Society, which helped young women in distress, was firmly allied in its outlook and its actions with the party of Lord Salisbury and Arthur Balfour.[291] But it is into the deeper areas of belief and thinking that the historian wishes to peer, into the whole relationship between the established Church and the Victorian cultural system. An inference is possible – did not the Conservative Party's defence of Anglicanism indicate an acknowledgement of the significant role the Church of England played in supporting Conservatism? In her portrayal of rural life Flora Thompson was keen to illustrate this point.[292]

The late-Victorian Conservative leadership was a repository of committed Anglicans. Lord Salisbury, Arthur Balfour (a Presbyterian) and Michael Hicks Beach were religious statesmen of a conventional Protestant hue. Balfour, indeed, was a theologian of high repute. From 1886 to 1914 the Conservative Party consistently and vigorously opposed any disestablishment of the Anglican Church in Wales.[293] In the 1890s a 'Church Parliamentary Committee' was established within the parliamentary party to co-ordinate opposition to the Liberal Party's plans.[294] Anti-disestablishmentarianism and anti-collectivism both found expression in the Tory Party. No doubt they had shared origins. Indeed, the establishment question was a property issue. The Right was resisting an attempt by the state to undermine the economic independence of a prominent institution. The defence of the Church was a further manifestation of Tory anti-statism. Concrete financial aid was given by the Conservatives to the Church by means of the reduction of rates on tithe receipts in 1899. Parsons were to be under less severe economic pressure in the discharge of their duties.[295] Earlier, in 1891, the Conservatives had made the Church of England less politically vulnerable by shifting the obligation of tithe payment from the occupier to the owner.[296]

The Conservative Party also sought to strengthen the position of the Church of England by supporting its educational ministry. There was a duality in the educational system. Voluntary schools existed side by side with the schools of the school boards. In the voluntary schools the Church of England found its special role. The late-Victorian and Edwardian educational question was one of considerable complexity, but reduced to essentials it involved two subjects: finance and religion. As Lord Salisbury said – 'there are two educational problems'.[297] The Anglican run voluntary schools were undergoing a financial crisis at the same time as the Church of England came to re-emphasise its educational mission. In 1897 the government gave central aid to the voluntary schools by special Act of Parliament. The 1902 Educational Act gave further funds as well as putting the voluntary schools under a new local authority. From 1906 to 1908 the Liberal government attempted to reverse this favouritism and to undermine Anglican educational influence. The House of Lords, true to its Tory colours, acted as a powerful obstacle.[298]

What of the Conservative Party's activities at a narrowly parliamentary level? A parliamentary tactic to which the Conservatives had long been habituated was obstructionism. The Irish Nationalists had paved the way in this form of political opposition and had provoked changes in the rules of parliamentary procedure. During the years 1892–1895 it was a tactic to which the Conservatives resorted. This was most especially seen in the opposition's treatment of Harcourt's 1894 budget. It was a sign of the hostility aroused on the Conservative benches by the new death duties on land that a campaign of obstruction was launched against them.[299] The vigour of the assault, and the nature of its object, were most revealing of the concerns of Conservatism. One Conservative MP remembered it as 'one of the most remarkable fights I ever witnessed in the House'; 'For nearly five weeks after the resumption of business, the Committee stage of the Bill was taken *de die in diem*.'[300] The Liberal Party condemned this Tory obstructionism in its propaganda.[301] Indicating Conservative concerns, the Tories were not to use such fierce methods again until the budget of 1909, which also provided for a reform of the taxation of land.

But obstructionism in the House of Commons was as of nothing compared to the rejection or moderation of legislation in the House of Lords. Between 1892 and 1895 the upper house proved itself a potent Conservative weapon. Even more anti-Liberal after the secession of the Whigs in 1886, the House of Lords was a force for anti-Liberalism and anti-Socialism. The Conservatives surrounded the House of Lords with a defensive barrage of doctrines and polemic.[302] Part of the influence of the House of Lords may well be seen in the legislation the Liberals did not introduce – it could have been thought that such legislation would never have a chance in the Other Place. Otherwise the Home Rule Bill and the Welsh Disestablishment Bill led a long list of casualties. Interventionism was checked: the Employers' Liability Bill, the Railway Hours Bill and the Parish Councils Bill all suffered at the hands of the nobility and the Liberals were loud in their complaints.[303] The ground was being prepared for the great constitutional crisis of 1909–1911.

The Conservative Party's method of winning the war over property rights and economic arrangements, which intensified between 1886 and 1906, was made up of various discernable responses and initiatives. A conservative approach to the world of wealth had its own appeal, and this was buttressed by an emphasis on other issues, especially those involving patriotic sentiments. The Left was frequently damned in combative fashion. At the same time the Conservative Party did its best to prevent a further democratisation of the national political process.[304] A promotion of opportunism for Conservative reasons was a major concern of certain prominent Unionists, and such pragmatism found expression in a series of legislative measures. These measures carried the imprint of their Tory provenance. Yet this opportunism was distinctly restrained, and may have courted political danger. Sympathy was expressed for the sufferings of the poor. The bulwark strategy did not progress beyond early stages of development. The agrarian sector was allowed to continue on its downward trend. The House of Lords was used to remedy the consequences of electoral rebuffs; obstructionism in the House of Commons showed that at times the constitutional party did not play the parliamentary game. Attempts at the reinforcement of Tory culture may be detected in the Right's creation of the Primrose League and its favoured treatment of the Church of England. At the end of this period there emerged from within the Unionist ranks a movement full of answers to the Left's challenge – the tariff reform campaign.

Three

Tariff Reform and the USRC

During the Edwardian period two forces arose which have been constantly cited as examples of the Tory Party's 'progressive' tendency.[1] Here, if anywhere, should be found the much canvassed leftist inheritance of British Conservatism. These Tory phenomena merit detailed and separate consideration. At first glance both the tariff reform movement and the Unionist Social Reform Committee seem to lend credence to the received view that there has always been an interventionist strand on the Right. They employed a great deal of anti-*laissez-faire* rhetoric and espoused policies which involved state expansion. Indeed, they would appear to invalidate that exposition of Conservative beliefs and attitudes presented in an earlier chapter. Yet a close examination reveals the opposite. Both may be seen, *inter alia*, as quintessential exercises in principled opportunism. Their ultimate aims were profoundly Conservative. Therein lay their true affinity. The tariff reform movement and the Unionist Social Reform Committee were, in part, Tory responses to the challenge of collectivism and democratisation – their very concerns indicated the way politics were going in Great Britain. They exemplify the truth that historians should not be misled by manufactured appearances.

I

The history of the tariff reform movement is familiar in outline. In 1903 Joseph Chamberlain launched his campaign for the introduction of a new system of tariffs. In a series of speeches around the country he called for the imposition of import duties to protect the domestic economy, secure additional government revenue, promote imperial welfare and solidarity, reduce certain food taxes, and finance measures of social reform. The Tariff Reform League (TRL) was created to direct the movement. It had a large army of speakers and lecturers, and engaged in advanced techniques of literary propaganda. A Tariff Commission was established under the guidance of the London School of Economics economist Professor Hewins to give intellectual and statistical support to the tariff programme. Its various committees produced detailed reports on a variety of economic subjects. By 1905 a majority of Unionist MPs were committed to Chamberlain's cause. By 1907 the National Union was giving its full endorsement to tariff reform and the Conservative Party had become officially committed to reforming the system of taxation on imports. A hard-core of some thirty to forty MPS was always at the centre of the campaign; other Unionists were antagonistic. The tariff reform movement was a heterogeneous collection of aspirations, interests, commitments and intentions which shifted over time. A mass of literature has grown up around Chamberlain's initiative and the pattern of events of the whole story is well described.[2] What needs to be done is to rise above the detail and to consider the true historical significance of this most studied of Conservative entities.

Chamberlain's movement appealed to Conservatives in a number of ways. Only by understanding this is it possible to understand the force of its appeal. First and foremost the tariff reform campaign was a Conservative creation. Indeed, it offered to solve certain pressing contemporary dilemmas and one of its most important characteristics was that it appeared in the 1900s. It seemed to square all kinds of Tory circles. In this it was an intelligent exercise in internal Conservative statesmanship. No doubt, to a certain extent, the man from the Midlands was aiming at control of the party. Most obviously, tariff reform appealed to the Conservatives at a national and imperial level. The Empire was to be strengthened and developed by a system of preferential tariffs. National power was to be increased by the expected rise in national wealth and the military strength derived from increased expenditure. Retaliatory tariffs and measures against the dumping of cheap foreign goods appealed to nationalist sentiments. Tariff reform may be seen as the last great exercise in positive British imperialism before the long march to concessive withdrawal.

Tariff reform also offered greater prosperity for the nation and the people. It was argued that protection, retaliation and the prevention of dumping would raise profits, incomes and wages. Imperial preference would have a productive effect by developing markets and stimulating trade within the Empire. By raising revenue from tariffs and not from internal taxes, it was asserted, the uneconomic burden on the domestic economy would be lightened. The working-classes would further benefit from a reduction in the taxes on their food. The fiscal appeal was also potent. Money was to be found for social reform, local taxation relief and national defence. The rising costs of government, so well revealed during the previous Tory administrations, were to be met (or partly met) by tariffs. In other words, this was a fiscal policy to rival the feared taxation proposals of the Left. More than this, an alternative was being offered to the collectivist means of making the people richer.

The tariff reform programme solved many Conservative problems and expressed important Conservative aims in a united and interlocking whole. All classes were to benefit in a great national and imperial crusade; power and prosperity were to accrue to a people bound together by a sense of their mission in the world. Tariff reform appeared to be a means of combating the Left without offending principles or injuring interests. Prosperity and social reform were to be given to the people; the taxation of the rich or the landed was not needed. Class conflict could be submerged. Protection could even appeal to some of the previously threatened interests. Yet there appeared to be no direct interference in the internal workings of the market, no overt transgression of property rights, and no immediate intrusion into economic liberty. Such proposals as statutory minimum wages, fixed rents, or nationalisation were absent. It was the foreigner who was to suffer. Tariff reform was presented as a defensive barrier, a massive shelter. The way things were was to be left the same but given protection from external and international forces. From all points of view, as an expression of Conservatism, Chamberlain's conception had a remarkable ingenuity.

There is much to suggest that tariff reform's chief appeal to Conservatives lay in its anti-collectivist possibilities. Seen in this light, the movement was a direct response to New Liberalism and new Labour. In this way it can be said that tariff reform carried on from Tory Democracy. Expressed intentions are very suggestive. What of Chamberlain himself? An examination of his career indicates that the tariff reform campaign followed on from the reform initiative of the 1890s and the Unauthorised Programme of the 1880s in being an exercise in principled opportunism. The Birmingham leopard had not changed his spots. Tariff reform seems, to a substantial extent, to have been an attempt to halt collectivism by undercutting its appeal and rivalling its social reform policies. This does not mean to say that it was not other things as well. In 1906 Chamberlain gave a private address to the 1900 Club of Unionist MPs. His arguments echoed those of the 1880s and 1890s. Away from the public spotlights Chamberlain could indulge in candour:

> We must not make the fatal mistake of thinking that we can or ought to ride back to power on a policy of mere negation. Speaking to you as a fighting club, I say, Give us or accept from us an effective, definite, fighting policy. The policy of resistance, of negation, is not sufficient answer to that Socialist opinion which is growing up amongst us – the Socialist opinion the objects of which are, after all, worthy of earnest and even favourable consideration. But the means by which these objects are promoted are open to serious objection. We can only meet Socialism...by pointing out in all true sympathy the impossibility, the impracticability of the methods chosen, and by suggesting other and better methods for securing all that is good in the object sought for...and as that policy, by whomsoever propounded, is a policy which means money, which means expenditure, it is closely connected with the third object of our party officially declared – that fiscal reform is the first constructive policy

of the Unionist Party...it is clear that, if great extension is to be given to social reform, the money can only be found by an extension of the basis of our taxation. It seems to me that it cannot be found in a less burden upon the people, a less interference with trade than by the moderate suggestions which the Unionist Party have made.[3]

The character and timing of the policy initiatives of the tariff reform activists bear witness to a desire to frustrate the social promises of the progressive alliance. In late 1907 Austen Chamberlain presented a provisional programme to Balfour. Old age pensions, land reform, housing and sweated industries all received a mention. This was not collectivist Conservatism but expedient Conservatism and one line said everything:'you would show the country that there is a definite constructive alternative to the wildcat and predatory schemes of the present Government and its Socialist allies'.[4] In 1908 the tariff reform leadership (including Milner, Bonar Law and Austen Chamberlain) published an 'unauthorised programme' in *The Morning Post*. One sentence indicated the extent to which tariff reform was conceived and promoted as a response to the social radicalism of the Left. 'As the only means of protecting employment, of increasing production, and of equitably providing additional revenue for national defence and social reform, it is essential to the union of classes.'[5] Shortly after the 1910 general election leading tariff reformers produced a list of policies. It was clearly a response to electoral pressure.[6] Later that year less important tariff reformers produced a 'Reveille manifesto'. Behind the advanced policies lay a conservative intent, as the following excerpts show. 'State credit and the great existing friendly societies will be used to assist insurance. So shall we avoid the ruin inherent in a Right to Work Bill.' More was to come. 'State credit will assist the purchase of land by small owners. So shall we avoid the risks of State ownership of the land.'[7]

The other leaders of the tariff reform movement shared the approach of their master. Andrew Bonar Law was a tariff reformer from the beginning. Yet his subsequent leadership of the party revealed an antipathy to the promotion of social reform. His earlier stances could be discarded now that they were of no use. Lord Henry Cavendish Bentinck, who was one of the very few Conservative MPs to be a genuine social reformer, wrote a book entitled *Tory Democracy* in 1918. In it he went out of his way to attack the Bonar Law leadership of the pre-war period for neglecting social reform.[8] Austen Chamberlain led the Tariff Reform League after the paralysis of his father. His attitude also exuded Conservative calculation. His 1907 letter to Balfour was permeated by fear and a desire to halt the Left. 'Labour-Socialism is making enormous strides among the working men and especially among the young men.' The Radicals were planning to use the land question to 'destroy' the Conservatives and the House of Lords.[9]

Alfred Milner (1854–1925) was one of the most prominent of the tariff reformers. A high position in the Inland Revenue and the Pro-Consulship in South Africa had led to a seat in the House of Lords and high national standing. Milner identified himself with the tariff reform movement's social programme and even came to play an important part in the enactment of the 1909 Trades Boards Act.[10] He, also, was in the business of frustration by concession. At heart Milner was an anti-statist. In December 1912 he delivered an address on 'The Two Nations' at Toynbee Hall. Milner confessed that as he grew older he tended 'more and more to trust to moral influences for the advancement of the mass of the people'.[11] In 1907 he gave a detailed speech on social reform to a Guildford audience. All sorts of policies were proposed: old age pensions, housing and town planning, small holdings, control of sweated labour. They were accompanied by a classic statement of principled opportunism. Social reform was necessary to halt the advance of Socialism:

> The true antidote to revolutionary Socialism is practical social reform...The revolutionary Socialist...would like to get rid of all private property... He is going absurdly too far; but what gave birth to his doctrine? The abuse of the rights of property, the cruelty and failure of the scramble for gain, which mark the reign of a one-sided Individualism. If we had not gone much too far in one direction, we should not have had this extravagant reaction in the other. But do not let us lose our heads in the face of that reaction. While resisting the revolutionary propaganda, let us be more, and not less, strenuous in removing the causes of it.[12]

Present in these sentences was the eminently Tory suggestion that moral shortcomings in economic relationships had contributed to the rise of Socialist ideas.

George Wyndham MP (1863–1913) was a country landowner and a member of the Cecil cousinhood. He had been a Cabinet member under Balfour and then a leading adherent of the Chamberlain movement. His motives, also, were tactical and strategic. In 1906 he thought that there were two chief ideals in politics. '(1) Imperialism, which demands Unity at Home, between classes, and Unity throughout the Empire; and which *prescribes* Fiscal Reform to secure both', and '(2) *Insular Socialism* and Class Antagonism...Between these two ideals a great battle will be fought.'[13] A year later, in a letter to his father, he declared that tariff reform was the only way of meeting the costs of inevitable collectivism. Left-wing taxation schemes could not be tolerated. The people could have state aid, but they would have to pay for it themselves. Pensions, small holdings, education, relief of the poor, and housing all required finance – 'there is no possible ultimate solution except that the people should pay for all this. And there is no way in which they pay except by broadening the basis of taxation.'[14] The leading lights of the tariff reform movement glittered with an enlightened Conservatism which often extended no further than hard-nosed political calculation.

What of the Conservative Party more generally? The evidence does not suggest that tariff reform was adopted out of a commitment to substantial social change. The National Union had for long adhered to the idea of import controls. Throughout the late-Victorian period mass party opinion endorsed differing kinds of protection at successive conferences.[15] The Fair Trade tradition had never died in British politics.[16] In 1905 the National Union came out in favour of an adjustment of tariffs.[17] In 1907 it passed a resolution which was confirmed for many years thereafter. The National Union declared that tariff reform was necessary to broaden the basis of taxation, safeguard domestic industry, strengthen the country's position in foreign markets, and improve imperial links.[18] In January 1907 the chief whip ascertained that the bulk of the party wanted a public statement from Balfour concerning the relationship of tariff reform to central and local finance, to closer commercial union with the colonies, and to the export of industrial goods. In addition, majority Tory opinion wanted a 'point made of the fact that schemes of social reform depending upon public money cannot be accomplished without that elasticity of revenue which alone can be obtained from a wider basis of taxation'.[19] This last gives a good indication of the extent to which tariff reform was bound up with the Tory response to the Liberal and Labour material challenge.

The point was made even more explicitly in official literature. *The Campaign Guide* of 1909 gave a detailed exposition of the official tariff reform case. The central idea was that import duties would raise popular standards of living and provide revenue for social reform. Clearly set out was the Right's answer to the Left's plans for achieving the same ends. The key section communicated Tory axioms about individual self-reliance, the folly of taxing the rich, and the need to allow free market mechanisms to operate to beneficial effect. Perhaps nowhere else is it so clearly suggested that tariff reform offered a right-wing solution to the rise of collectivism. Tariff reform not social reform – that was the motive spring:

> The difference between Tariff Reformers and the Radical-Socialists is that the latter believe that they can improve the condition of the poor by doles extracted by force from the pockets of the rich.
>
> This is a system of social reform which has been tried by all nations at greater times, and has always resulted in demoralisation and greater poverty and misery for the people. Tariff Reformers, on the other hand, believe in enabling people to earn by their own exertions the necessary competence on which they can support the standard of life and of comfort which we believe essential to national efficiency...The ambition of the State should be to enable its citizens to provide for all the chances of life out of the daily earnings of their

hand or brain...It makes no difference what name you give your
taxes - income tax, land tax, death duties, "taxes on windfalls"; all
in the end come out of the production of the country, and constitute
burdens upon industries, adding to "the cost of production"...Tariff
Reform will help to give the necessary scale of manufacture which
will make possible cheapness combined with better conditions'.[20]
Tariff reform countered collectivism in more general fashion. Its
broader physiognomy is equally suggestive. Tariff reform provided a
form of surrogate collectivism. It shared many of the features of its enemy
and thereby indicated its purpose. Activist politicians using modern
political methods promised that direct state action would increase popular
standards of welfare. One of the persistent features of British, European
and global statism has been the propensity of individual politicians to
present themselves as great benefactors of the people. The twentieth
century is crowded with such figures. Such a stance greatly appeals to self-
importance and the will to power. The chance to become the champion of
the people emerged as one of the prizes of the profession of politics.
Indeed, often these types have known of no other career than politics. One
of the commonest features of an increasingly political age has been the
willingness of political leaders to promise prosperity by means of the
manipulation of state levers. Herein lay one of the fatal attractions of
Keynesianism. In Great Britain Joseph Chamberlain was perhaps the first
great exponent of this modern style of politics. He certainly put Cobden
and Bright in the shade; and Gladstone proclaimed much more than he
offered. Others were to follow in the Birmingham manufacturer's foot-
steps. During the tariff reform campaign Chamberlain was at the centre of
the stage, and he recaptured many of the glories of his previous Radical
Campaign. In great speeches in large halls he promised a gleaming future.
The Tariff Reform League's propaganda, which often bore the imprint of
his monocled face, raised his profile to new heights. He was the Leader of
the Movement, the 'People's Joseph', the Prophet of a New Dawn.[21] This
leading star was surrounded by a number of lesser luminaries who
indulged in imitative activity.

The tariff reformers were in the business of promising raised levels of
mass prosperity, and like their left-wing counterparts they used advanced
campaigning techniques to comunicate their message. Chamberlain's
creation attested to materialisation. The tariff reform irruption was a
conspicuous part of a long-term development. It responded to, and
promoted, the increasing concern of public life with economic issues.
Linked to the promotion of the Empire was the promotion of prosperity.
Tariff reformers repeatedly promised that imperial preference, protection,
retaliation and tariff-funded welfare measures would work to the material
advantage of the people.[22] Necessarily, there was great scope for the
sympathy tactic and tariff reformers made clear that they cared. The other

aspects and appeals of tariff reform acted to support and buttress these more sharply defined anti-collectivist features. For some on the Right, notwithstanding the obvious political advantages, this approach was not acceptable. Lord Robert Cecil MP rejected what he saw as an assault on essential values: 'It appears to me to be utterly sordid and materialistic, not yet corrupt, but on the high road to corruption.'[23] A. Sykes concludes that, after 1907, tariff reform, under Balfour's direction, became a 'tactic to defend the *status quo*';[24] R.Jay affirms: 'tariff reform emerged as a form of minimal government interference in the market to fend off the threat of more drastic intervention from the left'.[25] Here one may detect the emergence of a future orthodoxy.

What can be made of the tariff reform solution to the challenge of collectivism? Certainly it was ingenious, but it was also somewhat ingenuous. The commitment to the imposition of certain new food taxes seems to have been a political error of the first magnitude. The history of the tariff reform movement was very much a history of attempts to remove this self-imposed millstone. The 1902 corn and flour duties had caused a furore and had had to be repealed a year later. The chief whip advised his colleagues at the time:'to face a General Election with this duty in existence would be to court defeat'.[26] In late 1903 Acland Hood submitted another memorandum about Chamberlain's new proposals which contained a very similar message.[27] Chamberlain himself recognised the 'prejudice against a food tax'.[28] Few doubted the widespread unpopularity of this aspect of the tariff reform programme. In 1910 Balfour declared that colonial wheat would not be taxed.[29] Later that year he promised a referendum on tariffs.[30] In January 1913 Bonar Law promised that food taxes would not be imposed by the next Conservative government.[31] As Chamberlain's duties were finally abandoned, and as it was widely recogised that they were electorally damaging, their original adoption must be considered a serious strategic mistake. The chief reason for their retention lay in the logistics of Chamberlain's plan – food taxes were an instrument for giving the colonies preference.

'I fear these social questions are destined to break up our party',[32] predicted Lord Salisbury in 1892. One of the themes of this study is that meeting the Left precipitated divisions within Conservatism over tactics and strategies rather than over goals. The tariff reform experience was an example of such divisions. Balfour regarded it as his duty to maintain the unity of his party. His unhappy leadership was much taken up with the difficulties of this task. In his endeavours he threw light upon the purpose of Conservatism. 'Our business is to prevent our divisions reaching a point which may convert them into a national disaster', he told the Duke of Devonshire in 1903, 'and may deprive the greatest interests of the guardianship by which since 1886 they have been protected';[33] 'my whole object is to restore the Unionist Party to the position of an effective fighting machine', he told Austen Chamberlain in 1907. One of the party's chief tasks, continued the Tory leader, was to 'resist the disintegrating forces of modern Radicalism'.[34] But all these divisions caused by Chamberlain's movement created a dispersion of forces, the image of disunity, the debility of internal strife, demoralisation and a lack of cohesion. All this must have worked against the Right.

A doubt, therefore, must be raised against Chamberlain's judgement and against the judgement of those who supported him. Food taxation and division were powerful anti-Tory factors. The timing of the campaign was also suspect. It was launched at the end of a long period of Unionist rule when another election loomed on the horizon. The situation required delicate handling. Chamberlain himself both admitted the unpopularity of the food taxes and anticipated electoral reversal in the short run. 'I do not expect, and indeed never have expected, to carry the country with a sweep at the next election', he wrote in April 1904, 'All my efforts and hopes are directed to the election after next.'[35] But a period of Liberal rule would pass the initiative to the Left and give it an opportunity to practise those policies Chamberlain and his followers believed to be so dangerous to the Conservative cause. This, in fact, is exactly what happened. The period 1906–1914 witnessed the first great exercise in statutory collectivism and seemed to work to the Left's electoral advantage. By 1914 the Right was still out of office and its immediate prospects did not appear to be bright. Viewed in this light, tariff reform may have aided the development it sought to frustrate. One eminent historian of the Conservative Party has expressed perplexed wonder at the Right's persistent support for a 'cause that was politically so calamitous'.[36] Was it not because so many Edwardian Tories believed they had found an answer to the appeal of New Liberalism and threatening Labour? It is almost as though traditionally hardened Conservatives were mesmerised by the glittering image of a painless and potent anti-collectivism.

II

The Unionist Social Reform Committee (USRC) was brought into being in 1911 and had a much narrower focus than the tariff reform movement. For one historian the USRC was a clear example of the Right's gaucheist inheritance;[37] for others it was an attempt to 'push the party in a collectivist direction'.[38] One recent observer has gone so far as to write that the USRC 'developed a distinctive ideology of social reform – a synthesis of traditional toryism, Fabian socialism and contemporary ideas about rural regneration'.[39] In fact, the USRC was a clear exercise in sincere expediency. It symbolised, perhaps more than any other Tory development, the readiness of Conservatives to adopt left-wing policies, and put on their opponents' clothes, to achieve right-wing ends. The Unionist Social Reform Committee came into existence in February 1911 when it commanded the allegiance of some fifty MPs;[40] by 1914 the figure had risen to over seventy – about a quarter of the parliamentary party.[41] Some peers and party sympathisers were also involved. The USRC organised its members in parliamentary debates; appointed committees to produce reports on prominent political topics; and introduced bills into the House of Commons.[42] As its name suggests, the USRC was largely concerned with social issues, and in this it was a sign of the times. It was an unofficial body but it had the tacit approval of the party leadership and located its office in party headquarters. The concerns of the USRC attested to the increasing materialisation of politics; the anxieties of the USRC derived from the rise of collectivism; the purpose of the USRC revealed the aims of Conservatism.

The leadership of the committee is a fitting vehicle for the analysis of its character. F.E.Smith (1874–1930), the future Lord Birkenhead, was the USRC's chairman.[43] Smith was a nationally famous barrister and one of the party's most popular speakers. He had made his mark with a brilliant maiden speech in the House of Commons and had subsequently vaulted his way to the front bench and the Privy Council. Perhaps ambition was behind his activity. The real guiding force behind the USRC was its vice-chairman, Arthur Steel-Maitland MP. Steel-Maitland (1876–1935), although a neglected figure, was a politician of distinct historical significance. He was a Scottish landowner, a fellow of All Souls, a member for Birmingham, and Alfred Milner's former private secretary. The Milner link is important – Steel-Maitland shared much of his former master's political outlook and Milner himself was an influential member of the USRC. In 1911, at a relatively early age, Steel-Maitland was appointed chairman of the party organisation and thus acquired a place in the shadow cabinet. Far from being a respectful and subordinate functionary, Steel-Maitland set out to transform the Conservative Party's methods and direction.

Steel-Maitland must be placed in the lineage of Joseph Chamberlain, Sir A.K.Rollit and Randolph Churchill. Like them he set out to tackle the problems that faced the Conservative Party in this period of increasing democratic and leftist pressure. Like them, also, he combined an emphasis on improved organisational techniques with the promotion of social reform policies. He was industrious, energetic and analytical, and he foreshadowed much of the political activism which so characterised the ensuing decades. This was no accident – Steel-Maitland was adapting to the demands of emergent mass politics. He conceived of himself as a moderniser, although his vision of what was modern differed from that of most of his colleagues. Perhaps more than any other Conservative of his time he had a distinct and detailed conception of how the Left's social radicalism could be frustrated. Steel-Maitland's activities brought out many of the problems which confronted the Conservative Party as the character of politics changed. Like many a talented young reformer he encountered resistance from those higher up the hierarchy. In 1913 he wrote 'our old buffers were not pleased with me';[44] Austen Chamberlain said that his colleague was 'still rather "young" and anxious to get things more cut and dried than I think they can be'. [45]

Steel-Maitland's general approach was expressed in a detailed memorandum he sent to Bonar Law after the latter had become leader of the party in 1911. The chairman called for a complete overhaul of organisation and the systematic production of policy. He especially emphasised the need to produce policies in the social sphere.[46] Steel-Maitland pressed ahead with modernising the party machinery and there was a marked improvement in the quality of party propaganda. He was altogether less successful on the policy front. Steel-Maitland was fond of memoranda which were a part of his professional vision. A series of such communications were submitted to his colleagues between 1911 and 1914. These documents repeatedly called for the production of policy, the debate of strategy, and the monitoring of public opinion.[47] Steel-Maitland often took independent initiatives in the creation of policy and drafted expert advisers to provide informed advice. Yet he was generally opposed by his fellow party leaders and gave vent to his frustration in private.

The Unionist Social Reform Committee bore the imprint of Maitland's mind. By 1911 the Conservative Party had lost three general elections in succession and the Left was reaping rewards from its social programme. The very timing of the USRC's foundation indicates its opportunistic character. If the committee's members were so inwardly committed to reform why had they not organised earlier? In January 1911 Steel-Maitland communicated with Balfour's private secretary. He wanted to co-ordinate and invigorate the party's backbench attacks on the government in the House of Commons and conduct an 'irregular warfare on the flank'. Social questions, in particular, would be concentrated upon.[48] Sandars approved of the idea and suggested the introduction of bills to gain electoral support.[49] Balfour, therefore, must have known and approved of Steel-Maitland's plan. The front bench, indeed, gave its support.[50] At this formative stage a fellow member of the committee told Steel-Maitland: 'I agree about acting with the knowledge & concurrence of the leaders.'[51] The USRC, therefore, was a product of the thinking of the party leadership and not only of its own members. It was an integral part of the Conservative Party's general strategy for defeating the government and its allies. It was autonomous and separate only in appearance. This is of crucial importance in understanding its significance. It was always unlikely that an independent unit would exist in the regimented ranks of the party's MPs. Steel-Maitland then turned to the Tory press. He asked Northcliffe to instruct his editors to call for the Conservative Party's adoption of social reform policies. In so doing he revealed the pragmatism that lay behind much of the USRC's purpose. Such policies would gain support for the party's imperialism, were desirable in themselves (probably an example of special pleading), and were an 'alternative to Socialistic measures which some people dread'.[52] Within a few weeks the Unionist Social Reform Committee had come into existence.

The USRC organised backbench attacks on Asquith's government and had a committee system for doing so. It did not confine itself only to social questions. In 1911, for example, the Osborne judgement and the Parliament Bill were discussed.[53] In such activity the USRC marked the movement towards a larger role for the ordinary Tory MP in parliamentary debates. But the USRC's main aim was to produce policy. Special committees were created, experts were consulted, and reports were published. The whole spectrum of social reform was covered and committees were established on agriculture, housing, education, public health, industrial unrest, imperial and local taxation, and the poor law. Both the agricultural and the housing committees introduced bills into the House of Commons.[54] The USRC was an intelligent and informed affair and was certainly no product of the dim party of legend. Its coherent organisation and systematic production of policy reflected Steel-Maitland's professionalising vision. In this it anticipated much of the Conservative Party's subsequent practice.

What were the members of the committee aiming at? No systematic survey of opinion is possible, but the available evidence suggests that these Tories were keen proponents of principled opportunism and the sympathy tactic. What the Conservatives held dear could be preserved by a stealing of some of their opponents' social thunder. 'Unless we rapidly reorganise on the lines of Disraelian Toryism, adapted of course to modern conditions, we cannot now stop revolution', reflected one member, 'It is not only the working classes we have to think of, revolutionary ideas are permeating all classes';[55] 'unless we do something, the Labour classes will be once again gulled by the promises of Lloyd George and Co.',[56] argued another. 'I still remain absolutely convinced as I have always been that unless you can put yourself straight with the people on Social questions', wrote Maurice Woods, the committee's secretary, 'all your Tariff, Home Rule or Constitutional thunderbolts will be discharged in vain'.[57] In 1913 Steel-Maitland corresponded with a friend in Canada. He argued that the modern electorate wanted social reform but that many Conservatives were still blind to the way things were. 'We cannot outbid the Liberals or the Socialists', he stressed, but it was important to show the electorate that 'we sympathise, and we are sincere in our desire to act along social lines'.[58] It was essential to 'try and convince some of the working-people of our sympathy with them'.[59] Earlier he had told the party leader that the USRC was 'useful in creating an atmosphere'.[60] In 1913 members of the agricultural committee put pressure on Bonar Law. A USRC member explained that his agricultural colleagues wanted the party commanders to 'give utterance to what everyone must feel is sympathy with the agricultural labourer'.[61]

The published reports carry the impress of their Conservative parent-
age. Once again Tory opportunism was constrained by Tory beliefs.
Although the USRC was not formulating official policy its policies were still
strikingly moderate and at times distinctly innocuous. There was a great
deal of talk about the abandonment of *laissez-faire* and a long tradition of
Tory social reform, but appearances concealed realities. These publications bear all the hallmarks of image projection, although it may be that
many of the committee's members had a less intense commitment to the
social order than other Conservative MPS. Once again a contextual perspective is illuminating. The reports which were the most radical – those
relating to industrial unrest and agriculture – were dealing with subjects
where the Left was making a great deal of running. Can it really be said
of the committee's housing policies that they demonstrated 'The latent
affinity between Tory étatisme and State Socialism'?[62] The committee on
the poor law advocated a general reorganisation of the system of poor
relief and suggested that the state might train the unemployed.[63] The
committee on industrial unrest called, in a cautious and limited fashion, for
voluntary minimum wages, an extension of the 1909 Trades Boards Act,
and the government enforcement of collectively bargained wage rates.[64]
The committee on health was almost exclusively concerned with the more
efficient organisation of the existing system.[65] The report on education
proposed increased central spending, the case for which was widely
accepted.[66] The housing committee introduced bills which provided for an
annual grant of first £500,000 and then £1 million, and which proposed increased powers for the Local Government Board.[67] The agricultural
committee was the most radical, but perhaps this was a response to the
expected radicalism of the impending Liberal land programme. It paralleled official party policy but also advocated a statutory minimum wage
for agricultural labourers.[68] The taxation committee failed to report.

From the outset it was clear that USRC policy would not become Conservative Party policy. Even the committee's highly moderate schemes
were too much for Conservatism. As Steel-Maitland admitted in private,
his committee's social reformism was not within the range of practical
Tory politics. This, in itself, was a powerful indicator of the character of
the Right. In 1912 this energetic moderniser submitted a memorandum to
the leadership which suggested that the shadow cabinet should establish
policy sub-committees on important political questions. The USRC could
not do the job because it was not a 'body to which we can give our adhesion
in advance'.[69] One year earlier, in his memorandum for Bonar Law, he had
called for a similar preparation of policy. The USRC could not be entrusted
with the task. It was helpful in influencing the climate of opinion but 'not
in working out a policy for which you could take responsibility'.[70] Not one
significant USRC policy was adopted by the Right between 1911 and 1914.

The party leadership, therefore, was both having its cake and eating it. It could garner votes by allowing the USRC to give the Conservative Party an image of social concern, but it could avoid sacrificing principle or offending allied interests by not making USRC policy official policy. This seems, indeed, to have been a deliberate intention on the part of the Tory leaders. In his original letter to Sandars Steel-Maitland had stressed that the activities of the backbench MPs could be 'made use of or disowned as occasion shows'.[71] To a substantial extent, therefore, the Unionist Social Reform Committee must be adjudged a Conservative anti-collectivist device.

Although the Unionist Social Reform Comittee did not leave much mark upon official party policy before 1914 its impact may have been delayed. The inter-war Conservative leadership was dominated by adherents of the USRC. Stanley Baldwin, Neville Chamberlain, and Edward Wood (Lord Halifax) had all been active associates. It is possible, therefore, that the USRC acted as a school for those who led Conservatism between 1918 and 1939. The success of the party in that period, and its accommodating attitude to interventionist change, may have been partly due to the experience of the pre-war years and to the tactics and strategies discussed and propounded in the Unionist Social Reform Committee. This gives some clues as to the thinking behind much of the leftward moves of the Right after the Labour Party had replaced the Liberal Party as the chief force on the Left. Was the Conservatism of Chamberlain and Baldwin another example of principled opportunism and the deliberate expression of sympathy? The Edwardian formative years merit serious consideration in the provision of an answer to this question.

☆

Both the tariff reform movement and the Unionist Social Reform Committee were Tory obstacles on the high road to collectivism. They were, in part, thoughtful attempts to halt the Left's drive towards economic change, and to achieve the success of traditional Conservative causes, by proffering a rival and Tory route to raised living standards. Although tariff reform had additional economic, national and imperial aims it is possible to assert that, just as British Radicalism was partly a product of the aristocracy and gentry, so these Edwardian forces were partly products of New Liberalism and new Labour. They overcame the frequent reluctance of Conservatives to adopt the methods of their opponents and employed modern styles of organisation, statist arguments and materialist rhetoric. But behind these facades there seems to have existed the same old Tory mansion constructed of individualism, voluntaryism and communitarianism. Both Chamberlain's movement and Steel-Maitland's brainchild were powerfully rooted in the orthodox desire to maintain the economic and social order, an order that was under attack. Tory conservation movement and Unionist Social Maintenance Committee are more suitable appellations. Yet, at the same time, they may have given an impetus to collectivism by giving credence to many of its ideas and ideals. This was a perpetual risk run by the Tory practitioners of pragmatism. How the Conservative Party met this attack between 1906 and 1914 forms the subject of the two succeeding chapters. Tariff reform and social reform were not enough.

Four

New Liberalism and New Labour

The general election of 1906 ushered in a new era in British political history. The domestic balance of power had changed. The Liberal landslide swept away old landmarks and introduced new features into the political landscape. The Liberal Party was installed in office and the approach of the previous Conservative governments was repudiated. The Labour Party became a significant parliamentary force and the trade unions flexed their political muscle. The years which preceded the land campaign of 1913–1914 witnessed substantial innovations in the role of the state. The statute book became distinctly more statist. This period brought to fruition many of the developments which had been underway during the previous decades. Collectivist ideas and attitudes gained new currency. An emphasis on material issues, a stress on the advantages of positive government action, and the practice of classist politics accompanied these first major steps in the construction of the collectivist state. In an acknowledgement of the importance of these last Liberal governments and these early Labour days a mass of literature has grown up on the activities of the Left. These early advances of their cause have aroused the interest of many collectivist historians.[1] But how did the Right respond to this eruption of interventionism? Its loss of power in the House of Commons meant that different forms of political behaviour were required. The techniques of British democratic opposition now come under scrutiny: this in itself is a separate subject for theoretical study.[2]

I

Much of the weight of the Liberal Party's effort went towards solving its own land question. This was a natural outcome of the composition and complexion of the new governing majority. British Radicalism had come in out of the cold: it was now an ascendant and not a dissentient force. David Lloyd George, its leading champion, was soon to become Chancellor of the Exchequer. The new House of Commons, observed one Tory MP in 1906, was full of members 'ready & willing to go to any lengths in the spoliation of the "squire"'.[3] The United Committee for the Taxation of Land Values, the new organising body for the Georgeite movement, claimed the allegiance of over 279 MPs (and thus a majority of the Liberal members), and proceeded to form the hard-core into the Land Values Group, (LVG).[4] 'The House of Commons as it assembled in 1906', records one historian, 'had the strongest contingent of land reformers yet'.[5] On the Right there was a sense of foreboding. 'It is to the land question', observed Austen Chamberlain in 1907, 'that the Radicals are looking to destroy both us and the House of Lords'.[6] Lord Onslow read the signs aright and warned of the 'dangers ahead of the landed interest'.[7]

One manifestation of the new condition of politics was the formation of a pressure group designed to protect landowners. The 1880s produced the Liberty and Property Defence League; the 1900s brought forth the Central Land Association (CLA). The CLA came into being in 1907[8] after Algernon Turnor, a Lincolnshire landlord and former secretary to Disraeli, circulated a memorandum to leading Tory landowners stressing that private landownership was in grave peril.[9] Onslow and Long reacted swiftly, becoming chairman and president respectively.[10] By 1910 the CLA had about a thousand members,[11] but it never mobilised its constituency and was subject to much criticism.[12] The CLA sought to represent all the agricultural classes and claimed party political neutrality. It concerned itself with agricultural issues and avoided more controversial subjects.[13] Here the Tory agriculturalist MPs found a home. But the intention was always, in Onslow's original and private words, to form a 'Landowners' Association'.[14] In this the CLA was a most significant organisation. It demonstrated the growing weakness of the landed interest within the political system. Landowners had to organise because they were losing their previous positions of political ascendancy. The peripheral Central Land Association was a revealing response to a new regime.

The governments of Campbell-Bannerman and Asquith sought to increase economic efficiency by reforming the land system. Anti-landlordism was given legislative expression; justice was to be done to the people. The famous People's Budget of 1909 introduced new taxes on land: a levy on the future unearned increment; a duty on undeveloped property; an impost on owners at the termination of long leases. A novel valuation of all real property was set in motion. In 1907 and 1908 the government attempted to prepare the ground for site value rating in Scotland by promoting legislation for a preliminary valuation. The 1906 Agricultural Holdings Act increased the rights of tenant farmers. The 1908 Small Holdings and Allotments Act sought to extend popular access to agricultural land. The Housing and Town Planning Act of 1909 attempted to improve urban habitation and sought in particular to put the novel provisions of the 1890 Act into practice. The Development Act of the same year established a central commission to stimulate agrarian development and provided a small grant to support its efforts. Taken as a whole these measures involved no significant financial outlay on the part of the Exchequer. This first stage of Liberal land reform was relatively costless.

Therein lay one of its attractions for its promoters.

Yet New Liberalism was not only concerned with the way things were in the world of land and buildings. State funded old age pensions were finally enacted in 1908. The National Insurance Act of 1911 provided for relief in times of unemployment and sickness, and relied upon contributions from the government, the employer and the worker. In 1909 labour exchanges set out to facilitate the workings of the labour market. The Trades Boards Act of the same year represented a new departure for the state. Wage rates in sweated industries were to be regulated by government agency. 'This is the first occasion, certainly in modern Parliamentary times', declared the Act's sponsor in the House of Commons', 'in which any Government has proposed machinery, first for deciding, and secondly for enforcing, a legal rate of wages'.[15] All this legislation was supported by such measures as the Shop Act, the Coal Mines Act, the Merchant Shipping Act, and the Workman's Compensation Act.

The Liberals also increased the taxation of personal wealth. In 1907 earned and unearned income were subjected to different levels of taxation. The People's Budget raised the income tax, introduced a super tax and increased the death duties. This general trend continued until the outbreak of war in 1914, and beyond. In 1914 a detailed statement of Liberal achievements and intentions observed that central government expenditure was almost double that of 1895.[16] The great 'Free Trade' party did not produce a free trade government. The Liberal administrations continued to raise substantial sums from customs and excise. But as time passed direct taxation accounted for an increasing share of central revenues, as the Conservatives unfailingly pointed out. After the 1914 budget was presented the Tariff Commission circulated a memorandum within the Tory Party. 'By the new Budget the proportion of direct to indirect taxation was 60 to 40 per cent. of the Imperial revenue', recorded Hewins, 'In the previous thirty years direct taxation had increased by 300 and indirect by less than 75 per cent.'[17] Thus did the Left repudiate Tory tariff reform. Redistributive taxation was well established on its long career. The state appropriated a larger proportion of the gross national product.[18] The future was signposted in these early years of the twentieth century.[19]

Underlying these Liberal initiatives were developments in the world of Labour. The Labour Party was now well established in the House of Commons and by 1910 it had forty MPs. Its manifestos promised a radical future. That of January 1910 concluded 'Vote for the Labour candidates. The land for the people. The wealth for the wealth producers. Down with privilege. Up with the people.'[20] Land reform was a major link between the two left-wing parties. Ramsay Macdonald's 'economic observations', writes one historian, 'were apt to comprise a castigation of the deadweight of landownership and rent upon industry rather than an economic critique of capitalism'.[21] The Labour Party gained from the continued growth in

trade union membership which more than doubled between 1900 and
1914, and in 1909 the powerful Miners' Federation affiliated to the Labour
Party.[22] Organised Labour was noted for its increased militancy. The
years 1911 to 1914 witnessed a sharp rise in industrial unrest.[23] Such
developments provoked alarm on the Conservative side of politics. 'What
is going on here', wrote Balfour in 1906, 'is the faint echo of the same
movement which has produced massacres in St.Petersburg, riots in Vienna, and Socialist processions in Berlin'.[24] The USRC's industrial committee reported that these disputes were 'uprisings of labour...against the condition of life, and indeed in some cases against the fact of employment
itself'.[25] To a certain extent Liberal social reform was an attempt to counter
the electoral threat from Labour. Concentration on the land system
involved a diversion of popular attention away from areas of the economic
order to which Liberalism was still committed. The rival parties of the Left
fought to establish the orientations of politics.

State growth, particularly in its centralist form, was thus one of the
cardinal features of the Edwardian Liberal experiment. An essential
aspect of this growth requires elucidation. The twentieth century has
witnessed a transformation in the legal environment of the British subject.
The provision to state officials of legislative and judicial powers has
increased by leaps and bounds. Administrative law has risen to be a major
feature of the legal landscape. Here, as in many other areas, Great Britain's
divergence from nineteenth century Europe was reversed by twentieth
century convergence. Great Britain has become a bureaucratic country,
with bureaucratic jurisdiction. This has important roots in late-Victorian
and Edwardian Liberalism. A select committee of the 1950s correctly
discerned the importance of the years 1886–1914 in the emergence of this
legal mushroom.[26] The movement away from the jury system towards
distant officials made society more impersonal. The cultural consequences of administrative law, like the history of administrative law itself,
provokes curiosity.

In much of their legislation the Liberals gave considerable discretion-
ary power to special central commissioners or government appointees.
Thus there were small holdings commissioners at the Board of Agriculture
or housing commissioners at the Local Government Board. Conservatives had expected that the chief threat to property would come from
taxation or statutory regulations. But in administrative law the Left had
found an equally potent weapon of attack. The Tories resisted the development and linked it to their attack on the installation of a patronage
system. Would not these administrators make decisions favourable to
their masters? The historian may detect another important motive in the
Liberal promotion of administrative law. The Liberals were taking the
administration of legislation out of the hands of local government. The
Liberals frequently charged that the urban and county councils, and

especially the latter, were often subject to the influence of local interests, most notably the landed interest.[27] Administrative law may be construed, in part, as being yet another attack on the political power of the aristocracy and gentry. In 1909 Lord Lansdowne gave voice to the Conservative critique. He discerned

> a tendency towards establishing a bureaucratic system in this coun-
> try. (Hear, hear). The tendency of many of the Bills which have
> passed through Parliament or which have come before Parliament,
> during this Government, has been to substitute for the established
> and trustworthy Courts of Law of this country the jurisdiction either
> of a Government Department or of a Government Board, or some
> special authority – some Commissioner or Commission, some
> Valuers or Referees, set up *ad hoc* for the purpose in the Bill. And
> these authorities which are to oust our Law Courts are given vast
> powers, powers which enable them, if so they will, positively to ruin
> the people who come under their jurisdiction. (Cheers). You will
> find that these powers are generally given without any appeal, or at
> any rate without anything which can be called a full and genuine
> appeal. I could multiply instances. We have had cases in the
> administration of the Education Acts...We have the same thing in
> the Old Age Pensions Act. We have the same thing in the Small
> Holdings Act of 1908; the same thing, again, in the Town Planning
> Bill now before the House of Commons, and in the Finance Bill you
> have this vast system of valuation, you have Commissioners ap-
> pointed by the Executive, acting for the Executive, and with plenary
> powers and the right of refusing an appeal to aggrieved persons if
> they think fit to refuse it. That is a very serious state of things...Where
> are you going to find the men to whom you are going to entrust these
> enormous powers, what guarantee will you have for their experi-
> ence, what guarantee will you have for their independence? (Hear,
> hear). Many of them will owe their position to Government patronage,
> and you will find that enthusiasm for the Government policy will be
> one of the principal qualifications insisted upon.'[28]

But when it came to bureaucratic power the Edwardians were not yet out of the nursery. The Conservatives, however, with their usual flair for prediction, could feel the way the gale was blowing.

Liberal land reform had always been linked to attacks upon the political power of the landed interest. The Edwardian Liberals did not fail to continue this tradition. One historian has used the phrase 'antilandlord state'[29] when writing about Asquith's government. Centralisation and administrative law by-passed the local authorities and thereby struck at the influence of the landed in local government. But the Liberals sought to undermine the aristocracy and gentry in a much more direct and dramatic fashion. Ever since the 1890s pressure had been building up for a reform of the House of Lords. After the rejection of the Finance Bill in 1909 the Liberal Party decided to take the plunge and to attempt major constitutional changes. After a sustained barrage of anti-aristocratic propaganda, which repeatedly (and characteristically) counterposed the landowners and the people in economic antagonism,[30] the Liberals removed the veto of the House of Lords in 1911. The Parliament Act brought to a climax the long nineteenth century Liberal assault on aristocratic influence; transformed the domestic distribution of political power; dismantled a potent barrier to land reform; and made Conservatives even more fearful for the future.

Collectivism stands in the Rationalist tradition and the Edwardians too had their *philosophes*. Planning required information. Liberal social reformism was supported by an impressive array of social investigators. Collectivism and the social sciences have had an intimate relationship. State growth has given economic support to the expansion of these disciplines, not least in the world of education. The social sciences, like politicians, came to be vested interests in collectivist society. These disciplines, in their turn, have often acted to support the idea that society can be improved by governmental direction. Many British social scientists have tended to subscribe to the materialistic and deterministic view that human advance can be achieved by the state directed alteration of socio-economic structures. They have thus belonged to the anti-Tory culture. This pattern was well apparent before 1914. In these early days it is possible to detect the early stirrings of a relationship which was to have a substantial impact. One historian has observed that Tories feel a distaste for social science,[31] and no doubt there is a consistent reluctance to focus attention on differences in wealth and levels of poverty. But it would perhaps be more accurate to say that Conservatives have often opposed left-wing investigations because such inquiries have been conducted in accordance with specifically left-wing perspectives of society. These inquiries have failed, for example, to appreciate much of the texture of social experience so much admired and valued by the Right. Aculturalism is not a characteristic of economics alone.

During the imperial age there was much exploration of the world. The territory of the British empire was mapped out. Yet the Victorians and Edwardians also turned inwards and investigated their own society. These investigations were either carried out officially by such means as royal commissions or departmental committees, or were conducted privately. This second avenue was the opportunity of the social reformer and it was widely used. The Left was well supported.[32] In 1890 General Booth published *In Darkest England and the Way Out*. One of his proffered exits was rural regeneration. His namesake Charles Booth pursued his own investigations. The Fabians and the Webbs made social analysis a *raison d'être*. Charles Masterman, who presented the public with *The Condition of England* in 1909, detected 'the first tentative effort towards the

construction of a sociology'.[33] William Beveridge was highly active
during this period and made a special study of unemployment. In the
future he was to have a major hand in that most prominent product of
British statism – the Welfare State. Perhaps the leading Liberal star was
Seebohm Rowntree who published a book on poverty in York in 1901. He
was especially interested in the land question and produced a number of
publications on the subject.[34] Rowntree inspired and directed the Liberal
Land Enquiry Committee of 1912–1914. This body symbolised the link
between the social investigators and social reform. It produced reports on
urban and rural conditions and formed a support for the ensuing land
campaign Lloyd George launched before the outbreak of hostilities in
1914.[35] Social investigators in the Beveridge–Rowntree mould displayed
the left-wing propensity to emphasise economic hardship rather than to
describe advances in prosperity.

The Liberal Party appealed to the electorate with collectivist arguments. It campaigned on issues relating to wealth and called attention to
the material benefits its interventionist legislation had brought to the
people. During the 1910 general elections Liberal candidates stressed
social questions;[36] in 1911 the Liberal Publication Department issued a
widely distributed leaflet entitled *The Liberal Party and Social Reform.
A Splendid Record.*[37] The existing economic system, and especially the
land system, were deemed unjust; landowners received moral opprobrium. Could not the Liberals claim that they were restructuring society
to beneficial effect? Lloyd George symbolised the approach. He followed
on from Joseph Chamberlain in his determination to appear as the People's
Benefactor, the generous operator of state levers. Was he also not the
'Radical agitator' of Salisbury's prediction? His intervention in, and settlement of, industrial disputes was an additional statist flourish. In 1909,
in a famous and infamous speech at Limehouse, Lloyd George presented
the Liberal collectivist case. After a vituperative attack upon landlords the
Chancellor of the Exchequer continued in the following vein:

> The provision for the aged and deserving poor – it was time it was
> done...It is rather hard that an old workman should have to find his
> way to the gates of the tomb, bleeding and footsore, through the
> brambles and thorns of poverty... We are raising money to provide
> against the evils and the sufferings that follow from unemployment
> (cheers). We are raising money for the purpose of assisting our great
> friendly societies to provide for the sick and the widows and
> orphans. We are providing money to enable us to develop the
> resources of our own land...We are placing the burdens on the broad
> shoulders (cheers). Why should I put burdens on the people? I am
> one of the children of the people...I know their trials; and God forbid
> that I should add one grain of trouble to the anxiety which they bear
> with such patience and fortitude.[38]

The widespread idea that the Liberal Party declined because it failed to adapt to mass politics, and that it continued to regard electoral conflict as a matter of rational debate with the voters cast in the role of a jury, has no validity. How did the Conservative Party respond to the Left's initiatives?

II

The parliamentary sphere commands initial attention. The formal enactment of legislation did not mean that it would have any real impact. Much of the previous century's social legislation had run into the sands of local government inertia and impotence. Finance was an abiding hindrance. More than this, legislation could encounter judicial difficulties in its implementation. Trade union legislation had received some suprises with the judgements of the courts.[39] The Agricultural Holdings Act of 1906 was moderated in its workings by the declaration of a county court judge.[40] Part of the attraction of administrative law must have lain in its ability to by-pass potentially hostile judges. The land taxes and the land valuation bristled with technical difficulties and the Conservatives sensed an opportunity to frustrate the Liberals' design at the level of execution. Ernest George Pretyman MP (1860–1931), a Suffolk and Lincolnshire landowner and a former Master of the Brocklesby Hounds, had taken a leading role in protesting against his party's failure to repeal the Harcout death duties in the 1890s.[41] Pretyman was a diehard and anti-opportunist in the Wemyss mould (although even he would come to learn pragmatism), and like Wemyss he sought to galvanise, mobilise and organise those of a similar persuasion. These two Tories were archetypical representatives of the unyielding conservative associates described by Lampedusa.

In 1910 Pretyman formed the Land Union. It was concerned solely with the land question, whose importance it thereby confirmed, and sought to unite 'all,who, either by property, profession or business, are in any way connected with Land and Building'.[42] This real property front thus acknowledged the force of the Liberal threat. The Land Union was a propaganda organisation which subjected Liberal land reform to continuous attack.[43] Like Pretyman it favoured a stance of resistance not concession. The Land Union, like the LPDL, espoused the unbending tenets of unreformed Conservatism. This militant society also set out to wreck Lloyd George's anti-landlord project by contesting the land taxes and the land valuation at every twist and turn. The *Land Union Guide* gave shrewd advice to owners on how to fill in the government's valuation forms,[44] and the Liberals described Pretyman and his followers as the 'New Law-Breakers'.[45] One historian has shown how the Duke of Bedford's officials attempted to sabotage the taxation of His Grace's properties by similar manipulation of the valuation. Their profesional expertise was used to the full.[46] The Land Union's executive committee was highly professional and informed, being composed of 'men engaged in the practical management of all kinds of property and in the industries dependent on it' and of

'leading members of the legal and surveying professions'.[47] This specialist force fought the taxes and the valuation in the courts and before the
specially appointed government referees. The Scrutton judgement and the
Marquis of Camden case nullified the undeveloped land duty and blunted
the teeth of the reversion duty. The land valuation became bogged down
in innumerable quicksands.[48] By the Finance Act of 1920 the whole
Liberal project was abandoned.[49] Conservative predictions about the im-
practicality of taxing land values were vindicated, but at considerable cost
to the taxpayer. Yet much Conservative energy went into the actual
prevention of legislation.

Consequently, His Majesty's Opposition was most active in the parliamentary sphere. The Conservatives may have lost their majority in the
House of Commons, but in the House of Lords they were supreme. The
leadership was aware of the new importance of the upper house and in
1906 it agreed to co-ordinate the party's activities in both Houses of
Parliament. Balfour stressed the need for a 'common plan of campaign'.[50]
But innovations in organisation did not stop there. The Earl of Onslow
immediately set out to form the active backbench Unionist peers into a
coherent and disciplined force. In 1906 he established an association
which absorbed the independent committees of Irish and Scottish members; secured the services of a barrister as secretary and expert adviser; and
established sub-committees to consider legislation introduced by the
Liberal ministry.[51] Some fifty members of the House of Lords appear to
have been involved in 1906 and some seventy-five in 1910.[52] Lord Lansdowne dubbed them the 'Apaches'[53] and in 1908 wrote 'verily the
Apaches have become a formidable nation'.[54] This association evolved
into the Association of Independent and Unionist Peers, about which
much more is known.[55] The House of Lords was thus being prepared as an
instrument of resistance to the Liberal programme.

The Right was not as obstructive as the Left often charged. The
achievements of the Campbell-Bannerman and Asquith governments
bore witness to that. The House of Lords succeeded in moderating a
number of measures such as the Housing and Town Planning Act or the
1908 Coal Mines Act and the Liberals were loud in their lament.[56] But the
Tory aristocracy would not countenance acceptance of what was most
controversial in the Liberals' schemes – the proposals concerning land
taxation. In this area Radicalism was in aggressive mood. In 1906, for
example, a land tax memorial signed by as many as four hundred Members
of Parliament was presented to the Prime Minister.[57] In 1907 and 1908 the
government sought to initiate a local site valuation in Scotland. This could
have prepared the ground for a radical reform of local taxation south of the
border. The House of Lords first rejected the measure and then insisted on
unacceptable amendments. The Liberals did not proceed with their
plans.[58] In 1914 Asquith's government introduced legislation which

rendered such previous obstruction obsolete. It was based upon the highly controversial provisions of Lloyd George's financial proposals of 1909. The People's Budget was rejected by the House of Lords and a constitutional crisis was precipitated. The evidence is not clear on the reasons for this decision. Much suggests that a profound hostility to the land taxes and the land valuation gave rise to a refusal to contemplate their enactment. This particular toad could not be swallowed. At the same time it appears as though the full weight of the greatest Tory interest of them all – the landed interest – was brought to bear on the Conservative response. Perhaps the Apaches were on an uncontrollable warpath: thus did the composition of the Conservative Party have major consequences. William Bridgeman MP, a Tory whip, maintained in his private diary that the decision of the peers was 'dictated by an honest and simple sense of duty which refused to agree to what was deemed to be wrong'.[59] Balfour's niece wrote a biography of her uncle in the 1930s. She may have received inside information from the great man. In Blanche Dugdale's view the refusal to pass the bill 'sprang from the irresistible instinct of self-preservation in the class from which the Party derived its tradition and much of its strength'.[60] Once again Tory principles and allied interests appear to have left a mark on the Right's handling of reform. But how intelligent a decision was this? As events turned out the Left was once again installed in power and the House of Lords came to lose its veto, with all that that implied for the propertied order. More than this the land taxes themselves, through their own technical complexity, quickly foundered, thus rendering their initial rejection unnecessary. In 1919 the Chancellor of the Exchequer reported that Lloyd George's project had reached a 'complete impasse'.[61] Was the fateful decision of November 1909 one of the great errors of late-Victorian and Edwardian Conservative politics?

Obstructionism came into its own as a political weapon. It was used with a vengeance against the Finance Bill of 1909. A committee of some fifty MPs, under the chairmanship of the shadow chancellor Austen Chamberlain, was established by the Conservative Party in the House of Commons.[62] It had four sub-committees. Its land tax committee was chaired by Ernest Pretyman and whipped by George Lane Fox MP.[63] The obstructionism consisted of endless speeches, continual amendments and the abandonment of all traditional co-operation. 'Old members & officials of the House', recorded Lane Fox in his diary, 'say there has never been so keen or so good a committee fight'.[64] The government replied with the guillotine, but all the same it took seventy days and over five hundred divisions to get the budget through the lower house. Much of the administration's other legislation was thus delayed.[65] Reflecting the Conservative Party's concerns, it was the land clauses which received the full force of the opposition's effort. But this had its disadvantages. 'We fought the land taxes too hard', recalled a participant, 'and the rest of the budget, when we

were tired out, not hard enough'.[66] Temperatures were rising as politics
became more controversial. What of the electoral sphere?

An essential element in the Conservative Party's method of resisting
collectivism between 1886 and 1914 lay in the Tory approach to political
reform. Constitutional history has gone out of vogue but constitutions are
often of decisive consequence. The Right realised that a prevention of
further democratisation could well aid its cause. The House of Lords was
well protected throughout the long years of Unionist ascendancy. Leaders
and party literature praised it without reservation.[67] In this area, as in
others, left-wing pressure led to shifts in the Right's position. After 1906
there were concessive stirrings. Lord Newton and others produced a
House of Lords reform bill in 1907. But it was opposed by the rest of the
party, and especially by the whips[68] (who no doubt foresaw a loss of party
revenue from the sale of honours), and was put to rest with the appointment
of a select committee.[69] With the onset of the constitutional crisis of 1910
and the Liberal government's preparation of reform the Conservative
Party's position changed rapidly. There was much Tory consideration of
policy and in 1911 Lansdowne introduced reform proposals into the upper
house.[70] Conservative divisions over the Parliament Bill were divisions
over tactics not goals and thereby belonged to a familiar pattern. Was it
better to provoke the creation of Liberal peers, and thus bring about a
Liberal House of Lords which would pass the bill anyway, or more
adviseable to concede the measure and retain a Tory majority in a second
chamber which would still have some powers?[71] In a memorandum of July
1911 Balfour made clear that a rejection of the Parliament Bill would
achieve little in the long run.[72]

The Conservative Party strove to control the nature of electoral power
and the importance of the electoral sphere. After the franchise reforms of
the 1880s the Right showed no desire to increase the number of voters. In
its public stance the party adopted a neutral stance on the enfranchisement
of women. Successive *Campaign Guides* sat on the fence.[73] But the period
1886–1906 saw no serious Tory moves towards change in this area and
Conservatives constituted the chief source of opposition to the feminine
franchise until the Representation of the People Act of 1918. Conversions
on the eve of the Great War seem to have been manifestations of
expediency.[74] The plural vote was considered by the Right to work in its
favour and was stoutly defended in print and in parliament. Party literature
never made any concessions.[75] In 1906 and 1913 the House of Lords
refused to pass the ministry's Plural Voting Bill.[76] Registration reform was
never seriously considered by the governments of Salisbury and Balfour.
The National Liberal Federation was in favour[77] but the Right was
unresponsive.[78] The Conservative Party constantly pressed for a reform in
the distribution of seats. It correctly argued that the Irish and celtic areas
were over-represented.[79] In 1905 Balfour's government mooted measures

which rectified this anomaly and also sought to reduce the number of rural constituencies.[80] But the plan was unpopular with the Tory MPs and agricultural pressure groups,[81] and was dropped. This was an error from a Conservative point of view – advantages accrued to the Liberal–Labour–Nationalist *entente* and the rural areas remained a large prize vulnerable to the Liberal land question. Overall, the Conservative Party resisted a further democratisation of the national political system. This must have been actuated by the fear that such a development would bring a further radicalisation of politics, legislation, and the role of the state. After the death of Salisbury, Salisburyian thoughts lived on.

The Conservative Party responded to the Liberals and Socialists with attacks on their policies and legislative achievements, although these attacks altered over time with the exigencies of expediency. The combative approach was not neglected. Party publications presented comprehensive denunciations of the general positions of the party's opponents. These followed traditional lines of attack. The whole gamut of Tory arguments was employed. Specific measures were described as harmful to the very interests they were meant to help. Local government was being undermined. An overweening bureaucracy was being established. Too much money was being taken out of the economy. Insecurity was inhibiting prosperity. The taxation of the rich would rebound to the disadvantage of the poor. All this was underpinned by an emphasis on the beneficial workings of the market and a rejection of statist methods.[82]

The Conservative Party's attack on the Left also found expression in the activities of the Anti-Socialist Union of Great Britain (ASU). Its very existence was a manifestation of Tory anxiety at political developments. This pressure group was founded in 1908, absorbed the Industrial Freedom League and was led by W.J.Ashley MP, an active tariff reformer.[83] The ASU was considered important enough to receive an 'enormous subsidy' from party funds.[84] The organisation sought to stop the spread of left-wing ideas. Its propaganda well reveals the conventional Conservative perspective.[85] The ASU stressed the tyranny and poverty which Socialism would bring, but also made familiar cultural predictions. Socialism would desocialise people by ending religion, undermining the family, and weakening moral character.[86] Thus, also, in typical right-wing fashion, the ASU laid great stress on 'the importance of maintaining existing social responsibilities, especially in the family context'.[87] Tory culture found an articulate exponent. Ashley's pressure group also reflected the tariff reform concessive method of combating New Liberalism and growing Labour by espousing moderate measures of social reform.

Much of the Liberal programme provoked much Conservative opportunism. Nowhere was this more clearly displayed than in the Right's public attitude to the new land taxes. There was a general feeling in Conservative circles that the Liberal fiscal and polemical attack on landownership had reaped handsome electoral rewards. In other words, collectivism was capable of great popularity. Democracy was prepared to support the most radical assault yet on private property rights. This sent tremors through the Right and informed much of its approach. The electors in London and Yorkshire, observed Austen Chamberlain, 'voted against the Lords and above all, against Landlords'. 'In Scotland', he continued, 'the class hatred was very bitter and the animosity against landlords extreme'.[88] F.E.Smith, Goulding and Storey believed that in the 'English towns we were beaten by the Land Taxes of the Budget'.[89] Acland Hood, the chief whip, advised his leaders that the party would not carry the towns if it promised the repeal of the taxes.[90] Balfour and his colleagues confronted a dilemma. The Conservative Party had obstructed, vetoed and condemned the taxes, but to promise their repeal would mean risking further electoral defeat and installing the Left once again in power. For a while the Tory leaders did not know what to do and said nothing. Party propaganda tried to avoid the subject. This was an example of diversion tactics.[91]

But as 1910 progressed and another general election loomed on the horizon the rank and file began to protest against this silence. Acland Hood reported that he was being bombarded with letters. Some Conservatives wanted repeal, some wanted partial repeal, some wanted inaction.[92] Hood conducted a survey of Tory opinion and concluded that in the rural areas the feeling was in favour of repeal but such was not the case in the urban districts. 'In many of the industrial towns there are very large ground landlords', he reported, 'and our men fear they will have once more to fight the battle of these owners in places where the taxes are popular'.[93] Pretyman, who had manned the obstructionist committee against the land taxes, pressed for repeal.[94] Percival Hughes, the Principal Agent, reported that many party candidates had publicly declared themselves for Pretyman's line. But this kept alive the 'political prejudice against landowners' and saddled the Tories 'with the same burden which they bore with such difficulty at the general election'.[95] In November 1910 Acland Hood said that a decision had to be reached.[96]

The Conservative Party decided against a public commitment to repeal. In part the leadership did not like making promises as to future taxation policies whilst out of office. Balfour constantly reiterated this principle of constitutional opposition.[97] But a far more important reason related to expediency. Such a commitment would lose votes and risk another period of left-wing ascendancy. Austen Chamberlain summed up the leadership's thinking when writing to Pretyman. The land taxes were popular and it would not serve the Conservative cause to 'rouse again the bitter feeling against the great urban landlords which did us so much injury at the last general election'. A commitment to repeal would 'be bad electoral tactics as well as a very rash promise for anyone to make who may have to share the responsibility for a Unionist budget'.[98] In time even Pretyman came round to this view. In 1913 he privately advised Bonar Law against a promise of repeal.[99] In the same year the party leaders were counselled by an internal policy committee to promise drastic amendment but not outright repeal.[100] The arch-diehards in the Land Union were not interested in such hedging and called for a removal of Lloyd George's creations from the statute book. [101]

A great measure of expediency marked the Conservative Party's treatment of much of the rest of the Liberal Party's programme. This was anticipated in the readiness of the House of Lords to tolerate much of that programme's enactment. The Conservatives failed to vote in favour of old age pensions in the House of Commons, as the Liberals never tired of pointing out.[102] But in time they became committed to this most popular item of Liberal legislation.[103] Only the National Insurance Act, of the Liberals' major items of legislation, was earmarked for Tory reform. This was partly attributable to that Act's initial unpopularity. Voluntaryism, obstructionism and opportunism characterised the Conservative Party's treatment of this prominent collectivist measure. In the House of Commons a USRC committee under Worthington-Evans was used to combat and obstruct the provisions of the bill which the Right did not like. Once again the USRC was not so distant from the party leadership as appearances indicated.[104]

This parliamentary campaign continued after 1911 and there emerged from the committee's activities the Insurance Act Amendment Association which took the campaign to the country.[105] As Steel-Maitland had advised,[106] the Unionist Party criticised much of the working of the scheme and argued against its compulsory provisons but was careful to avoid condemnation of its popular aspects.[107] The Tory vision of progress was involved and the good old cause of voluntaryism was championed. Friendly societies were an example of the independent action and mutual aid which the Conservatives so admired. In November 1913 the National Union resolved for a purely voluntary scheme.[108] Bonar Law advocated an impartial inquiry and was sympathetic to a voluntary system.[109] Steel-Maitland had also advised that in its attitude to the industrial disputes which arose after 1911 the Conservative Party should hold the government responsible and express sympathy for legitimate industrial grievances.[110] Such was the Right's approach.[111] Overall the Conservative Party continued to claim that it was the true friend of the working classes; invoked its previous legislation as evidence; and declared that it empathised with the tribulations of the poor.[112]

Conservative support for the bulwark strategy increased as the threat to the existing order intensified. Indeed, the more the Left menaced, the more the Right turned to owner-occupation. But this strategy, like opportunistic reform, was constrained by the axioms of the right-wing outlook. It was to the countryside that Tory attention was turned. Urban freeholding or leasehold enfranchisement did not arouse interest. The idea was to turn labourers into peasant proprietors and farmers into yeomen. From 1906 to 1910 the chief support for the strategy, apart from the inevitable Collings, came from the tariff reform movement, the Central Land Association, and a high level trio consisting of Walter Long, Lord Onslow and Austen Chamberlain. All were captivated by the vision of a solid bloc of agrarian small owners. Arthur Balfour led the doubters and sceptics, and voiced objections anchored in rightist thinking. These years showed that as collectivism progressed the concept of a property owning democracy gained in Tory favour.

In 1906 the Agricultural Committee of the Tariff Commission endorsed Collings' bill and stressed that in the past peasant proprietors had 'added to the stability of the social system'.[113] The tariff reform Unauthorised Programme of 1908 had similar ideas and declared 'a large class of freeholders gives stability to the institutions of the State, and in particular is an impediment to the progress of crude Socialism'.[114] Sir Gilbert Parker MP, a devoted tariff reformer, published a much publicised pamphlet on the subject in 1909.[115] In his CLA memorandum Algernon Turnor argued that the inheritance of a larger number of owner occupiers would have made property more secure, strengthened the position of every landowner, and increased the 'Conservative instincts of the Nation'.[116] At the inaugural meeting of the CLA its chairman called for the creation of 'small freeholders all over the country'.[117] The CLA's programme came down firmly on the side of extending rural owner-occupation.[118] In 1907 both Austen Chamberlain[119] and Walter Long[120] urged Balfour to embrace occupying ownership. In March 1909 Onslow drew up an agricultural programme in which small ownership figured prominently.[121] All of these proponents of increased owner-occupation produced numerous schemes designed to aid the economic success of the projected small proprietors.

Balfour was consistent in his opposition. He seems to have been sceptical as to the economic viability of small ownerships, attached to the existing way of doing things in the agricultural world, and anxious about the financial costs to the state of the whole policy. At Dumfries on 6 October 1908 Balfour spoke in favour of small holders but emphasised their economic vulnerability. Only the magic of ownership could allow of success.[122] Onslow had asked Sir Horace Plunkett (1854–1932), a landowner, former Unionist MP, and the inspiration of the Irish co-operative movement, to send some of his pamphlets to the leader of the party, but Balfour merely presented the author with some 'difficult conundrums'.[123] He also wrote a preface to Parker's pamphlet, but it was powerfully noncommittal.[124] On 22 September 1909 the leader of the Conservative Party made a major policy speech which involved a vague commitment to an extension of agricultural small ownership. 'Depend upon it, it is not so very easy or light a task to make a living out of the small holding in this country'. What would increase the prospect of success? 'A feeling of ownership, and nothing else.'[125] The policy, such as it was, was relayed to the electorate through party propaganda.[126] Collings was not very impressed and detected Balfour's hesitancy.[127] In November 1909 Balfour went a little further in another public declaration.[128]

The ferocity of the People's Budget and the adverse results of the 1910 general elections increased Tory fears and gave a further impetus to the development of the bulwark strategy. It became widely supported throughout the party, although Balfour still dragged his feet. Long, Onslow and Austen Chamberlain were keener than ever. 'You would go far before you could find a small owner who was a radical',[129] observed Onslow; Chamberlain replied that ownership would make the best of 'both the land and the man and will give stability to our institutions as nothing else will'.[130] Long had been a keen advocate of the rejection of the 1909 Finance Bill by the House of Lords[131] and feared the end of private landownership. He told Collings that a system of small ownerships was the only way to stop the advance of Socialism 'as exemplified, not by Snowden and Keir Hardie, but by the present financial policy of the Government'.[132] In early 1910 Balfour appointed a small ownerships policy committee chaired by Parker.[133] It produced a report in June 1910 after much friction between Collings and Parker who were two of its members.[134] On 14 April 1910 over a hundred Conservative MPs gathered in a room in the House of Commons and declared themselves in favour of 'creating an extended system of cultivating ownerships in land'.[135]

On 5 October 1910, during a major speech at Edinburgh, Balfour called for an increase in the number of agricultural owner-occupiers. Central state loans, administered either directly by the government or indirectly by a state land bank, would bring about the creation of landowning peasants and yeomen. Technical advice from a government department and organised co-operation would facilitate economic success. The Tory approach left its mark – the whole scheme was voluntary and would neither displace farmers nor transgress property rights. The credit of the state was not put at risk nor great sums projected. The whole plan was couched in cautious and general terms.[136] On no account was Balfour applying his party's Irish policies to the mainland. Earlier the leader of the Conservative Party had written that the Irish analogy was 'apt to mislead the ignorant'.[137] In his Edinburgh speech Balfour went out of his way to praise the landlord–tenant–labourer system; expressed the hope that everything valuable in it would be preserved; and stressed that there was a 'fundamental difference between the British question and the Irish question'.[138] By 1912 a commitment to an extension of agricultural owner-occupation was a prominent feature of the party programme.[139] Steel-Maitland reported that the 'doctrine of small ownership is being very widely preached on our side'.[140] But still there was a vagueness and nebulousness at the level of concrete detail which Collings and his associates found irksome.[141] Two parliamentary debates on the subject in 1912,[142] in the words of one informed observer, revealed only 'vacillation and havering' on the part of the party leaders.[143] Tory beliefs were acting as both an engine and a brake.

British Liberalism attempted to discredit landowners much as British Socialism attempted to discredit capitalists. Both forms of collectivism revealed a readiness to categorise certain individuals in relation to their socio-economic location; to separate them out from the rest of the community; and to make them objects of popular hatred. The reform of a perceived economic system appeared to necessitate an attack upon its most obvious benefactors. The Left was united in its practice of polemical classism. This was an integral feature of Salisbury's projected disintegration. Many Conservatives believed that the Liberals had indeed succeeded in creating fractures in the national community. 'The whole political atmosphere has been changed since Limehouse, Newcastle, etc.', reflected one observant Tory in 1912, 'and I suppose it is a fact in history that when once the respect of one class for another class is gone, there is no halting place'.[144] In such a context an obvious option open to the Conservatives was to secure a legitimation of the landed classes by involving them more in agricultural and local affairs.

Notwithstanding much canvassing of this idea between 1886 and 1914, it was an option that was largely ignored. In 1897 the Duke of Bedford published a book about the management of his estates. He sought to show how enlightened and energetic landowners could make a substantial contribution to rural prosperity. He wanted to demonstrate 'the service done to the country by the working of the existing system'[145] and called on other landowners to provide an answer to the gathering Radical attack by following his example:

> An agitation has been set on foot, and assiduously encouraged by political leaders, that landlords are a parasitical class, feasting on others' labour, reaping where others sow...Readers of the following pages will be enabled to judge how far these views are borne out by the Story of the Bedford Estate.[146]

The Agricultural Organisation Society (AOS) came into existence in 1901. Landowner activists helped farmers to create and maintain co-operative societies. The AOS drew much of its inspiration from Sir Horace Plunkett whose *Noblesse Oblige* of 1908 gave forceful expression to the legitimation strategy. In 1909 Plunkett told a Welsh member of the CLA that 'the prospect of the Landlord Class in not very bright'. He advised Welsh landlords to meet the crisis by entering 'into the lives of their poorer neighbours'.[147] Plunkett was a member of the executive committee of the CLA and at the association's inaugural meeting its chairman declared 'if we are going to make a common stand against the threatened attack we must accept duties and privileges in the most liberal minded spirit possible'.[148] The Duke of Bedford was subsequently asked to be the organisation's chairman but he declined.[149] The CLA failed to promote activity in this area.

After the Finance Bill of 1909 more Conservatives came to consider this option. In September of that year R.A.Yerburgh MP (1853–1916), one of the AOS's leading spirits, wrote to eminent landowners. He wanted the nation's landowners to create and finance an agricultural credit bank which would fund local co-operative and credit societies. Yerburgh believed that his scheme would help a 'class that is now being held up to the masses as parasites on social progress' by giving 'unchallengeable evidence of their real interest in any sound movement to get more people on the land'.[150] Long, in particular, was opposed.[151] The project remained on the drawing board. In 1911 *Land Problems and National Welfare* was published by C.Turnor. Its author wanted the aristocracy and gentry to take a guiding role in the development of the agricultural industry and the movement for land reform 'so that Socialists and extreme Radicals may be given no opportunity of asserting that property owners are pursuing a merely selfish policy'.[152] The legitimation strategy became even more pertinent after the launching of the land campaign in 1913. Lloyd George declared that landowners were about as necessary to agriculture as a gold watchchain to a watch.[153] In October 1913 Turnor proposed to the Tory leaders a great landowners' society which would carry out all sorts of local schemes. He hoped that it would 'supply an effective answer to Radical attacks'.[154] Lansdowne was sceptical.[155] This scheme, also, remained a mere blueprint.

Why was the legitimation strategy never adopted in systematic fashion by the Conservative Party in these years of anti-landlordism? Perhaps a raising of the profile of the landowners even more would have exposed them to further political abuse. Perhaps there was a lack of will on the part of the landowners themselves, as Turnor himself charged.[156] If they were not already sufficiently involved would it not be too much of an effort to secure a change of attitude? In addition, there was the habitual lack of interest in agriculture by the politically active landowners. Any Tory agriculturalist who supported the idea did not have available a powerful group of allies. However the strategy did bear fruit after the First World War when the Central Land Association converted into the Central Landowners' Association, an organisation for owners only. The new CLA preached that the owners of landed estates should move away from public affairs and devote themselves to agriculture.[157] 'Back to the land' was now an aristocratic injunction. This was an obvious response to the continued rise of the Socialist Party and constituted a neglected aspect of the impact of Labour: landowners were altogether less vulnerable when engaged in activity down on the farm.

As in the period of Salisbury's ascendancy the Conservative Party sought to frustrate collectivism by campaigning on other issues. All this while the Right beat the tariff reform drum.[158] The constitution was upheld.[159] The Conservative Party continued to focus attention on Ireland and to play the Unionist card.[160] The established Church was still protected.[161] The Empire was praised.[162] It was in the area of defence that Balfour's party concentrated much of its attention. The German threat provoked a Tory emphasis on the need to increase naval strength. 'We want eight, and we won't wait' was the Right's platform slogan for an increase in the number of British dreadnoughts.[163] Before the First World War, as before the Second World War, it was from the right side of politics that the most appropriate warnings about Germany chiefly came. The Conservative Party also emphasised the need to strengthen the army.[164] Collectivism was thus to be countered with patriotism, nationalism and imperialism. With the loss of the Empire, national grandeur, the Union with Ireland, and the importance of the Church of England, the Conservative Party was to lose many of its anti-collectivist causes. International and religious decline hastened the materialisation of public life.

Perhaps the forces of Conservatism had another form of opposition up their sleeve. High society was a part of the Victorian and Edwardian political landscape.[165] Country estates and metropolitan great houses were the focal points of a world which participants often recalled with nostalgia in their post-war memoirs.[166] This narrow world resonant with aristocratic tone was woven into the Tory experience. Bonar Law lived in an out-of-the-way London house which sometimes could not be found by his high-born visitors.[167] He lacked the appropriate contacts. Lady Londonderry was commissioned to act as his social aide.[168] High society facilitated intra party communication; gave the parliamentary party a unifying milieu; and encouraged respectful attitudes towards the leadership on the part of the party faithful. When Alderman Stanley Salvidge, the Liverpool party boss, stayed at Welbeck Abbey whilst attending the 1910 conference, he exuded admiration for the Duke and Duchess of Portland.[169] But high society was not exclusively Tory and leading Liberals and their families participated in the social whirl. Thus the Right had a weapon in its hand – ostracism. Liberalism attacked high society's leading personages. Earl Carrington, an aristocratic member of the Liberal Cabinet, reported that there was great "'Society'" opposition to the 1909 Finance Bill;[170] Arthur Lee MP, the man who gave Chequers to the nation, recalled that at the time 'Mayfair was full of foreboding'.[171] There are signs that from the People's Budget until the Great War high society put pressure on the Liberals by means of exclusion. Samuel Hoare MP recalled how 'Party feeling being very high, we never met a Liberal at any dinner to which we went.'[172] It seems as though Westminster Liberals were being sent to Coventry.

Another possibility for the Right's armoury may be detected in the party political conflict which took place between 1886 and 1914. Truces, negotiations and alliances belonged to war and politics alike. The Conservative Party could always moderate the proposals of its opponents by striking deals. 'Moderationism' even took regular institutional form in the round-table conferences which occurred at moments of especial political disagreement.[173] The Tories had gained much from the accession of the Liberal Unionists and this amounted to an alliance with a section of their previous opponents. In 1910 a round-table conference on the House of Lords was convened. Balfour and his colleagues took part and attempted to secure special powers for the House of Lords over penal taxation.[174] During the conference Lloyd George floated the idea of a coalition. His proposed common programme was strikingly moderate with regard to land.[175] Perhaps the Right missed a moderationist opportunity. In 1913 Steel-Maitland urged a round-table conference on the land question – he believed that delay and a moderation of the Liberal programme might be possible.[176] In 1914 Long offered the government the opposition's co-operation in passing legislation to remove the grievances of town tenants.[177] Later that year Bonar Law and his fellow leaders sat down with Asquith and leading Liberals to come to an agreement over Ireland.[178] Yet the great point about moderationism was that it was usually a sign of weakness. It depended on the consent of those with power. The Liberals were shrewd political operators and rarely gave anything away. Moderationism had very moderate possibilities for a Conservative Party in opposition.

What of the pressure groups? The Anti-Socialist Union, the Central Land Association and the Land Union have all been described. But the Conservative Party also gained support from a neglected corner of professional England. The study of the professions has become one of the vogues of anglo-saxon historiography.[179] Historians have yet to inquire into the part played by the professions in the creation of the collectivist state. George Bernard Shaw remarked that professions were a conspiracy against the general public.[180] Certainly the public organisation of the professions has been motivated by a strong impulse towards material reward and social prestige. Government has played an indispensable part in the professionalisation process. State recognition and legitimation seem to have been central aims; government financial support a common intention. Doctors and teachers, for example, have become parts of the state apparatus. In 1914 a writer of Tory persuasion maintained that the National Insurance Act had converted medical practitioners into government officials.[181] To go through the list of lawyers, architects, engineers, academics, teachers, doctors and the rest is to perceive bodies which at times have been drawn towards the state like moths to a flame. Government, by laws, employment and funding has been a font of gain which at times has conferred its mantle of authority. Towering above them all is the civil service, the profession which gained enormously from state expansion. Having acquired all the trappings of professionalisation by the Edwardian period, perhaps this profession often served as a model and an inspiration for the rest.[182] Many of the professions became some of the most conspicuous entrenched beneficiaries of collectivist Britain.

Yet during the Victorian and Edwardian period there was one corner of professional England which lined up with the Conservative Party in opposing the Left. Here we encounter some of the neglected social supports of the Right. A cluster of professionals connected with real property produced organisations which entered the political fray to oppose Liberal land reform. Surveyors, estate agents, land agents and auctioneers were small in number but energetic in activity. In their formidable expertise they were able to exercise an influence disproportionate to their numbers. They gave a cutting edge to the Right's polemical assaults. Leading the pack was the Surveyors' Institution (SI), which was positioned impressively and strategically in Parliament Square. The 1911 census maintained that there were some 4,000 land, house and ship surveyors in England and Wales.[183] The introduction of qualifying exams and the imposition of a code of practice attested to the Institution's success in organising, improving and promoting its profession.[184] 'Whenever new ideas were expressed about the ownership, management, or taxation of land and property at any time before 1914', observes Professor F.M.L.Thompson, 'the great bulk of the membership almost instinctively showed its attachment to the existing order of things'.[185] The Liberal MP E.Davies declared in the House of Commons that the SI could not be called a 'Radical society'.[186]

In 1912 the Auctioneers' Institute fused with the Estate Agents' Institute to produce the Auctioneers' and Estate Agents' Institute (AEAI) of the United Kingdom.[187] The 1911 census estimated that there were some 18,000 auctioneers, appraisers, valuers and house agents in England and Wales.[188] The AEAI did not match the prestige of its big surveying brother but its attitude to the land system was equally Tory. In 1901 the Land Agents' Society (LAS) came into existence. Its primary aim was to secure a specific place for agricultural land agents in the professional sun.[189] The Society's founders wanted to end the endemic overlapping. 'Applicants must be bona fide Landed Estate Agents', it was decided at the outset, 'and not professional gentlemen, surveyors, auctioneers or others who undertake the management of agricultural estates as an adjunct to their other business'.[190] The LAS was Conservative to the core, much to the discomfort of Lord Carrington, the Liberal President of the Board of Agriculture in the Edwardian period. Sometimes, however, there were surprises. On 3 July 1907 Carrington recorded in his diary 'Dined at the Land Agents' Dinner...better received than I expected from so Tory a body.'[191]

The People's Budget well exemplified the help the Right received from these property professionals in resisting the forces for change. Austen Chamberlain persuaded the Surveyors' Institution to publish a memorandum hostile to the land taxes.[192] The other associations joined in the polemic and Lord Lansdowne kept a number of their publications to aid him in his work.[193] The Earl of Onslow had additional ideas. Public protest meetings are a neglected feature of British political life before the First World War. In a sense they illustrated weakness. When the Chartists gathered on Kennington Common in 1848, or when feminists protested at Greenham Common in 1983, they unwittingly proclaimed their lack of political power. If protesters had real influence there would be no need to protest. In 1909 W. Cornwallis-West, a Welsh landowner and former Unionist MP, suggested to the secretary of the CLA that a great protest meeting of aristocrats and landed gentlemen be held in the Albert Hall. In his belief that a 'general protest from so influential a class could not fail to impress the government' Cornwallis-West was expressing the realities of an extinct political structure. If he had thought about it, his very proposal attested to the fact that the landowning class was not 'so influential' as it once was.[194] When speaking in favour of Bonar Law in 1911, after not becoming the party's leader, Walter Long declared that it had been 'a drawback to our Party that we have seemed to be always identified in our high posts with the land'.[195] The vulnerability and increasing debility of the landed interest was further confirmed in 1909. 'I am trying to organise a big meeting of protest against the land clauses', Onslow told Austen Chamberlain, '*not* by the landowners' but 'by all the professional classes who live by or out of the land'.[196] The property professional organisations co-operated and the meeting took place on 13 July 1909.[197] Another professional meeting was organised by J.Boyton MP (1855–1926), a Tory auctioneer, four months later.[198]

The world of pressure was not always so friendly. What was the Conservative attitude to the trade unions? Once again the Tories proceeded in politic fashion. The Unionist government had not taken steps to reverse the implications of the 1901 Taff Vale case. But no sustained Conservative opposition was offered to the 1906 Trade Disputes Bill which greatly extended trade union privileges and erected a wall of immunity against civil actions for damages.[199] The Conservatives were hostile to a repeal of the 1909 Osborne judgement.[200] This ruling made it illegal for unions to levy compulsory sums from their members for the sake of parliamentary representation. But the Right softpedalled over the 1913 Trade Union Bill which reversed the decision and established a contracting-out system.[201] The payment of MPs, which was introduced in 1911, impinged on the whole question. Conservatives resented the innovation but were reluctant to make public promises of repeal.[202] The Edwardian period witnessed a major entrenchment of trade union legal rights which the Right was unwilling to combat with full force. The subject was to prove one of the great dificulties of Conservative politics for the rest of the century.

An alternative to this concessive approach was to enter into the world of trade unionism and to deny leftist hegemony. On the Continent the English monolithic model came to be repudiated, not least by the formation of Catholic trade unions. There were some stirrings in this direction. The Tariff Reform League created the Trade Union Tariff Reform Association. By 1910 it was said to have some ten thousand members and to be devoting especial attention to the industrial heartland of Lancashire.[203] But this never constituted a serious assault and the Conservative Party failed to establish a significant Tory bridgehead in organised labour. From 1900 onwards the Labour Party could rely upon the trade unions as a solid base of organisational, financial and cultural support. This vital force in political life had become powerfully sectionalised and the Right was to be excluded from some of the nation's most important organisations. Conservative working-class electoral support failed to be translated into institutional representation – this was a non-event of incalculable consequences.

☆

The new regime which gained power in 1906 was not congenial to the Conservative mind. It pressed ahead with its reformist plans. True to their colours the Tories offered opposition. The House of Lords acted as a powerful brake on the Left, but overreached itself in 1909. No doubt many Unionist peers thought they were being responsible in rejecting Lloyd George's land taxes. Perhaps they found that particular toad unswallowable. But to be good in politics is often not good enough. In these years, as throughout the period 1886–1914, the Right was not keen to extend democracy. Obstructionism was used to the utmost against the People's Budget. There was much polemical attack on the Liberal–Labour programme and a central theme was that the poorer sections of society were being injured. Opportunism was once again in evidence and the rural bulwark strategy made rapid progress. Attempts to moderate the government through compromise came to nothing. High society may have revealed itself as a rightist weapon. Pressure groups came to the aid of the Tory cause but trade unions became entrenched on the other side of politics. The Land Union sought to cripple the land taxes and valuation through litigation; the property professionals engaged in expert denunciations. At the same time the Conservative Party relied on its familiar planks and slogans. This first stage of left-wing reform brought out the electoral dangers that awaited the Conservative Party on the social reform front. The second stage was even more threatening to the party of preservation.

Five

Towards the Radical State

On the eve of the Great War the Liberal Party drew up plans for collectivist advance which were never implemented. This is one of the reasons for their neglect by historians. But in their scope and range these Liberal schemes were unprecedented in the levels of state intervention they envisaged. Many subsequent aspects of government activity were foreshadowed. The Liberal Party was seeking to construct the Radical state. Home Rule, Welsh disestablishment, democracy and free trade were essential components of this brave new world. A solution to the land question was perhaps the most dominant feature of the architecture. The land campaign, which has all too often been dismissed as the irrelevant expression of an outdated Radicalism, felt the future in its bones. Liberalism hoped for much from its land programme and from its abortive 1914 budget, and put land reform at the centre of its social policy. British Radicalism was reaching its climax: the tradition of Cobden and Bright, Henry George and his followers, the Radical Campaign of the 1880s, and the emphases of the National Liberal Federation, was being given concrete expression. The land campaign bears witness to the extent to which the Liberal land question forms an important part of the historical patrimony of British collectivism. It also illustrates the extent to which national politics were becoming increasingly preoccupied with material issues. What was the detailed character of the Liberal onslaught?

I

The Liberal land programme was outlined in major speeches and party publications during the course of the campaign,[1] which was formally launched by Lloyd George in October 1913. The programme was statist, centralist and interventionist. The government proposed to bring into existence a new 'Ministry of Land'. This new department would be equipped with specially appointed land commissioners. These commissioners would have broad-ranging powers throughout the world of land and buildings. They would be able to interfere in contracts between owners and occupiers, and between farmers and labourers, and would have such other duties as directing local authority housing, securing afforestation, bringing about the creation of small holdings, and preventing the misuse of land. Against the decisions of these bureaucrats there was to be no appeal. Administrative law was to take a great leap forward. This most notable of Edwardian Liberal innovations was continued with a vengeance. 'It is not, of course, a new thing for the judicial determination of questions to be entrusted by Statute to a Government Department or Commissioners', the Cabinet was told, but in no previous case 'are the judicial duties nearly so extensive as they will be under the new Ministry'.[2] This new government department was also to take over land valuation and registration, and to absorb many of the functions of other ministries and boards.

The dominant Liberal idea was that market mechanisms were not to be relied upon. Individual economic relationships required active government guidance. 'Abuses of the present system show themselves in unfairness of contract between landlord and tenant or between tenant and labourers or workmen', explained some Cabinet proponents of the programme,

> and the cardinal point of the present proposals is that a Commission should have discretionary power to intervene in any case in which it was alleged that an unfairness of contract existed which prevented land being used in the best interests of the community.[3]

The Tory concept of economic liberty was not to be respected; the Liberal notion that the land laws needed reform was given expression. The whole scheme amounted to a massive intervention in property rights in the name of the collective good. 'What he sees in his Land Department & what he gloats over, is the prospect of an omnipotent bureaucracy interfering with private rights as much as possible', Milner wrote of Lloyd George, 'not as an occasional & regrettable necessity, but as the main object of its existence, & independent apparently of all control by the Courts of Law'.[4]

What was the land programme to mean in practice? In the countryside the land commissioners would be able to fix rents, to nullify eviction notices, to determine rates of compensation for improvements, disturbance, and game damage; to fix wage rates (although the Liberals also considered the idea of setting up wage boards), and in so doing to give an abatement of rent to farmers in compensation, to revise hours of labour, to help in the provison of small holdings and allotments, and in the supply of houses – for which there were to be central grants; to acquire land by compulsion for the purposes of afforestation and reclamation, and to take over land which was not being used correctly. The essential features of the rural policy were clear. The labourers were offered higher wages, shorter working hours, improved housing, and better access to the land; the farmers were promised lower rents, security of tenure, and improved tenancy arrangements. The landowners were to lose all along the line.

The urban section of the programme was similarly radical although some of its features were not as clearly worked out. The land commissioners were to have extensive control over tenancy in the towns. Every holder of a lease granted for more than twenty-one years would be entitled to ask the land commissioners to renew the lease for such a time, at such a rent, and on such conditions as they saw fit. In fixing the rent the owner's reversionary interest in any buildings or improvements made before the passage of the proposed legislation would be recognised. If the lease were not renewed, for reasons of public interest, the lessee would receive compensation for those improvements made after the legislation, and compensation for disturbance. The commissioners were also to be able to abrogate restrictive covenants and to override the lessor's refusal to make improvements or assign leases. All commercial tenants, irrespective of the lease's length, were to receive these benefits, and for them compensation for disturbance included compensation for loss of goodwill and deterioration of stock. 'It is the leasehold system – presumably urban – that he intends to hammer hardest',[5] Lansdowne had predicted of Lloyd George.

A comprehensive survey of housing conditions and an inventory of the nation's housing stock were to prepare the ground for a reform of urban housing. The cost of building land to the municipalities was to be lowered by the employment of the 1910 land valuation by the land commissioners to fix prices, and by the replacement of the property professionals by the commissioners in the administration of the sale. Constraints on cost were also to be eased by central grants and revenue from the local taxation of land values. The central authorities would direct the local authorities to engage in schemes of urban development and housing. Less clearly elaborated was the idea to extend the provisions of the Trades Boards Act in the towns to secure an urban minimum wage. This threatened to offend a potential Liberal constituency of employers. In the towns, unlike in the countryside, there was no opportunity of making landowners bear the cost. As a result, the government avoided controversial details.

A reform of local taxation, and of the entire relationship between local and national government, was a component part of the whole Liberal project. The Liberals aimed at nothing less than a repudiation of the Victorian tradition of independent local government. Centralism, not localism, was the order of these statist days. There were compelling reasons for aiding the town and county councils, and successive governments had refused to grasp the nettle. The valuation system was as chaotic as ever; central grants had failed to keep pace with rising local expenditure; rate demands had grown steadily since 1900; and the local authority associations declared that British local government was in a state of crisis.[6] The Liberals had already run into trouble with their land taxes. The Association of Municipal Corporations had stressed that revenues from the taxation of urban land values belonged to the urban councils.[7] Lloyd George ignored such claims in the Finance Bill but soon came to realise the error of his ways. In June 1909 he declared that one half of the sums derived from the new taxes would be allocated to the local authorities.[8] Three weeks later he told the still smarting AMC that the following fiscal year would see increased grants-in-aid.[9] Neither promise was kept and the local authorities kept up their pressure.[10]

The Georgeite organisations were in euphoric mood and believed that with the new land valuation their hour had come. Could it not be used to implement their general programme? The United Committee for the Taxation of Land Values was buoyant with optimism. 'The good result of the year's work is marked in the wider and deeper understanding of our policy', declared its annual report for 1911–1912, 'the enthusiasm with which it is accepted when explained, and the growing demand for a prompt and radical instalment of the reform'.[11] In May and July 1912 two keen land taxers won by-elections at North West Norfolk and Hanley.[12] In May 1911 the 173 Liberal and Labour MPs who adhered to the Land Values Group presented a great land tax programme to the Prime Minister. They asked for a speeding up of the 1910 valuation and its use by the local authorities as a basis for site value rating. They further demanded the imposition of a national tax on land values. Its proceeds were to be distributed to the local authorities as grants towards the national services and to the Exchequer to relieve the existing duties on food.[13] Once again landowners were to be on the receiving end of Liberal reform. Earlier in the year a departmental committee on local taxation had been appointed and Asquith asked the land taxers to present it with their views.[14] In April 1913 the programme was presented again and this time it called for an alteration in the land valuation as it applied to agricultural land.[15] The 1913 Revenue Bill complied with this request.[16]

In May 1914 Lloyd George unveiled the government's plans for local taxation reform in his budget speech. At the centre of the scheme was a replacement of the assigned revenues system and the special grants of 1896 and 1899 with direct grants linked to specific services. These subventions were to be increased by £9 million. This sum was intended to relieve the ratepayers, but the procedure by which this relief was to be distributed was complicated. It would only go in relief of that rate burden which fell on the improvement to the site rather than the site itself; it would be allocated according to local needs and resources; and it would be linked to the efficiency of each local authority. Separate from this plan was another proposal to give special grants, amounting to an additional £1.5 million, for certain special services. Centralisation was the great order of the day; Whitehall was to take a major step forward. Henceforth all central grants in their local expenditure would be subject to central control. Separate again was the provision to local authorities of the ability to rate site values. The land valuation office would so adjust the 1910 valuation as to allow the relief to improvements to be distributed and to create a basis of assessment for SVR. The department, in another centralising provision, was also to replace the local assessment committees in the drawing up of valuations for rating purposes. The grants would cost money and Liberal needs required a further raid on personal wealth. The 1914 budget must be accounted a major milestone in redistributive finance.[17]

Rural land campaigns were a salient feature of the British Radical tradition. The Anti-Corn Law League had agitated the countryside;[18] Joseph Chamberlain had promised 'three acres and a cow' to the country labourers in the 1880s;[19] and the land reform pressure groups had set off into the countryside in coloured vans in the last years of the previous century.[20] But Lloyd George's effort was the greatest land campaign of them all and aimed at both town and country alike. It was launched by the Welsh Wizard in the autumn of 1913 and was co-ordinated by a special organisation set up for the purpose – the Central Land and Housing Council.[21] A great army of lecturers, speakers and enthusiasts held innumerable meetings and distributed millions of leaflets and pamphlets. By May 1914 ninety to a hundred and twenty such meetings were being held each day and over three million handbills had been distributed.[22] Lloyd George was the man of the hour, promising the populace that with correct government action the people would never have it so good. He was the subject of a plethora of political cartoons.[23] Once again anti-landlordism was all the rage. The campaign sought to concentrate popular attention on the land system; to direct antipathy towards the aristocracy and gentry; to win popular support for the Liberal programme; and to give Liberalism a secure electoral future.

Asquith's government, it appears, was planning to fight a general election in 1915, and to fight it chiefly on the land question and the reforming budget. The Home Rule Bill was scheduled to become law in the autumn of 1914, thus clearing the decks for a redoubled effort on the real property front. There was an aspect of this strategy which made very good political sense. No doubt the Liberals hoped to repeat the urban successes of their foray of 1909–1910, but the countryside held out especially enticing prospects. The agrarian sector was over-represented in the House of Commons; no redistribution of seats had taken place to take account of rural decline after 1885. A large prize presented itself to the Liberal Party, and it was a prize within reach. In December 1910 about two-thirds of the English rural seats had been won by the Conservative Party, but this base had always been insecure.[24] 'Half of the seats in England which the Liberals could hope to win in 1915', maintains one historian, 'were rural in character'.[25] To put it another way, the Liberals were aiming at the soft underbelly of electoral Conservatism. There was anxiety on the Right. 'I have always thought', opined Balfour in 1913, 'that our hold upon the rural counties was more or less precarious'.[26] 'The present strength of our party in the House of Commons', Acland Hood hurried to tell Bonar Law in 1912, 'comes largely from the agricultural districts'.[27] The Liberal Party, therefore, was looking to its own version of collectivism to put it back into Downing Street. A governing party had never previously run on such an interventionist platform and the redistributive inclinations of the Democracy had never before been so thoroughly tested. How did the Conservative Party respond to this eminently modern initiative? A mass of hitherto unused material survives and it is thus possible to give a detailed answer to this question. The Right's response to the land campaign may be taken as a case study in Conservative method and this case study can be subjected to microscopic examination. General and familiar patterns are discerned – this miniature has similar outlines to much larger canvasses already examined.

II

At a parliamentary level the forces of anti-collectivism found themselves in a novel situation. The Parliament Act of 1911 had abolished the veto of the House of Lords. A powerful obstacle to the establishment of the Radical state had been removed. Here the constitutional history of the nation had a profound impact. Indeed, the relationship of the British constitution to the rise of collectivism gains illumination. With no Bill of Rights, no set of written guarantees, no significant powers vested in the head of state, and now an emasculated second chamber, the collectivists had before them only the need to gain a majority of seats in the House of Commons. In this respect the British experience has been unique among major Western nations. It is no accident that the New Conservatives of the 1980s mooted ideas of re-establishing constitutional safeguards.[28] Both Left and Right realised what had happened in 1911. 'The ending of the Lords' veto', exulted the United Committee for the Taxation of Land Values, 'has left the way clear for those political reforms that have been demanded for a generation'.[29] At the time of the Parliament Bill Long warned that landowners would suffer from legislation over which the second chamber had no control.[30] Pretyman observed the land campaign and the debilitated House of Lords and concluded that the outlook was 'about as black as it can be'.[31] There was no possibility, therefore, of the Conservative Party relying upon the nobility to offer substantial checks to the Liberals. There was to be no repeat of 1906–1910.

There remained, however, the option of obstructionism in the House of Commons. Land taxation was especially feared by the Conservatives. Pretyman's 1909 land tax sub-committee was expanded and strengthened. Austen Chamberlain became its chairman, Pretyman was its whip, and its other members included Balfour, Fitzroy, Royds, Pollock, Mason, Peel, Cassell and Helmsley, all of whom could bring to bear specialist knowledge. The committee's secretary was Crofton Black of the Land Union. A rich source of expertise was thereby tapped. One insider recalled how an 'immense amount of work was done by this committee during the years 1910–1914'; 'amendment after amendment was moved at the opening of

various Parliaments' and 'numerous clauses in the Finance and Revenue
Bills introduced by the Government were bitterly contested'.[32] The
committee's activities were part of a wider obstructionist effort attempted
by the opposition on the eve of the Great War. The House of Commons
became a battlefield.[33] 'Party feeling ran higher than I have ever known it
to', recalled one old parliamentary hand in the 1920s, 'before and
since'.[34] These years showed that obstructionism was a tactic which could
bring rewards.

The 1913 Revenue Bill was precisely what Chamberlain's committee
existed to attack. Pretyman suggested to Bonar Law that the party put
down an amendment to the bill repealing Part I of the 1910 Finance Act
as it applied to land of a purely agricultural value.[35] It seems, however, that
Bonar Law was already satisfied with a concession won from the Chancellor. Lloyd George had agreed to drop clause 11 of the Revenue Bill if
the opposition gave the rest of the bill a clear run. Here, it appears, was one
of the fruits of obstructionism – clause 11 contained the LVG's proposals
for the adjustment of the site valuation. The land taxers were furious at this
perceived betrayal and in their anger succeeded in wrecking the entire
bill.[36] The 1914 budget was also the object of the committee's methods.
New constitutional requirements worked to the Right's advantage. It had
been decided in the courts, in a case brought by the Tory MP Gibson
Bowles, that the collection of taxes prescribed in the 1909 Finance Bill
before that bill's enactment had been illegal. The Provisional Collection
of Taxes Act of 1913 laid down rigid rules of procedure for future
reference.[37] As applied to the 1914 budget the Act required that the taxes
be passed into law by 6 August.[38] In his budget speech Lloyd George
declared that his reforms would be divided between a Finance Bill and a
Revenue Bill. The former was to deal with the taxes levied; the latter was
concerned with their expenditure and contained all the local taxation
proposals. The Conservatives realised that if they could delay the Finance
Bill the government might be forced to jettison the Revenue Bill to meet
the August deadline. The whole project of local government reform could
be delayed.

From May onwards the opposition put up a formidable barrage of
amendments, procedural objections, and interminable speeches. Legislation was not an occupation for the tender hearted. Such behaviour had the
desired effect. In early June Lloyd George attempted to save time by
altering the respective contents of the two bills,[39] but this did not suffice.
In June Asquith and the Cabinet decided that the local taxation legislation
would have to be put off to an autumn session – in part, the king was told,
'in view of the exigencies of time'.[40] By its delaying tactics, therefore, the
opposition had ensured that the rating reforms would have to be introduced after 6 August. Notwithstanding backbench Liberal rebellion, the
government decided to persevere. The grants would be available in April

1915 and a new revenue bill would create a basis of assessment for SVR and allow the grants to relieve buildings and improvements.[41] But internal Cabinet deliberation revealed that the whole project of site value rating was full of technical difficulties and there was an ominous degree of apprehension.[42] The great point about delay, as Salisbury was so fond of pointing out, is that you can always hope that something will turn up. In August 1914 international hostilities broke out, ministerial priorities changed, and Lloyd George's programme failed to be realised. SVR has never been implemented in Great Britain.

What of the electoral sphere? The Conservatives had always placed much reliance on the Irish card and now they played it for all it was worth. The Right wanted to focus popular attention not on property but on the Union. In October 1913, after the launching of the land campaign, the party was instructed by the Central Office and the chief whip to concentrate on the Irish question to the deliberate exclusion of the land question.[43] Similar instructions, it appears, were issued to the Tory press.[44] This diversion tactic was pursued until the outbreak of the First World War. The action was most significant: the Conservative Party was not willing to fight the Liberal Party on the latter's chosen ground, and thereby admitted its vulnerability on questions relating to property redistribution. Yet the Right was not rigid in its diversion tactic and both attacked the Liberal programme and presented rival policies of its own. But these approaches were contradictory and worked against each other. 'The more we defend', Steel-Maitland accurately perceived in June 1914, 'the more we play their game by shifting the venue from our most favourable ground to theirs'.[45] The party also relied on familiar stalwarts such as tariff reform, defence and disestablishment.[46] In the House of Commons Samuel Hoare and Alfred Lyttelton led the fight to defend the property of the Welsh Church.[47] The Marconi scandal supplied the party with additional ammunition for polemical attack and tied in well with the emphasis on the corrupting consequences of Liberal statism.[48]

The Conservative Party sought to turn the people against the campaign by denouncing its proposals. The Tory arguments were most revealing about the nature of Conservatism and therefore merit extensive consideration. The Right warned the people that they would be subjected to dictatorial bureaucratic control. Orwell's *Animal Farm* prediction was anticipated: there would be 'new landlords for old'.[49] Property rights and economic liberty were to be curtailed. 'Mr. Lloyd George had started a wild anti-landlord campaign in support of a scheme for setting up a vast beaurocracy [sic] under the control of a "Ministry of Lands"', described the *Campaign Guide* of 1914, 'which was to interfere in every contract between owner and occupier of land or buildings and between farmers and labourers'.[50] The party journal gave the Tory perspective on Lloyd George's programme:

His panacea to solve all urban and rural difficulties is "to send a man down" from a Government office in London to settle everybody's affairs. Mr.Lloyd George's officials are to settle what rent the farmer is to pay the landlord, what wage he is to pay the labourer, how long the labourer shall work, what holidays he is to have, and whether he is physically fit to earn the minimum wage when it is fixed. More than that, he is to tell the farmer how to cultivate the land...

In the town the Government officials will decide the terms upon which shopkeepers, business men, and even private residents are to occupy their premises or houses, and when they are so daring as to enter into a contract for themselves the Government officials will decide what the contract means and whether it is fair, and tear it up if they do not like it...

All this is of a piece with the new Liberalism.[51]

The centralisation of the 1914 plan was also condemned.[52] In this the Conservative Party received the support of the Association of Municipal Corporations.[53] The local authorities were lining up behind the localist party and the alignments of the years of high municipalism were being reversed.

The Conservative Party went on to charge that the Liberal Party's land policies were injuring, and would further injure, popular welfare and prosperity. For the Right the Left was upsetting beneficial market mechanisms and destroying business confidence. The People's Budget had already received a substantial amount of flak and land value taxation was constantly condemned.[54] A building slump took place as the Edwardian era drew to a close.[55] The Conservative Party held the Liberal land taxation schemes to be responsible. The opposition repeatedly blamed the government for the shortage of houses, the high level of rents, and the depressed state of the construction industry. It was argued that the land taxes and the threat of future taxation were inhibiting investment in bricks and mortar. Builders themselves were having their enterprise taxed.[56] The Lumsden case, which was sponsored by the Land Union, went through the High Court and the Court of Appeal to the House of Lords. The case was lost, but the law lords made clear that the increment value duty taxed builders' profits.[57] The Conservative Party attacked in a way which fully revealed its anti-interventionism, as the following propaganda leaflet well illustrates:

YOU WANT A CHEAP HOUSE?

Well, the way to get it is to induce plenty of people to put their money into the housing and building trade, then there will be plenty of people competing for tenants and you will get a house as cheap as it can be made. People will not put money into the building trade if they think vindictive taxes are going to be put upon them. Mr Lloyd

George's "Land Taxes" in the "People's Budget" have hit the
builders, because when builders have been successful and sold their
houses and made a profit it is called "unearned increment" and part
of it is confiscated. The result is that fewer people will put money
into that trade. Fewer people are building houses and so rents are
going up...Land and houses used to be regarded as the safest form
of investment and, therefore, people could lend money to build
houses and develop land at the lowest possible rates of interest. This
meant comparatively cheap houses and low rents. Now money can
only be got for this purpose at a higher rate of interest, which means
higher priced houses and higher rents, simply because the Radicals
have made people regard land and houses as a dangerous investment.[58]

The Confidence Party had spoken.

The Conservatives also blamed the Liberals for a new anxiety which
afflicted the farmers. After 1909 agricultural estates came onto the market
(which did not mean that they were necessarily sold) in increasing
numbers.[59] After the Great War this stream turned into a torrent.[60] Lights
were beginning to go out all over landed England. Tenant farmers could
receive notices to quit on the sale of the estate. From the Right came the
charge that the Liberal attack had driven apprehensive landowners into the
auction room. The farmers could blame the Liberals for their plight.[61] In
1911 Asquith's administration appointed a departmental committee on
tenant farmers and sales of estates. Its report was a classic statement of
conventional Tory views. It paid handsome tribute to the landlord–tenant
system and observed that most witnesses believed that it was partly the
Liberal attack which had led most owners to sell. [62]

In February 1914 the Conservative Party moved an amendment to the
Address which well captured its approach to Liberal land policy. The idea
that the land system was benevolent and progressive permeated the
pronouncements of the opposition. Tories could hardly say otherwise.
Fitzroy argued that the weathering of the agricultural depression was
'entirely due to the land system of this country'.[63] Royds declared that the
nation should look to private enterprise to 'house the population'.[64] Not
one significant measure of reform was proposed by the opposition; it was
clear that the *status quo* was regarded as valuable. Speaker after speaker
rose to charge that the government was by its own actions having an
adverse effect on the economy. The amendment is well worth reading, not
least because it was such a clear statement of anti-collectivism:

> But humbly regrets that no legislation is foreshadowed to restore the
> credit and security of land and house property which has been
> undermined by the Finance (1909–10) Act 1910, and by recent
> public utterances of Ministers suggesting further land legislation
> based on the Report of a secret and partisan Committee, thus causing

the withdrawal of capital, a shortage in the supply of houses and cottages for the working classes, serious loss to the building and allied trades, an arrest of agricultural development, and a check to the natural rise in labourers' wages. [65]

Liberal policies were condemned as injurious to the very people they were intended to help: the rural minimum wage would cause unemployment amongst the agricultural labourers;[66] rent fixing would rebound to the disadvantage of the occupiers.[67] The overall Tory message was simple – collectivism did not conduce to the collective good.

For the Conservatives the land programme and the accompanying budget were further steps towards the creation of a bureaucratic state dominated by the politics of patronage. The most coherent statement of this view is to be found in a review article of 1914 entitled 'The Encroaching Bureaucracy'. 'The trend of government in England of late years has been towards bureaucracy and centralisation', the article began, 'with a constant widening of the area of control and increasing interference with the functions of daily life'.[68] This Conservative perceived administrative law as a threat to the liberty of the subject and observed that democracy involved the subordination of taxpayers and ratepayers to the electoral power of those 'many who pay little or nothing'.[69] Further social legislation would only increase the number of officials and these would become a great vested interest. 'It is appalling to contemplate the possibility of several millions of men and women receiving salaries and wages from the Exchequer or from the rates', it was concluded, 'and using electoral influence for personal benefit'.[70] The emergence of directive bureaucrats in the Edwardian period heightened Conservative apprehensions. The left-wing Beveridge was director of the labour exchanges from 1909 to 1916. Edgar Harper (1860–1934), a land tax enthusiast who had been Statistical officer at the LCC before becoming chief of Lloyd George's land valuation in 1911, was the Tories' leading bureaucratic *bête noire*.

The Conservative Party's attack on the Liberal land policies, and its emphasis on the error of Home Rule, corresponded to the tactical thinking of the new leader of the opposition. Andrew Bonar Law favoured a militant and combative form of politics which his opponents termed 'the new style'.[71] He was uninterested in a concessive approach and repeatedly affirmed Tory principles. The Liberals and Socialists may have been making the running on social issues but there was no great readiness to run after them. Lansdowne agreed with Law's view that it was 'better tactics to make capital out of the mistakes of our adversaries than to compete with them by producing rival proposals of our own'.[72] Austen Chamberlain noted that Bonar Law was unconcerned with such subjects as land and housing and probably knew very little about them.[73] The man from Birmingham also recorded his leader's view that 'if we are united we can win on the faults of our opponents'.[74] In 1913 Bonar Law met members of the

Unionist Social Reform Committee and his lack of enthusiasm for their policies was made apparent.[75] The leader of His Majesty's Opposition continued his advocacy of tariff reform,[76] but there was no idea that the leader of the Conservative Party had a sympathy or affinity with the Left's social inclinations. The chain-smoking Bonar Law was the combative approach made flesh.

The Conservative Party also engaged in one of its most favoured forms of political response – principled opportunism – and developed the bulwark strategy. The land campaign provoked a flurry of policy formulation as answers were sought to the Liberal challenge. Committees sprang up where previously there had been silence. In June 1912, on his own initiative, Steel-Maitland appointed a two man committee of Lord Milner and Herbert Trustram Eve to produce a land policy for country districts.[77] Their report, which Milner wrote in the first person singular, was presented in March 1913.[78] In July 1912 Bonar Law and Walter Long set up a land policy committee composed of the three Conservative MPS C.Bathurst, B.Peto and C.Mills.[79] The resultant report appeared in August 1912.[80] In the same year a high-powered committee on imperial and local taxation was called into being under the chairmanship of W.Hayes Fisher. It produced a series of reports during the course of the next two years.[81] Hayes Fisher also set up his own private committee on town tenancies.[82] In July 1913 Salisbury was asked to preside over a committee representative of a broad spectrum of internal opinion.[83] This committee produced a general report on party land policy in August 1913[84] and a special report on agricultural wages in February 1914.[85] Steel-Maitland also brought in special experts to advise the party: Eve, Howard Frank, Rowland Prothero, Edmund Strutt and Bevill Tollemache. A great deal of informed thought and considered effort went into the production of the Conservative Party's policy response.

The chronology of the Conservative Party's actions brought out the extent to which the Tories were reacting to the Liberal challenge. The first major move towards a land programme was made in June 1913 when Lord Lansdowne gave a major policy speech at Matlock Bath.[86] This was the outcome of much internal discussion[87] and was clearly meant to pre-empt Lloyd George. It was presented in party propaganda as a coherent statement of official policy.[88] But the programme was lacking in substance and a motion was presented to the National Union demanding a clear Conservative answer to the impending Liberal campaign.[89] Immediately after the launching of the campaign, but not before, the diversion tactic was promoted. A number of hectic months followed before the party came up with an alternative wage policy. In June 1914 an expanded programme was presented to the electorate in party propaganda.[90] During these months, also, the party responded to pressure to produce alterations in its policies towards urban and rural tenancies.[91] The Conservative Party was reacting to events and Steel-Maitland's pleas for a planned and systematic approach fell on deaf ears.

With the new Liberal menace the bulwark strategy cast an even greater spell over anxious Tory minds. Milner and Eve gave a good description of that strategy and held up the mirage which so attracted troubled Conservatives:

> There can be no manner of doubt that the institution of private property is seriously menaced at the present time – more seriously menaced perhaps in Great Britain than anywhere else in the world... If the present Social Order is to endure, it is simply necessary, at whatever cost, to effect a great increase in the number of people who have a direct interest in the maintenance of private property.
>
> There is no bulwark against communism at all equal to that provided by a large number of small property owners and especially small owners of land...One man may own 5,000 acres, another only five, but as long as he owns anything, he will, in 99 cases out of 100, be on the side of private property against nationalisation. And there is no form of property which has anything like the same steadying effect upon its owners as land.[92]

Milner and Eve endorsed the ideas of Collings' bill, suggested that where possible small owners should be grouped together in farm colonies to give them greater economic viability, and talked of village reconstruction.[93] Lansdowne was sceptical but did not withhold his blessing.[94] Salisbury's committee was more enthusiastic.[95] The Unionist Social Reform Committee displayed similar keeness.[96] The National Union resolved itself in favour of rural owner-occupation.[97] Party propaganda declared that loans would be extended to farmers to enable them to purchase their holdings; that ownership would be promoted under the 1907 Small Holdings Act; that farm colonies of owner-occupiers would be created; that villagers would come to own gardens and allotments; and that common livestock pastures would be created. The farm colonies were Israeli *kibbutzim* Edwardian Tory style: agrarian co-operative communes without the communal ownership of land. Compulsory purchase and central loans were the means to this propertied end.[98]

The urban world was deemed less favourable territory for such Conservative social engineering. The Peto committee of August 1912 advocated a scheme of leasehold enfranchisement. Such a policy would increase the 'number of persons interested as Proprietors in defending the community against Robbery by Act of Parliament'.[99] Steel-Maitland was drawn towards leasehold enfranchisement,[100] consulted the Surveyors' Institution on the subject,[101] and circulated a plan drawn up by a Welsh section of the National Union.[102] Party propaganda adopted a rather unconvincing neutral stance towards LE.[103] In truth, such an interference in property rights could not be accepted by the Right. Steel-Maitland also floated the idea of expanding the provisions of the 1899 Housing Act. 'I certainly think', replied his urban adviser Howard Frank of Knight, Frank and Rutley, 'it would be a step towards settling many of the social troubles and lead to greater stability if a percentage of the workers could become their own freeholders'.[104] But the proposal never saw the light of day.

The rural bulwark strategy involved reform and thus came into conflict with the Conservative beliefs and instincts of the party that embraced it. For this reason caution and hesitation mark its consideration in internal correspondence and in the party's policy committees. Five factors lay behind this lack of full commitment and all were rooted in the nature of Conservatism itself. First, there was the great question of economic viability. Many Tories believed that the existing estate system was efficient and productive, and doubted if a system of small ownerships was as effective or even capable of success.[105] Bevil Tollemache was a proponent and in 1913 set out the case for viability in *The Occupying Ownership of Land*. Milner and Eve enlisted his aid in setting up a farm colony but the project was abandoned.[106] There was also the major question of cost. The Conservative leaders were determined not to squander the resources of government or to injure the fiscal health of the state. In addition, there was the habitual Tory antipathy to increasing state expenditure.[107] On top of this was a marked reluctance to further undermine property rights with compulsory purchase.[108] Finally, there was an emotional adherence to the old order. The party of landed society had a natural attachment to landed society – peasant plots or yeoman farms were not landed estates. Collings thought this last factor lay behind the Conservative Party's marked reserve towards its own proposals. 'I am afraid that you and some others connected with the landed interest', he complained to Lord Robert Cecil in 1914, 'are in favour of letting things abide as they are'.[109] Change was not easy for the party of maintenance. By an act of historical irony, the subsequent success of the Left prepared the ground for a substantial implementation of the bulwark strategy. In the 1980s Mrs Thatcher was able to secure the private ownership of over a million council houses.[110] State growth had facilitated the realisation of an anti-statist strategy.

Opportunism, also, had its difficulties. What was most significant about the Right's response to the urban land campaign was that its chief innovations lay in an area where the Liberal promises were believed to have had an electoral impact. Until May 1914 both political parties recognised that the first stage of the urban land campaign had had very mixed results in the towns. In the area of local taxation the Conservative Party was strikingly inert. Perhaps a more innovative response would have been prompted by the actual passage of the 1914 reforms. The great left-wing idea was to shift the incidence of taxation and thus to secure a greater payment from the landowner. Could the collectivists not be frustrated by moving in their direction? In the middle of 1910 the tariff reform leaders

surveyed the scene and came up with a solution. They proposed the policy
of 'permitting Municipalities to rate vacant plots at their real letting
value'.[111] The policy's proponents argued that it would gain the support of
the town councils, increase the number of Tory votes, and prevent the state
from raising the existing land taxes to penal or confiscatory levels – 'if this
source of revenue, such as it is, is once given to municipalities, the
Treasury will never be able to put its finger in the pie again'.[112] The
Conservative Party had already sought to woo the urban councils and the
ratepayers by supporting the local claim on the 1909 land taxes.[113]
Lansdowne thought it was a good idea to show that landowners were not
arresting the development of their districts.[114] But the suggestion was not
carried into effect.

During the summer of 1910 Pretyman and his associates also drew up
a scheme. 'There can be be no doubt that L.G. will shortly announce a
policy of rating reform based on Land Values', wrote the prophetic
Pretyman, 'and we must have an alternative to put before the country'.[115]
Pretyman was deviating from his usual diehardism. He proposed a special
tax on urban building land. It would be levied when land was sold for
building purposes and would amount to either 5% of the purchase money
or a sum equal to one year's rent. It would be a national tax though
Pretyman did not specify whether its revenues would go to national or to
local coffers.[116] Salisbury's 1913 committee called for measures which
would prevent the withholding of land but was vague on detail.[117] All of
these three initiatives bore witness to the force of the Liberal emphasis on
vacant, underdeveloped, or unrated, urban or suburban property. The
programme of Hayes Fisher's committee does not survive. An interim
report on land value taxation was issued in 1912 but it merely gave a
comprehensive account and condemnation of the activities and policies of
the land tax movement.[118] The Conservative Party, therefore, continued
with its traditional incidence policy and subjected the Left's ideas to a
barrage of denunciations. The Hayes Fisher interim report was distributed
to the party faithful.[119] A special pamphlet on land taxation was issued by
the National Union.[120] Lloyd George's SVR plans received short shrift.[121]
There was to be no opportunism on the incidence front, notwithstanding
a number of internal moves in that direction. From 1886 to 1914 the
Conservative Party's powerful commitment to landed property meant that
it had an intense aversion to any proposal, however moderate, to tax land
values.

Nor was the Conservative Party's general policy of national grants
towards locally administered national services developed. Pretyman's
plan proposed that a national rating tax on incomes should be used to pay
for the locally administered national services. The tax was to be graduated
and PAYE was anticipated – where wages were involved a deduction was
to be made by the employer. Relief of the poor and education were still to

be administered locally but henceforth they would be under the supervision of a Treasury 'financial adviser'. Some £25 million to £30 million was to be raised in this way.[122] As the national services in 1910 in England and Wales alone cost over £60 million.[123] Pretyman was not advocating total relief for land and buildings. But this former artillery officer was seeking to pay for the national services more in accordance with the principle of ability to pay than the existing rating system. As Pretyman himself said: 'It is really a new basis for the old principle of "ability to pay".'[124] The leadership did not act on Pretyman's suggestion. The programme of the Hayes Fisher committee was never made public. This avoided certain obvious pitfalls, not least the question of distribution. This had flared up again in 1913 when Bonar Law promised the farmers that they would receive special rate relief to compensate them for the loss of benefits from the abandoned food taxes.[125] Austen Chamberlain reported how the promise had 'set every municipality buzzing angrily'.[126]

From a certain point of view the 1914 grants appealed to the Tory approach to local taxation. The new subventions were to be financed from an increase in the taxation of income. As Chamberlain conceded, this acknowledged personal property's debt to real property.[127] Yet the Right would have no truck with the centralisation and argued that Whitehall's new powers would subvert valuable local sovereignty, help to construct a parasitical bureaucracy, and work against economy.[128] Thus did the Conservative Party and the municipalities join hands to resist Liberal centralism. The town councils themselves looked askance on their proposed subjection and further aided the Right by deploring Lloyd George's linking of his grants to a reform of incidence.[129] 'The unfettered power of government departments to attach conditions to the grants', Steel-Maitland was told by the clerk to the Birmingham town council, 'is against all accepted ideas of local self-government'.[130] The Conservatives merely repeated their vague promise of greater grants-in-aid in party propaganda[131] or by amendments to the Address.[132] 'At present the Unionist Party has no rating policy', an observer told *The Land Union Journal* in 1914, 'other than that of asking for increased Imperial grants in aid of local expenses for purposes of national interest'.[133] Once again the whole degree of Conservative commitment to increasing Treasury grants is called into question. It was quite natural that the anti-statist party lacked enthusiasm for anything that could augment government taxation and expenditure.

The Conservative Party was equally unchanging in its urban housing policy. There was no sign that the government's housing promises had won many votes and so the Right did nothing. The USRC's bill was praised by party propaganda[134] but was never officially endorsed. Walter Long was once again opportunistic when it came to the urban world – he unsuccessfully advised Bonar Law to advocate state aid for housing along the lines of the bill.[135] The party leader asked the USRC's secretary to produce a book on housing.[136] The National Union published *The History of Housing Reform* without acknowledging Woods' authorship. The collusion of the party leadership with the supposedly independent USRC was demonstrated once again. This publication did not endorse any specific housing policy but gave vent to some typical USRC thinking. 'The maintenance of the principle of property, and of that stability of the body politic without which that principle cannot be maintained', depended on the people 'living under social conditions which, negatively at least, permit them to believe in and practice [sic] the ordinary civic virtues'.[137] But such politic Conservatism had no effect. The Conservative Party would not even consider the idea of a Tory urban minimum wage – it was beyond the ideological pale.

With regard to urban tenancy, however, the Right moved leftwards rapidly. This was a direct outcome of perceived electoral pressure. Yet once again Tory opportunism produced policies which by their moderation bore witness to their origins. W. Hayes Fisher (1853–1920) was a London MP, a barrister, a London County Council activist, and an influential backbencher. In December 1913 he sent a series of proposals which had been drawn up by his own private commmittee to the leaders of his party. Hayes Fisher argued that it was not possible to make town tenants vote on Home Rule only when they were being given strong material inducements to do otherwise. He called for a sound policy initiative on town tenancies.[138] Lansdowne was in favour of a moderate change in the party's stance.[139] Long agreed on the need for a counter attraction to the Liberal promises.[140] Hayes Fisher sounded the alarm bell: 'Mr.Lloyd George's promise to town tenants has proved a big bait and is seriously disturbing the allegiance of hundreds of our supporters.'[141] A by-election was pending in Islington. A London Tory MP warned against allowing the Liberals to monopolise the policy and win the seat.[142] On 18 January 1914 Long presented the new party policy on town tenants in a major speech in Islington.[143] Party propaganda trumpeted this substantial concession.[144] Major steps were made towards Lloyd George's position, but an independent tribunal was to take the place of executive officials. Long did not specify whether existing contracts were to be broken, as a deprecating Land Union correctly observed.[145] This diehard organisation opposed the party – 'Are we no longer to be left to settle rules of contract for ourselves, or to carry on our own business in our own way?'[146]

From a Tory point of view the rural campaign was altogether more problematic. One manifestation of the difficulties the Conservative Party faced was the appearance among the county and landed MPs of two opposing factions. Both agreed on fundamental aims but disagreed on means. They thus symbolised the process of division that frequently arose within the party's ranks when the Left posed a real threat – these two factions do not represent a conflict between the alleged collectivist and libertarian strands of British Conservatism. They may also have been manifestations of a new taste for backbench activity which was developing amongst the Tory MPs. On the Right was the 'land group', or 'Land Union group' as it was sometimes called. This appears to have been a fusion of some of the members of the old agricultural committee and the MPs attached to Pretyman's organisation.[147] It seems to have been established in February 1913,[148] and its chief aim appears to have been a stiffening of the Right's resistance to the Liberal land programme. The land group had a traditional approach to the rural order and the defence of property rights seems to have been its primary aim. Its leaders were E.Fitzroy MP, the heir to a landed title and the future Speaker, and the old campaigner himself, Ernest Pretyman. On the Left was the 'social reform group' (SRG), a collection of some twenty MPs, peers and agriculturalists associated with the agricultural committee of the Unionist Social Reform Committee. Its leaders were L.Scott MP, J.Hills MP and C.Turnor.[149] They had rural regenerative aspirations and favoured meeting the Liberal challenge with reformist policies. They even tried to do a moderationist deal with the rampaging Welshman. Scott told Lloyd George that if he ceased his 'Limehouse' style attacks on landlords the SRG would give significant support to his policies the Tory intent was crystal clear.[150] Representatives of these two factions were placed on Salisbury's land policy committee. Here the affinity of belief of these two groupings was made apparent – the Liberal menace secured a temporary agreement on tactics.[151]

The land question served to reveal the social bases of Victorian and Edwardian Conservatism. The landed interest was an important support. The property professions, it seemed, belonged to the Tory nation. In 1911 there were some 210,000 farmers in England and Wales.[152] No peasantry on the Continental model existed – only 12.4% of holdings of over one acre were owner-occupied.[153] Contemporary received wisdom asserted that in the main farmers were a Tory class. Henry Chaplin said that they were the 'best supporters of Unionist candidates and members'.[154] Organised opinion confirmed this judgement. In 1904 a group of Lincolnshire farmers sheltered out of the rain at a hunt puppy show, formed the Lincolnshire Farmers' Union, and made history.[155] This organisation evolved into the National Farmers' Union and by 1914 the NFU was claiming a membership of nearly 25,000.[156] By seeking independent representation this organisation broke away from the domination of agricultural politics by landowners. It thereby further confirmed the waning power of the landed interest. But informed Conservatives knew that the NFU was on their side of national politics. Onslow referred to his party's 'control of, & influence, with this body'.[157] In 1913 Bonar Law and Steel-Maitland considered inviting the NFU's leaders to stand as Tory candidates,[158] a sure sign of their congeniality. Despite a strong desire for separate parliamentary representation,[159] the NFU was quite content to allow a Unionist continued tenure in

Lincolnshire,[160] its most favourable territory. The Liberals were trying to undermine an incorrigibly Tory constituency.

Many Conservatives feared that the 1913 decision to abandon the tariff reform food taxes had dislodged many farmers from their conventional electoral resting place. Chaplin said that the policy would 'alienate "vast numbers" of farmers'.[161] In September 1913 Turnor declared 'the farmers are getting more and more angry with the Unionist leaders'.[162] The Lincolnshire Farmers' Union passed a resolution antagonistic to the Conservative Party.[163] Bernard Gilbert launched the Farmers' Tariff Union in direct opposition to the January decision[164] and published two condemnatory pamphlets.[165] But these were all Lincolnshire phenomena and people, and Lincolnshire was a county with a long and rather idiosyncratic protectionist tradition.[166] National behaviour was at variance with this local experience. The National Farmers' Union, for example, did not follow the example of its Lincolnshire branch but kept up correct relations with the Tory leaders.[167] The Farmers' Tariff Union failed to break out of its county boundaries and secured the support of only one Tory MP.[168] The Conservative leaders did display some anxiety: Lansdowne reported Turnor's warnings to Bonar Law;[169] Bonar Law sent the whip R. Sanders MP to mollify the Lincolnshire Farmers' Union;[170] and Steel-Maitland was worried about the solidity of the farming vote[171] But Bonar Law had sweetened the pill by promising the farmers extra rate relief[172] and after October 1913 the party leaders showed no signs of thinking that the January 1913 decision had caused them significant damage.

The Conservative Party did not believe that the land campaign was eroding its support amongst the farmers – its policies thus lacked a substantial opportunistic content. A commitment to national grants in relief of local taxation and promises of loans to aid in farm purchase were the opposition's chief offerings to its traditional supporters.[173] A brief moment of alarm, however, provoked the expedient production of minor concessions. The Central Chamber of Agriculture had for some time demanded compensation for disturbance on the sale of the estate.[174] The Right had not responded. On 28 October 1913 Prothero warned that some Radicals were attempting to capture the CCA by exploiting this issue and the issue of compensation for continuous good tillage.[175] He wanted the Conservative Party to concede both these rights.[176] Steel-Maitland wrote 'I am frightened at the prospect of the farmers being turned against us.'[177] Lansdowne consented to the change.[178] Both rights came to be conceded by the Conservative Party.[179] In Parliament the Conservatives offered no opposition to the 1914 Agricultural Holdings Bill and thus temporarily suspended their continuous obstructionism. This measure provided for compensation for disturbance on the sale of an estate.[180] As with urban tenancy, official Tory policy had responded to perceived electoral pressure.

It was the agricultural labourer who was the chief object of the Liberals' rural campaign, and of party political desire, as a *Punch* cartoon well recognised.[181] The promised minimum wage was the central means by which the farm workers were to be induced to vote for the governing party. The Conservative Party promised central loans to local authorities, associations and private individuals for the improvement and supply of rural housing.[182] A group of Conservative landowners set up the Landowners' Rural Housing Society to stimulate activity under the provisions of the 1909 Housing and Town Planning Act.[183] The Right also developed its access to land policies. But these subjects were submerged in importance by the question of wages. The Conservative Party's handling of the wage question between 1912 and 1914 was a classic example of opportunism and may be taken as representative of behaviour to which this study has constantly drawn attention. The Conservative Party did not want to upset market forces or infringe the rights of property. At the same time it was reluctant to offend its traditional allied interests in the countryside – the farmers and landowners. Equally, it did not want to provoke the emergence of a strong agricultural labourers' union with all its radical potentialities. But the success of the Liberal appeal to the labourers was widely recognised. The diversion tactic was not working. The Right feared a loss of seats and a consequent defeat at the impending general election. It responded by moving towards the Liberal position, but in so doing it was constantly inhibited by its own concerns, cares and convictions.

A chronological perspective on the Conservative Party's treatment of the wages question is most revealing. Before the genesis of the land campaign the subject was very little discussed within the party. After the campaign's inception Tory apprehensions precipitated greater consideration. After the launching of the Liberal effort, and the perception that the prospect of higher wages was turning the campaign into a success, the Conservative leadership searched for an effective and rival policy. One Tory insider acutely observed of the Liberal idea of a minimum wage: 'If that had not been started no one would be thinking about Agricultural Labourers Wages.'[184] Of the first stage there is very little to say. The Right's commitment to non-intervention was at work. Ever since 1886 the Conservatives had refused to regulate rural wages by state means; the policy continued to be espoused. The next two stages will now be considered in succession. The Tory Party will be observed bending with the breeze.

The appointment of the Liberal land enquiry in 1912 prompted Bonar Law and Long to establish a policy committee which was to devote especial attention to the agricultural labourer.[185] The committee predicted the future. 'We regard it as evident', its members wrote in August 1912, 'that the Chancellor of the Exchequer has his attention directed to the question of Agricultural Wages, and contemplates steps to raise them by Act of Parliament'.[186] The committee was in opportunistic mood. Basil

Peto and his colleagues proposed a rival policy. Given Conservative beliefs it was rather ingenious. Wage boards would link agricultural wage rates to local market prices and achieve a minimum wage by establishing a datum line. Tariffs and bounties would act to buoy up market prices. The policy intruded upon economic liberty but attempted to avoid unemployment and redistribution by funding the wage increase indirectly from subsidies and import duties.[187] There were immediate protests from within the party. Acland Hood reported this opposition, argued that a minimum wage would cause unemployment, and condemned such an idea as reckless opportunism. Peto and his friends were playing the 'discredited game of going one better than the Radicals'.[188] One West Country MP recorded in his diary 'Our "social reformers" have been thinking of outbidding the Rads.'[189] Bonar Law informed Peto that his committee's policy was 'indistinguishable from a minimum wage, and could not be proposed by a Conservative party'.[190] Milner and Eve stressed that a minimum wage would cause unemployment. They suggested that state bounties on agricultural produce might be used to raise wages indirectly.[191] Otherwise they recommended profit-sharing schemes.[192]

In May 1913 members of the social reform group introduced a minimum wage bill into the House of Commons.[193] The other Conservatives displayed a conspicuous lack of enthusiasm. Francis Mildmay MP, a Devon and Kent landowner, expressed what must have been a common judgement. He believed that such 'ultra-socialist' legislation would have 'far-reaching consequences', was unworkable, and would alienate the farmers in his constituency.[194] This last concern was the constant preoccupation of Walter Long, the country gentlemen's country gentleman. Long may have been concessive on the urban front but when it came to the countryside he was a ditcher of the first order. He too was a Lampedusan conservative associate. In April 1913 he told Bathurst that it was essential not to give 'offence to our best supporters in the country, namely the smaller country gentlemen and the farmers'.[195] In October 1913 he wrote a letter to his leader 'I am sure you recognise the danger of estranging or even alarming the Land owner & Farmer who are the backbone of our Party.'[196] The SRG learnt of Lansdowne's forthcoming Matlock Bath speech and applied pressure to the Marquess.[197] But a Tory minimum wage could not be embraced. In his public declaration of policy Lansdowne first said that his mind was open on the subject of a minimum wage and then proceeded to produce a number of hostile arguments.[198] By June 1913 the Conservative Party had not changed its position.

In August 1913 Salisbury's committee reported that in some areas agricultural wages were 'too low for a proper standard of decent and healthy living', and made two suggestions. The committee observed that landowners and farmers could be persuaded to raise wages voluntarily and argued that compulsory wage fixing was not impossible. If wages were to be raised by legislative means then agriculture would have to receive corresponding relief from local taxation. The committee also suggested that it should reconsider the wages question later in the year.[199] Lord Alexander Thynne MP, a landowner and moderate member of the SRG, took up the idea of a voluntary wage rise and pressed it upon his leaders. He believed that it was wise to secure an increase in agricultural wage rates 'before the new land policy has caught hold'. He rejected wage boards because they would aid in the growth of a dangerous trade union. Thynne wanted his party to persuade landowners to join with their tenants in raising wage rates and suggested a number of leading Tory magnates who could set the movement in motion.[200] The new chief whip, Edmund Talbot, was enthusiastic.[201] But Lansdowne voiced a number of objections: it was better to wait until the Liberals had presented their policy and the reaction to it had been gauged; such an initiative would lend credence to the impending land campaign by making it appear as though the landowners and farmers were pleading guilty; and anyway wage rates would come to be raised naturally as the rural economy continued to revive.[202] Thynne was told that although official party backing for his plan was not possible private intiatives were always welcome.[203] The Conservative leadership was waiting on events. In late September 1913 Lansdowne wrote to Bonar Law about the Liberal minimum wage. No outright objection should be given; it was best to 'see what form the proposal takes and what kind of reception it meets with'.[204] The second stage was about to begin.

After Lloyd George's Swindon speech of 22 October 1913 it became clear that the Liberal minimum wage proposal was turning the rural campaign into a success; that the diversion tactic was not working ; and that the absence of an effective Conservative wage policy was dividing the party and causing consternation in its ranks. Once again electoral pressure precipitated divisions on the Right as to the appropriate means for maintaining the established order. On 29 October Steel-Maitland circulated a memorandum on the Liberal effort. 'Our own men are already going in all directions like foxes in the cornfield', he reported. The chairman agreed that attention should be focused on the Irish question but warned that the Conservative Party had to be aware of the danger on its land flank.[205] R.A. Sanders MP recorded that there was great unease in the West Country about the campaign's impact and noticed the divisions that were appearing within the party.[206] In early December 1913 Steel-Maitland received a report from one of his officials – it was bleak. The Liberal minimum wage policy was winning votes and 'we must face a loss of votes in districts hitherto favourable'.[207] In the same month Charles Bathurst MP told Bonar Law that in the South of England and to a certain extent in the West the government promises were 'carrying off their feet a considerable number of Conservative labourers who have voted Conservative all their lives'.[208] Acland Hood, a Somerset landlord, believed that the Liberal initiative would 'tell in his parts & further west'.[209] In late 1913 and early 1914 the party leaders came under pressure from their followers to produce a wages policy which would halt the slide to the Left in the countryside.[210]

Certain members of the social reform group thought that they had the answer and continued to advocate a Conservative compulsory minimum wage for agricultural labourers. But even amongst these concessive Tories there were divisions – some of the adherents of the USRC's agricultural committee were opposed to a mandatory farm wage. The SRG's manifesto, *A Unionist Agricultural Policy*, which appeared in September 1913, praised the May 1913 bill.[211] This bill was also commended by a book commissioned by some of the SRG which appeared in February 1914.[212] A new version of this measure was introduced into the House of Commons in April 1914. Even this policy had some traces of Conservatism – compulsion was only involved after voluntary rates had not been implemented.[213] The underlying motives of the agricultural committee of the Unionist Social Reform Committee were well revealed in a letter which was sent by many of its members to Bonar Law in November 1913. These were not collectivists but tactical anti-collectivists. They argued that the Liberal minimum wage policy was popular, that the diversion strategy could not work because the labourers were much more interested in their pockets than the maintenance of the Union, and that the Conservative Party was in real electoral trouble. These 'social reformers' recognised party opposition to their principal policy and suggested that Bonar Law might express sympathy for the plight of the farmworkers and commit the party to carrying out inquiries in low wage districts to discover the best means of raising labourers' incomes.[214] Another eminently conservative motive was that expressed by the SRG leader C.Turnor. He defended the 1914 bill to a hostile fellow Tory with the following sentence: 'with the threatened development of labourers' Unions it is important that something should be done'.[215] The tone was hardly left-wing. On 13 November, at Norwich, Bonar Law declared that in many areas wages were 'so low' that they had to be raised. But all he could offer was an official inquiry into the effects of a minimum wage.[216] This was the first, albeit minor, shift in the party's official position.

The Conservative Party as a whole rejected the SRG's minimum wage response. The land group denounced the SRG's ideas and actions in no uncertain terms. Pretyman wrote an angry letter to Bonar Law: 'you cannot expect your agricultural followers to accept such a policy as these "social reformers" are putting forward'.[217] At an agricultural show in November 1913 Long declared that a mandatory minimum wage would be a 'disaster'.[218] Members of the SRG reacted angrily.[219] Bristolian Conservatives maintained that Long's line would spell electoral ruin for the Right.[220] Steel-Maitland, the vice-chairman of the USRC, floated the idea of a minimum wage in low wage districts which excluded old and infirm labourers.[221] He pressed the policy on his colleagues in late October 1913 and declared: 'It enables us to condemn Lloyd George's scheme outright, and to produce a quite distinct and better alternative'.[222] But such enthusiasm met with no response. A compulsory miniumum wage for farm labourers, reported Salisbury in February 1914, was opposed by a large section, if not a considerable majority, of the Conservative Party.[223]

The Central Land Association had its own ideas about how to frustrate Lloyd George and these were rooted deep in Tory voluntaryism. On 10 December 1913 its executive committee decided to ask its members to secure a voluntary increase in farm wages.[224] A week later a circular was dispatched.[225] The CLA was able to use a national network of country landowners and Tory politicians. In effect, the Right had its own extra-governmental machinery for raising wages. This was a sign of the socio-economic times. In Hertfordshire A.H. Smith, a landowner and former MP, invited his aristocratic neighbour Lord Salisbury to participate in the scheme.[226] Early in the new year Bathurst told Long that the CLA's proposal was 'being adopted by all the larger and more enlightened landowners of my acquaintance in Gloucestershire, S.Wiltshire, & Dorset'.[227] But even this mild initiative could cause offence to arch-diehards. Long resented the circular's assertion that rural wages were too low, and threatened to resign the presidency.[228]

The Conservative Party tried to blunt the appeal of the Liberal wage policy with hostile propaganda. The chief line of argument was that a minimum wage would injure the labourers; state regulated incomes were said not to be in the interest of 'Hodge' and his brethren. Although Lansdowne and Bonar Law tried to avoid a direct rejection of the proposal, party literature stressed that farm workers would be harmed by a fixed wage.[229] Another favourite theme of the party's propaganda was that Conservative agricultural rate relief would act to raise wage rates indirectly. The claim was that the party's 1896 Agricultural Rates Act had had this effect and that future legislation would repeat the process.[230] Steel-Maitland backed this horse quite strongly and corresponded with Acland Hood in December 1913. The chairman of the party reported that the idea was well received at public meetings. Could the policy not be developed?[231] Acland Hood was not encouraging. 'I think', he wrote, 'it would be very difficult for our Members and Candidates in Boroughs, and so-called County areas which are really urban, to justify such a measure'.[232] This was to return to the drawbacks of the Tory local taxation policy.

By early 1914 the party leadership was agreed that the party needed a rival wage policy. Political circumstances and Conservative beliefs required a policy which appealed to labourers without offending farmers or landowners; which did not subvert economic liberty or transgress property rights; and which did not cause unemployment. Thus the Right moved towards a voluntary minimum wage : wage rates would be suggested in low wage districts which would then be voluntarily implemented by owners and occupiers. Of course the presentation of such a scheme would allow of a great expression of sympathy for the poverty which existed amongst the agricultural labourers. The policy was a clear product of the Tory mould. Salisbury was invited by Lansdowne and Bonar Law to consider whether the policy was within the 'compass of our convictions'.[233] In January 1914 the owner of Hatfield House produced two weighty memoranda. Salisbury dwelt at length upon the proper wage fixing body.[234] This was an anti-centralist party and both Lansdowne and Long favoured local committees.[235] Steel-Maitland still had faith in the diversion tactic but stressed that the rank and file would clamour for a policy when Parliament reassembled. He wanted the Salisbury committee to be recalled to prepare a wage policy.[236] In February 1914 the committee met at Central Office and advocated a voluntary minimum wage in low-wage districts. The wage-fixing body would be a committee appointed by the Board of Agriculture on the recommendation of the local county council.[237] The two factions then clashed – the land group was opposed to the centralist involvement of the Board of Agriculture.[238] They agreed to disagree and to leave the question open.[239] Steel-Maitland circulated yet another memorandum in April 1914. He warned that if the Irish question was solved the land question would come to the forefront of politics, and with damaging results for the party. A rival wage policy needed to be presented to the electorate.[240]

On 21 April 1914 Lansdowne and Salisbury declared for the policy of Salisbury's committee in the House of Lords. They also argued that a compulsory minimum wage would injure agriculture. These two Tory grandees maintained that local public opinion would ensure that the recommended rate was paid. Communal bonds would secure voluntary action.[241] The idea was characteristic of Tory thinking. But for the rest of 1914 the policy was not propagated by the Conservatives. The party's *Gleanings and Memoranda*, a regular publication which kept the faithful informed about political developments, referred to the policy but did not endorse it.[242] The rural programme presented by Lord Lansdowne in party propaganda in June 1914 merely promised inquiries into agricultural wage rates.[243] A party leaflet for farm workers only advocated inquiries in low wage districts into proper wage rates and the means by which they could be achieved.[244] Great effort and thought had gone into the creation of a wages policy. Why was it not propagated? The answer is simple: during the summer months of 1914 the Irish question came to dominate national politics and the diversion tactic acquired a new viability. 'Our party is certainly planning for a general election on the Ulster question of exclusion',[245] a Tory MP observed to his diary in March 1914. It was now expedient to abandon a policy which it had been opportune to adopt. This particular toad could be regurgitated. No doubt 1915 would have seen the policy's resurrection. A similar policy was enacted in the early 1920s, when Labour was pressing, but proved ineffective.[246]

A polemical attack on field sports was a salient feature of the land campaign and accompanied the myriad of Liberal policies. The attack was a part of an overall attempt to discredit the aristocracy and gentry. It involved the idea that landowners neither toiled nor span but engaged in the economically wasteful and damaging recreational pursuits of hunting and shooting.[247] Once again one returns to the Liberal idea that the land system was economically inhibiting. The land commissioners would act to curb such injurious activity. On the Right there were jokes. Lord Malmesbury told a friend in 1913 that he was going to do a little shooting before the pheasant was abolished.[248] In his memoirs Lord Willoughby de Broke remembered an anti-Radical poem which included the words 'I read the Book of Fate, And saw Fox-hunting abolished by an order from the State.'[249] But in the long run the Left would indeed threaten to use the state to hinder or prevent field sports. Certainly the Liberals were aiming at a large target. Before the Great War hunting and shooting reached their zenith. 'Those were the spacious days', recalled one Tory MP, 'when at some places you were invited down for the week, arriving on Monday, shooting the four intervening days, and leaving on the Saturday'.[250] Lord Henry Cavendish Bentinck MP recalled the 'easy-going extravagance, the fox-hunting, the huge slaughter of pheasants, the 60-horse-power motors, the incessant golf of pre-War days'.[251]

To what extent was sport in Victorian and Edwardian England a force for social cohesion? The Conservatives often saw it as an integral part of the British way of life. All classes could take part in shared forms of recreation; common tastes could bind the nation together. Tory communitarianism here found expression. Did not the Primrose League place great emphasis on individuals from different backgrounds participating together in social events? The Conservative emphasis on freedom of activity and antipathy to state interference agreed very well with these beliefs. Thus right-wingers led the opposition to Liberal plans to use governmental powers to further curb drinking or gambling. Perhaps horse racing, boxing, football, cricket and blood sports (in many of which the aristocracy took a leading and patronising part) acted to encourage Tory sympathies. The Left could be described as killjoys, spoilsports and authoritarian puritans. Lord Willoughby de Broke, for all his social elevation, may have expressed sentiments which brought out a link between popular recreation and Tory anti-statism:

> If there be any one who is temperamentally opposed to sport, and would injure it if he could, he is hardly worth considering. His whole outlook would probably be anti-social and un-English in whatever rank of life he is to be found. He can perhaps best be described as the

spiritual descendant of that often-quoted band of reformers who
wished to put a stop to bear-baiting not because it gave pain to the
bear, but because it gave pleasure to the spectators.[252]
Surely in these lines one gains insight into what it was to be a Victorian or
Edwardian Tory?

One of the ways in which Victorian and Edwardian landowners gained
legitimacy was by participating in the armed forces. The landed interest
was closely connected with the services and thus displayed a sense of
public duty. About three-quarters of the landed Unionist MPs of the period
1900–1914 were consistently connected with the regular or irregular
forces.[253] The army and navy may themselves have served to encourage
Tory values amongst their members and to have given weight to Conservative nationalism. British Liberalism was characterised by a hostility to
landowners, but in this sphere there was a marked confirmation of their
role. Haldane's territorial army reforms placed the landed interest at the
centre of the new organisation. One Tory MP asserted that the People's
Budget had provoked many landowners into a stance of non-co-opera-
tion.[254] Did the experience of the First World War act to further discredit
the landed interest by undermining its military rationale?

It was often argued that field sports trained landowners in skills
appropriate to their military duties. In 1913 E.A.Alderson published *Pink
and Scarlet, or Hunting as a School for Soldiering*. In 1908 H.Martin
presented this line of defence in his presidential address to the Surveyors'
Institution. *The Land Union Journal* reprinted much of this lecture on the
value of field sports in its issue of April 1914.[255] Martin also said that
hunting and shooting aided the agricultural economy and brought wealth
to the rural districts.[256] But the Conservative Party eschewed such sophis-
ticated arguments in responding to the land campaign. On the one hand
the Liberals were mocked over their attitude towards game. Speakers had
been instructed to engage in ridicule in the October circular.[257] Bonar Law
set the tone with his denigration of this 'game-destroying Government'.[258] On the other hand the Liberals were accused of hypocrisy. Many
a government politician enjoyed the pleasures of the chase. The leader of
the Conservative Party received special information to sustain this charge
in public.[259] A typical party propaganda leaflet asked *Do Liberals Practice*
[sic] *What They Preach?*[260]

The final Conservative rural programme of June 1914 was comprehensive and detailed.[261] Did this mean that the Conservative Party had a desire
to maintain old rural England? This bears on M. Wiener's thesis. Certainly
the SRG was in favour of rural regeneration. Its manifesto talked of 500,000
people being returned to the land.[262] C. Turnor, one of its leaders, told
Milner that another million labourers could inhabit the countryside.[263] But
the official party programme bore all the signs of being a response to the
Liberal challenge rather than a product of an inner desire to achieve

agrarian expansion. Certainly there were no more Tory agriculturalists in 1914 than there had been in 1900 or 1886. It is most telling that the land group, the repository of the non-opportunist agriculturalists, was never moved to produce an agricultural programme. Indeed, the Conservative Party's whole economic approach consisted in allowing the existing economic machine to function smoothly and to give it a secure and stable environment in which to operate. The Right both accepted the way things were and the dynamics of economic development. One of these dynamics was a move away from the villages and hamlets.

A hostility to industrial and commercial growth cannot be detected in the late-Victorian and Edwardian Conservative Party's general attitude towards the economy. After all, had not abundant wealth and global power resulted from the existing system? The nationalist party would be unlikely to repudiate the economic bases of national greatness. Wiener's thesis may also be contested with regard to the Liberals. The assertion that the appealing values of landed society came to dominate the British elite sits unevenly with Liberal anti-landlordism. The Liberal Party's land policies were intended to increase economic growth, not least in the countryside, by setting the people free from retardative and regressive land laws. Both Conservatives and Liberals promised that their policies would encourage industrial, commercial, financial and agricultural prosperity and progress. There is no evidence that in the period 1886–1914 mainstream Conservatism or Liberalism sustained an anti-industrial or anti-growth political culture. It is certainly tempting to observe a common love of the countryside amongst the Victorian politically active and to invoke it as evidence for an anti-industrialism. But to admire rivers, trees or mountains did not mean to reject cities, factories or banking-houses. Ecologism is a rather recent force.

How did the familiar pressure groups aid the Conservative Party in these threatening days? Liberal radicalism finally brought the agricultural and property professional associations out into the political open. They revealed themselves in their true political colours. Herbert Trustram Eve, (1865–1936), was a land agent and surveyor, an enthusiastic Conservative, one of Steel-Maitland's most used advisers, and an active member of these organisations. He was a symbol of the Conservatism of the property professionals and said of himself 'I love the Unionist Party and loathe L.G. and all his single taxers.'[264] This phrase reveals all about Eve. He was also an active polemicist and published a number of anti-Georgeite pamphlets.[265] But Eve wanted to go beyond words into the world of action. In early 1912 he prompted the formation of the 'Land Conference',[266] a front body representing

The Central and Associated Chambers of Agriculture,
The Central Land Association,
The National Farmers' Union,

The Land Agents' Society,
The Farmers' Club,
The Surveyors' Institution,
The Auctioneers' and Estate Agents' Institute,
The Rating Surveyors' Association,
The Central Association of Agricultural and Tenant Right Valuers,
The 1894 Club, and
The Land Union.

The property professionals had good reason to campaign against the government. The projected land commissioners would take away much of their business. Lloyd George spoke of the 'fees for surveyors, architects, solicitors, counsel, arbitrators, umpires, expert witnesses' who 'never showed their expertness greater than when they came to draft the bill of costs'.[267] The Liberal government had done a 'great deal to alienate our profession by seeking to appoint commissioners to carry out all sorts of difficult duties', a leading member of Knight, Frank and Rutley told Steel-Maitland in May 1914, 'instead of employing practical men with the necessary training'.[268] This leading firm of estate agents itself published an anti-Liberal pamphlet on the land question.[269] In addition, would not the predicted nationalisation of land abolish private property and thus the precondition to property professional livelihoods? The Tories hoped to surround the landed interest with a firm defensive wall of small freeholders. These professionals already acted as such bulwarks. The Liberal land question had a marked capacity to disadvantage landowners to the immediate benefit of other social groups. But Eve and his kind constituted a small hornets' nest which the Liberals could not fail to infuriate.

The Land Conference well illustrated this point. Its president was the Unionist landowner Lord Clinton; its secretary was Trustram Eve. Steel-Maitland was kept closely informed by Eve and recognised a good political opportunity when he saw one. 'I have reason to believe', he told Lansdowne in September 1913, 'that we could use this body for our purpose'.[270] The Land Union proved to be too partisan and by 1914 it had ceased to be a member.[271] At first the Land Conference sought to obstruct the land taxers by presenting contrary evidence to the departmental committee on local taxation.[272] It then drew up a memorandum on the 1910 Finance Act in its relation to agricultural land. This document was expertly critical and called for a repeal of the land clauses as they applied to agricultural land. This memorandum was published at the time of the 1913 Revenue Bill, much to Pretyman's delight,[273] and opposed the land taxers' demand for changes in the valuation of agricultural land.[274] In May 1914 Eve presented a memorandum on that year's budget to the party's Central Office. He warned that Lloyd George and his followers were aiming at the ultimate nationalisation of land and regarded their land taxes as the means to this end. Eve gave a critical assessment of the budget and asked the

Conservatives to reserve judgement until the Land Conference had published its evaluation.[275] No such publication appeared.

The Liberal land enquiry was an intelligent political move and the Right required an answer. When it came to the land question the Tory agricultural and property professional associations were the Conservative obverse of the Left's array of social investigators. The former favoured official inquiries, the latter engaged in private explorations. The Left may have had the Webbs and Rowntrees; but the Right had the Trustram Eves and Rowland Protheros. The Conservative Party had a great deal of expertise on its side. A war of facts raged and interesting alignments were revealed. The leaders of the Conservative Party called for an official inquiry into urban and rural conditions.[276] No doubt they hoped that these organisations would secure a Tory report. In 1914 Lloyd George responded to criticism by declaring that established rural interests were always well able to put their case across to a royal commission.[277] Pretyman came up with the idea of a rival Conservative inquiry. It would, he told Bonar Law, call upon 'representative bodies such as Surveyors' Institution, Farmers' Union, Land Union etc. etc.'.[278] In November 1913 the Land Conference called for the appointment of a royal commission on land.[279] Steel-Maitland encouraged Eve to proceed with a 'non-party deputation to Asquith in order to get a proper enquiry made'.[280] In February 1914 the Prime Minister told the Land Conference that its wish could not be granted.[281]

The Right could also go independent. In January 1914 the Land Conference published a critique of the land enquiry's report without revealing that it had been drawn up by Eve.[282] 'The Unionist office is in love with this reply', exulted Eve, 'and will circulate it widely and boom it in the Press'.[283] This is exactly what happened.[284] Earlier Steel-Maitland had supplied a platform answer to the Liberal rural report to his party workers.[285] Lansdowne correctly observed that this ran counter to the diversion tactic.[286] Now copies of Eve's *The Land Problem* were distributed to the constituency associations.[287] In November 1913 the Land Agents' Society asked its members for their views on the Liberal publication.[288] Rowland Prothero (1851–1937), a former review editor, the Duke of Bedford's land agent, and the author of the famous *English Farming Past and Present* (1912), collated the replies and prepared them for publication.[289] *Facts About Land* appeared in 1915. It was a systematic destruction of Rowntree's publication. 'no body of evidence on the condition of the agricultural industry in 1913', Prothero later argued, 'at once so detailed, so practical...so authoritative, is to be found elsewhere'.[290] The Central Land Association conducted its own inquiry into rural wage rates.[291] The Surveyors' Institution drew up a critique of the Liberal urban report,[292] but war broke out before it could be published.

The Land Conference also planned an anti-Liberal 'Land Congress'.

This was to be a meeting where the Liberal land programme was condemned and a rival (and quasi-Tory) programme was proposed in its stead.[293] It followed on from Onslow's public protest of 1909. Steel-Maitland constantly called for these organisations to be used by the party and perhaps he had a hand in the Congress's conception. Resolutions were printed and secretly distributed to the Conservative leaders.[294] The motions were typically Tory. Minimum wages and rent fixing, for example, were forcefully condemned. Indeed, the Land Congress well anticipated the completed Conservative programme of June 1914. But the Land Congress was called off for reasons which are not clear. Perhaps Steel-Maitland and the other party leaders did not want to draw public attention to the land question now that Ireland was coming to dominate political concerns. Other pressure groups such as the Land Union and the Anti-Socialist Union continued their anti-collectivist activity.

What were the likely electoral consequences of the great land campaign and the accompanying budget of 1914? Conservatives had for long feared that an expanded franchise would involve attacks on property and these Liberal initiatives were the most formidable attacks yet. Would the Democracy support the most advanced collectivist programme that any government had ever presented to the electorate? This question bears on an important historiographical debate which has commanded a great deal of attention – the origins of the decline of the British Liberal Party. Nothwithstanding an extensive literature on the subject, historians have tended to be uninterested in the possibilities of the land campaign.[295] This is despite the fact that the Liberal Party was looking to the land programme and the 1914 budget to secure it success at the impending general election. The land campaign was British Liberalism's bid for a future and it requires serious consideration. Dr Tanner's discovery that the Edwardian electoral system was not greatly biased against working-class representation has already been noted.

Any evaluation of the likely consequences of the land campaign is a hazardous undertaking. The perils of prediction are compounded by the problems of evidence. The 1915 general election never took place. By-elections are notoriously unreliable indicators of electoral opinion. Contemporary commentary is plagued by the partiality of partisanship. But there are good reasons for suggesting that the Liberal Party's strategy was well conceived. The Conservative Party's alarm at the appeal of the Liberal minimum wage for farm labourers has already been recorded. For what it is worth, three by-elections in the English counties which took place between October 1913 and August 1914 showed a marginal swing away from the Conservative Party. But the presence of Labour candidates complicates interpretation.[296] In the eyes of the Right the government had achieved much success in its bid for the votes of town tenants. Steel-Maitland, as chairman of the party organisation, was perfectly placed to gauge the assessments of the rank and file. On 23 June 1914 he drew up a memorandum for the party leadership. Steel-Maitland warned that when the Home Rule Bill was passed at the end of the year the land question would come to the forefront of politics. The Liberals were planning a rejuvenation of their campaign and he was not optimistic about the outcome. 'I think, therefore, that *unless* some act or situation occurs which will again draw the public imagination to the Home Rule question', he concluded, 'the Autumn may see rather a set back than an improvement in our position'.[297] The most informed member of the Conservative Party believed that the land campaign posed a real threat to his party. This raises an interesting point. Was the Right's mobilisation of Ulster, and its support for armed resistance, partly animated by a desire to divert attention away from a subject which threatened to deprive it of office?

The most systematic analysis of the progress of the land campaign was undertaken by the Liberals themselves in May 1914. G.Wallace Carter, the secretary of the Central Land and Housing Council, provided Lloyd George with two sources of evidence: his own survey derived from the reports of the campaign workers, and the assessments of the regional Liberal associations. Wallace Carter reported that the 'Government's proposals are arousing unprecedented enthusiasm in the rural constituencies'. He anticipated major electoral successes in the countryside. The urban campaign had not gone so well. 'In the north-east counties, Lancashire, Eastern counties, Devon and Cornwall, the urban campaign has gone fairly well' but 'for the rest of the country the campaign in the boroughs has been disappointing'.[298] From the Liberal federations of the North, the Midlands, and Lancashire, Cheshire and the North West, came the news that the campaign was succeeding in both town and country.[299] From Yorkshire, Devon and Cornwall, and the Home Counties it was reported that the campaign was only achieving success in the rural districts.[300] But even here there were favourable signs. W.Crook of the Home Counties observed that at the end of May the urban effort had begun to catch on in certain urban centres, most notably Portsmouth, Southampton and Reading.[301]

After taking stock of the situation the Liberal Party proceeded to strengthen the campaign with appropriate policies and renewed propaganda.[302] Lloyd George was advised to make his urban policies less vague, to emphasise SVR and the full rating of vacant and undeveloped land, and to advocate a minimum wage for all low paid urban workers.[303] Wallace Carter stressed that an urban minimum wage would win votes in the towns.[304] In late June Steel-Maitland noticed that the Liberals had recently redoubled their efforts on 'a *very* large and costly scale and it is very well done...That such a process should go on throughout the Autumn is a serious prospect.'[305] The 1914 budget involved the suggested changes in the basis of local taxation and also promised substantial grants. As has been noted, the government planned to start distributing these subventions in April 1915 – a date full of tactical implications. Before the outbreak of international hostilities the Liberal Party was already making substantial appeals to the ratepayers on the basis of the subventions promised in that year's budget.[306] The urban minimum wage was also developed. In June the Chancellor of the Exchequer proclaimed that his government's urban policy would achieve 'a living wage to the worker'.[307] But the entire Liberal plan was frustrated by the outbreak of the Great War.

Given the evidence, therefore, there are good grounds for contesting the view that the Liberal Party was in a state of short-term decline in 1914. This pessimistic view is widely held, and is well expressed by J.Ramsden's statement 'by 1914 the Liberals were on the ropes'.[308] One of the most eminent Liberal historians asserts that 'Lloyd George's new land campaign offered no clear way forward'[309] for the party. Yet Liberalism's peculiar brand of collectivism, which centred around its plans for the land system, appeared to give it an electoral future. If this is accurate, Salisbury's fears about the expropriating tendencies of the people were being proved correct. Churchill's 'trust the people' rang a little hollow. It also raises doubts as to Mr Pelling's judgement on late-Victorian and Edwardian politics: 'there is no evidence that social reform was in fact popular with the electorate as a whole until *after* it had been carried out'.[310] A general neglect of the land question has thus led to misapprehensions concerning the prospects for Liberalism on the eve of the First World War.

It becomes much easier, therefore, to understand the frequent opportunism of the Right and to discern a reality behind Tory anxieties about the prospects for property. Collectivism, it seems, posed a real electoral threat to the Conservative Party. Between 1886 and 1914 those Tories who stressed that the Left's social radicalism was a substantial danger were not taking fright at shadows. It required the radicalisation of the Left to put collectivism to the electoral test. In 1914 it appeared as though the Welsh Wizard had released the dreaded genie from the bottle, but to what extent it is difficult to determine. A whole host of Conservative apprehensions were confirmed. The long-term prospects for Liberalism are a different matter. The 1918 Franchise Act, and subsequent demographic changes, would make the countryside increasingly unimportant in national politics. The Liberal Party would not be able to gain much from its rural land question. The reasons for the decline of the Liberal Party after the First World War, however, fall outside the scope of this study. But given the experience of these pre-war years it comes as no surprise that the Labour Party's more extensive version of collectivism came to secure substantial popular support. When Labour members frequently cheered Lloyd George long after his fall they were paying tribute to one who had greatly prepared the ground for Socialism.

☆

The Liberal moves towards the construction of the Radical state were fiercely resisted by the Conservative Party. Land reform figured prominently in these moves and the Right used a host of weapons. The House of Lords could no longer achieve much but in the Commons obstructionism reaped rewards. A diversion tactic was employed but the material draw of the Liberals' promises was not to be removed by Ireland. Thus the Right turned to attacks, opportunism, the bulwark strategy, ridicule, rate relief, voluntary initiatives, and its allied pressure groups. A variety of standard Tory causes and familiar policies were employed to win votes. Once again the Conservative Party was reactive and responsive rather than planned and unyielding. There are good reasons for supposing that Princip's bullet rescued the British Tories from an unwelcome fate at the hands of New Liberalism's distinctive form of collectivism. Long standing Conservative fears about the redistributive propensities of the expanded electorate were not without foundation.

Conclusion: Victorian Values

The impulse to collectivisation in the late-Victorian and Edwardian period, therefore, came from areas other than the British Conservative Party. It was located in a Left that was divided in its orientations. The Liberal Party, far from being a prisoner of Victorian *laissez-faire*, stoked the accelerating engine. Liberalism concentrated on reforming the relationship of the people to land and buildings, and made especial use of administrative law. A reduction in the political power of landed proprietors was a central feature of the Liberal initiative. The Labour Party, which was always a minor force whose importance can be much exaggerated with the benefit of hindsight, sought more general changes and aimed at deeper shifts in political power. For a period the town halls added to the pressure with their own localist plans. Reformers of the Left anticipated major themes of the twentieth century - they held up the possibility of changing socio-economic structures, using the active powers of the state to achieve prosperity, and advancing civilisation by government intervention. New vistas are opened up on the origins of collectivism in Great Britain.

But collectivisation was not only rooted in politicians, it was sanctioned by the popular will. Democratisation underlay left-wing advances. The post-1885 electorate made possible measures which the pre-1867 electorate would never have countenanced. The Left promoted, explored and tested popular desires for a transformation of the world of property. By 1910 a reforming Lib–Lab bloc was sustained by 50% of the electorate. Commentary on the general elections of 1910 and responses to the land campaign of 1913–1914 suggest that the Liberal and Labour emphasis on material issues was well founded in electoral support. It may be, therefore, that the Liberal Party had found the key to its future. The land question could have been the vehicle by which Liberalism continued to adapt to the emerging demands of a developing democracy. It contained a range of policies, such as the urban minimum wage or large-scale grants-in-aid, which could have eased the party into much of the terrain Labour aspired to occupy. The Kaiser's Germany reduced all this to an intriguing might-have-been. But one gains a very different picture of how collectivism could have advanced after 1914. It is often asserted that the intervention required by the First World War discredited Liberalism. But was not such government activity foreshadowed by the pre-war initiatives of Asquith and his followers?

It seems a reasonable supposition that popular support for left-wing measures was animated by a demand for immediate improvements in individual material well-being. But there is another dimension which should not be overlooked – that many Englishmen came to believe that this could be achieved through government. Collectivisation may also have had origins in expectations engendered by the achievements of the system it was replacing. Fiscal rectitude, bureaucratic efficiency, public spirit, political highmindedness, uncorrupt statesmen, the whole apparatus of the Italian dream of *buon governo* – all these could have given plausibility to the idea that the state could be trusted to carry out great tasks. Did not the prestige of politics provoke faith in political cures for society's ills? The very success of the Victorian system of low government may have created a popular receptivity to proposals as to its enlargement. The Left invoked the legitimacy of state institutions as arguments for their transformation. An eminently anti-statist past, by a variety of routes, could thus have encouraged the construction of a pre-eminently statist future. Did the tradition of Peel, Gladstone and Salisbury pave the way for the lineage of Macdonald, Attlee and Kinnock?

The Conservative Party, indeed, manifested a continual hostility to nascent collectivism. Tory centrism, anti-capitalism, or paternalist interventionism, at least with regard to this period, appear to be phantoms of the historiographical imagination. The Conservatives who most conspicuously advocated reform policies seem to have done so in order to weaken collectivism by moving towards its proposals. A detailed study of the Churchill–Chamberlain–Rollit–Steel–Maitland line, and a close investigation of the tariff reform movement and the Unionist Social Reform Committee, reveal right-wingers struggling to find ways of thwarting the Left's social challenge. They also embraced modern means of organisation and campaigning, and thereby revealed how aware they were of the demands of democratisation. To take their professions of interventionism seriously is to mistake the deliberate image for the calculating reality – face value should not be overvalued. Those Conservatives of the 1970s and 1980s who discern in their nineteenth century and early-twentieth century antecedents evidence for a long tradition of left-wing Conservatism are in error.[1] In order to differentiate the Tories of this period, and to construct a Left–Right spectrum, it will be necessary to go beyond the opportunist-resistance divide and to consider attitudes towards such great issues as the franchise, defence, Ireland, the Empire and the Church.

All the indicators suggest, rather, that the Conservative Party was a non-interventionist party. The evidence piles up: the inability to promote a substantial grants-in-aid policy despite an attitude towards rating which provided an apparently favourable point of departure; the marked reluctance to take any steps to halt agrarian contraction notwithstanding profound economic, cultural and electoral links with the countryside; the admiration of voluntary methods with regard to employers' liability in the 1890s, national insurance in 1911, and rural wages in 1913–14; the striking inaction, reluctance and resistance of the Salisbury and Balfour governments when it came to proposals to expand the role of government in the economic and social spheres; the whole thrust of Tory polemical attacks on leftist policies from the 1880s to the Great War; the need for the party to be put under electoral pressure before it would move towards the positions of its opponents. The observer is drawn towards the conclusion that the Conservative Party was the expression of an outlook which was not attracted by the idea that society could be improved by positive government action. Peering below the surface of political activity, one seems to detect a culture which rejected the social engineering vision of progress and believed that the advance of civilisation in England derived, in large measure, from individual face-to-face action guided by Christian concepts.

The Conservative Party's method of resistance took many forms – nearly all of which, in some way or another, illustrated the fundamental conservatism of Conservatism. The Tories relied upon a maintenance of the existing constitution; the power of the House of Lords and the possibilities of obstructionism in the House of Commmons; the anti-Liberal activity of a myriad of allied pressure groups; polemical attacks upon the Left's proposals; the support of traditional social adherents; the force of stock-in-trade causes and rallying cries; a succession of voluntaryist initiatives; appeals to Conservative cultural values; the idea of creating a solid bloc of right-wing small freeholders; the expedient adoption of policies which belonged to, or were in the direction of, the Liberal and Labour position; the expression of regret at the presence of poverty; and the progressive dynamics of market economics.

But the Conservative Party's resistance was not marked by systematic planning, regular deliberations of strategy and tactics, or the drawing up of contingency plans. A retrospective analysis of Conservative method is apt to give the impression that leading Tories made a selection of the available options and then decided on the correct course of action. But many of the Right's responses arose naturally, almost spontaneously, and were not the product of a controlling mind: Conservative method was not methodical. This lack of a systematic approach was not the product of a lack of time. The Tory leaders were drawn from the leisured classes and workloads bore no comparison to modern burdens. Tennis games, bird-shoots and fox-hunts symbolised the opportunities that existed for reflection. Nor was it because of any lack of intelligence or insight. Another phantom must be laid to rest – here was no 'Stupid Party'. There has always been a tendency by the Left to denigrate the intellectual ability of its opponents. J.M.Keynes wrote that 'With a little stupidity and a few prejudices dashed in' Asquith would have been a Tory.[2] The Conservative Party consistently displayed a perception and an expertise which helped to make it what it was – a formidable political force. Such leading lights as Salisbury, Balfour and Bonar Law were statesmen of real intellectual power and political understanding. Electoral success made the Conservative Party even more informed – it brought the habit and instruction of government. In addition, there was always the expert advice of the party's specialist counsellors.

The party's propensity to wait on events stemmed, rather, from the nature of Conservatism itself, which it thereby helped to illuminate. Asquith's famous 'wait and see' should have been coined by a Tory leader. The Left made the running and the Conservatives had to respond accordingly. It seems that the Tories were unwilling to take pre-emptive action because it involved uncongenial measures which might turn out to be avoidable. Precisely because they were reactionaries the Conservatives were conspicuous for their adaptability – *ad hoc* was *à la mode*. Thus also did the Tories not study the methods of their counterparts on the Continent. Bismarckian practices and French peasant proprietorship filtered through, but otherwise the Right was characterised by a remarkable parochialism. Perhaps, in addition, the rulers of the British Empire believed they had little to learn from European politicos. Some Unionists, such as Steel-Maitland or Joseph Chamberlain, who constantly advised early opportunism, naturally counselled a planned approach to politics. Their frustration bore witness to their frequent failure. Steel-Maitland later lamented 'we were never anything else but a scratch lot of individuals under Balfour'.[3]

Principled opportunism was the centrepiece of Conservative method. The pressure of electoral realities forced the Tory leopard to change its spots. 'If we want things to stay as they are, things must change'– Prince Lampedusa's famous phrase could have been the right-wing motto. The party, notwithstanding its own preferences, had to recognise that a large part of the electorate favoured measures it found unpalatable. This simple fact could be managed but it could never be wished away. Thus it was that the official Tory programme of 1885 had been transformed by 1914.[4] In this way the Right had the peculiar historical characteristic of being a sensitive indicator of shifting consensus. The Conservatives found it necessary to conduct a salvage operation on the socio-economic established order. Divisions often arose within the party as to the utility, nature and extent of the concessions of that operation. They were not divisons over its objects. Intra-party thunder was generated by fundamental agreement. The Conservatives, therefore, were maximisers who frequently sought to achieve as much as they could in the circumstances. It appears as though the descendants of the opponents of J.S.Mill MP were distinctly utilitarian. One thing is certain: the Tories did not forbear to stoop to conquer. Conservative opportunism was not animated by a mere desire for places and power. The party's policies in office, and the inhibitions it experienced when producing proposals in response to electoral needs, indicated that it was powerfully motivated by belief. Again and again, whether they were dealing with workmen's compensation or farm workers' wages, urban housing or town tenancies, the Tories left the impress of their outlook on the expedient policies they produced. Similarly, the bulwark strategy was constrained by the thinking of its originators. Thus the Conservatives were principled in their opportunism, even sincere. Indeed, many more votes could have been gathered by more collectivistic measures, but these were ruled out by Tory convictions. During Balfour's government, for example, old age pensions were forsworn. As Steel-Maitland noted in 1913: 'while we are opportunists in small things, we are really not so much so in bigger things'.[5] Tory interests were also an ever present potential check on the promotion of reform. Certainly the Right did not suffer the debilitation of moral doubt. Tories believed in what they were doing – a frequently unobserved source of strength. Byzantinism was not a characteristic of those late-Victorian and Edwardian Conservative politicians who inhabited upper England.

A dominant feature of the Conservative Party's behaviour was, therefore, a readiness to concede to collectivism's legislative demands. This painful process of compromise with the Left was well described in a memorandum submitted to Steel-Maitland in 1909. No doubt there was an affinity of outlook between the chairman of the party and his correspondent. The author of 'Upon the Necessity, the Method and the Limits of Social Reform Considered as a Part of Unionist Policy' recognised that social questions were now the substance of politics; stressed the danger from New Liberalism and Labour; and urged the Conservative Party to adopt reform policies and thereby avoid 'Revolution through the ballot box'.[6] This articulate exponent of principled opportunism correctly discerned the Tory dilemma: the promotion of reform would offend the party's beliefs and injure its allied interests. But he made clear that the Conservative Party would have to make some concessions in order to prevent more radical change and pointed to past achievements in the adoption of this method. The idea that collectivism would change cultural attitudes was given predictable emphasis:

> In dealing with Social Reform the Unionist Party, (especially as now composed after absorbing the Whigs,) is peculiarly embarassed by difficulties both of principle and situation.
>
> (A). *Upon grounds of principle* it is objected that the operations of enterprise are fettered and burthened; that State aid and supervision

weaken the springs of self-activity in the masses, and therefore diminish their productive power; that the growth of capital is discouraged, and the stock of capital may be actually diminished; that the whole tendency is towards the corruption and enfeeblement of national character.

(B). *Upon the point of political expediency* it is urged that for the Unionist Party to take up such measures, say, as "insurance against unemployment" or certain features of the Development Bill, or Poor Law reconstruction, may be injurious and obnoxious to some of its best and most powerful adherents, especially in the industrial constituencies...

That there is some truth in the first and some force in the second class of objections, it would be in vain to deny. Taking the question of party expediency, however, the Conservative Party for generations has been and it must remain, under the necessity of sacrificing a proportion of Conservative interests to save the rest. This method of gradual concession, so familiar in the field of political rights, was adopted in the sphere of economic legislation since shortly after the Reform Bill. It is an essentially English method. The battle has hitherto proved well worth fighting on these dilatory lines, which have enabled the ground to be disputed obstinately. *We have constantly prevented a revolution in forms from becoming a revolution in reality.* The Unionist party has been held together, in spite of measures like the Compensation Act, because the concessions only became more extensive as the danger of far worse things under Radical supremacy becomes plain and urgent.[7]

There was metamorphosis in the Conservative Party's method. Official stances and commitments shifted over time. In a way collectivism had a vampire effect: it drew out the true Tory blood and transferred its characteristics. Thus the Conservative Party came to be an integral part of the means by which Liberalism and Socialism progressed – it was a political carrier of previously resisted proposals. At the same time, by adopting leftist policies, the Conservative Party promoted and gave credence to the perspectives and proposals of its opponents. Sir John Simon, in his memoirs, reflected on changes in the nature of the Conservative Party. 'The present-day Conservative is a very different person, in outlook and ideals, from the Tory of forty years ago', he wrote in 1952, 'The truth is that he has become liberalised.'[8] This raises another question. The Conservative Party may have come to accept many of the Left's measures, but did it absorb, both in the period 1886–1914 and in the long run, the mentality of collectivism? The historical myth that before the First World War the Right had a substantial receptivity to interventionism, and the party's celebration of previous radical measures, may have served to promote such a process. The immense hostility to the ideas of the Left on the eve of the Great War suggests that this mutation was not yet underway by 1914.

If this Tory method of principled opportunism to collectivist change was carried on until 1945 (and beyond), it casts much light on the origins of a key feature of the nation's political experience. Steel-Maitland's correspondent used the significant phrase 'English method'. The British political system has been habitually praised for its capacity to accommodate change and achieve compromise. Certainly (at least until recently), Great Britain has avoided those lurches to political or totalitarian extremes which have so disrupted other parts of Europe. An integral part of this move towards moderation has been the Right's readiness to concede. Its opportunism indicated a realism in the face of political pressure. In this area also was the Conservative Party a cohesive force. In examining the origins of the famous 'peaceable kingdom' great attention must be given to the pragmatism of the nation's most successful political party. To a certain extent the Right has been a shock-absorber. Much of the British 'liberal tradition' is rooted in Conservatism and its political sense.

But although the late-Victorian and Edwardian Conservative Party combated the Left with concessions at an institutional level, it failed to devote substantial thought and effort to resistance at the level of ideas and attitudes. This was especially appropriate because the New Liberals and Socialists represented a new departure in beliefs and visions. The materialist, determinist and classist way of thinking which increasingly underlay their legislative proposals threatened to undermine the Tory vision. There was the Primrose League, support for the Church of England's educational mission, and day to day espousals of Conservative thinking, but there was no systematic attempt to meet the Left's cultural challenge. The reasons for this are a matter for speculation. Perhaps the Conservatives were constrained by what they thought was the proper province of the politician; perhaps they did not appreciate the danger; perhaps they did not think sufficiently in cultural terms. Whatever the reasons, the Right by its refusal hastened the progress of its opponents. By such means were foundations not laid for a subsequent movement towards the Continental 'Christian Democratic' strategy for Conservatism.

The employment of the theoretical notion of 'Conservative method' has acted to give a productive analytical framework to a broad range of complicated activity. Information has been supplied which may serve as material for the investigation of Conservative behaviour in a variety of contexts. Most obviously, the hypothetical options may be applied to the Conservative Party's handling of other political subjects in Victorian and Edwardian Britain. Consider the Irish question, certainly Tory beliefs were at work here. A cursory glance is most informative. There was the use of the House of Lords (against Gladstone's Home Rule Bill); obstructionism in the House of Commons (against Asquith's Home Rule Bill); an attempt at moderationism (during the round table conference of 1914); the implementation of the bulwark strategy (through the land purchase acts); and the practice of expediency (by an acceptance of successive measures of tenancy reform). But there is also room for a wider sweep. Looking, for example, towards Bismarck's Germany, or Stolypin's Russia, or Giolitti's Italy, it is possible to perceive the adoption of courses of political action not alien to the late-Victorian and Edwardian experience of the British Conservative Party. Central to any investigation of Conservative method should be the theoretical question: how do Conservatives conserve what they regard as valuable?

This study has also observed profound changes that were taking place in the nation's political system. Power was being more widely distributed amongst the people. Anybody who reads the correspondence of the leading Tories cannot fail to notice an increasing awareness of the general will. Elections were getting more and more on Conservative minds. All this was quite natural. Mass political parties, trade unions, newspapers, the platform, campaigns, armies of party speakers, extensions of the franchise, local government reform, the mending of the House of Lords, and a seemingly ever-expanding number of pressure groups were all phenomena of democratisation. The mounting Conservative concern with policy, the formulation of which often provoked heated internal controversy, attested to a need to come to terms with the increasing power of the people.

A concomitant of democratisation was a decline in the influence of the landed interest. The existence of the Central Land Association, the reform of the House of Lords, the changing complexion of the House of Commons, the exclusion of landowners from a 1909 meeting of public protest, and the emergence of the National Farmers' Union all pointed to a major shift of power away from those with broad acres. The fact that after the First World War the Central Landowners' Association came to urge landowners to devote themselves to their estates is full of significance. Farming, not public affairs, was to command their attention. From governing elite to agricultural profession – perhaps that is the essential story of the aristocracy and gentry in modern Britain.

The other great feature of the political system which confronts the observer of the struggle between Conservatism and collectivism was the determining influence of beliefs. 'Conviction politics' is a more descriptive phrase than 'high politics'. Day to day tribulations, the orientations of office, the pursuit of personal power, and shifts in platforms and planks, all tend to conceal a fundamental reality: there was a notable symmetry in the legislation and proposals of the political parties. It is crystal clear, for example, that attitudes towards land acted to delineate the Liberal and Tory camps. By perceiving the Conservative Party as a repository of Tory culture it has been possible to uncover the true meaning of the Right's behaviour. There is also the question of the temperature of politics. Many of the legislative proposals of the years 1886–1914 touched on little of consequence in terms of belief and raised not a whisper of smoke. Other measures, however, provoked a volcano. The eruptions which accompanied such measures as the People's Budget attested to a conflict of ideas which animated politics. It comes as no suprise that the radical years of 1909–1914 brought politics to boiling point. 'It is not easy', recalled one Conservative MP,

> for anyone who was not in the House of Commons at the time to appreciate the extraordinary state of affairs that existed down at Westminster the last two years before the Great War. The atmosphere was just charged with electricity and scenes of uncontrollable anger were continually breaking out. Neither side was on speaking terms with the other, and we were forbidden to give any pairs.[9]

Politicians cared. If the conclusions of this study are anything to go by, high politics, for the top Tories, was the management of belief.

A principal function of the Conservative Party in the formative years which preceded the First World War was resistance to state intervention. In this respect, Mrs Thatcher and her followers are connected to their roots. It is possible to discern a distinct continuity of outlook between the Conservative Party of the 1880s and the Conservative Party of the 1980s. The New Conservatism which came to the fore after the demise of Edward Heath has involved a determined attempt to reverse a development which gathered such powerful strength in the period 1886–1914. The impulse to privatisation, to lower taxation, to deregulation, to controlling local government expenditure, to eliminating inflation, to council house ownership, to reducing bureaucracy, to a social diffusion of company shares, and above all else to market forces, represents a repudiation of previous collectivist advance.[10] In October 1986 the Prime Minister told the party faithful that Conservatives 'believe in popular capitalism, in a property-owning democracy. And it works'.[11] This anti-statist stance has involved a rejection of the previous Tory habit of concessions to collectivism. Conservative governments of the post-Second World War period have been berated for not turning the clock back, and thus for allowing a 'ratchet' effect towards full Socialism.[12] But even the New Conservatives have displayed principled opportunism – many of their plans and ideals have been compromised by electoral pressure. As Ian Gilmour MP reflected as early as 1978 'In the past, Conservatives "trimmed" in favour of the state and against *laissez-faire*. Today they "trim" against the state and in favour of the individual.'[13] Democracy, once again, is certainly an influential thing.

This affinity of outlook has been matched by an affinity of method. Similar activity is being provoked by similar beliefs. Many a modern course of action was anticipated by the Tories in the years 1886–1914. A strong Nationalist and defence stance, an opposition to electoral reform, and the 'resolute approach', all have their conspicuous precursors. Salisbury's weakening of the LCC has been carried on by the abolition of the GLC and other urban authorities. Indeed, the need to control left-wing councils has led the Conservative Party to become the centralist party and thus to break with its Edwardian past. The legitimation strategy has found echoes in the Tory attempt to build up the prestige of such figures as Sinclair, Laker and Edwardes. Expediency is not neglected: many popular collectivist achievements have been maintained and electoral risks have not been run. The Conservative Party still strives to present itself as the Caring Party. The bulwark strategy has come to fruition with a vengeance. The sale of council houses and of shares in privatised industries has given electoral flesh to the old dream of a property owning democracy. This has been made possible by previous extensions of state control. Twentieth century collectivists could little have realised that the more they were successful in their municipalisation and nationalisation plans they more they may have been digging their own graves. Precisely because of the success of the Left, Mrs Thatcher has resources to implement this strategy which were never remotely available to Salisbury and his heirs. Bulwarks constructed with stone taken from statist edifices may turn out to be some of the significant features (and supports) of post-collectivist society. The installation of the local poll tax should finally relieve real property of the injustice perceived far back into the nineteenth century.

What is especially interesting about the contemporary Conservative Party is that it often attacks a cultural state of affairs which the late-Victorian and Edwardian Conservatives predicted would arise with the success of collectivism. It is almost as though many contemporary right-wingers believe that the expectations of their forerunners have been confirmed. It seems as if the Right is seeking to emphasise, or even in part to return to, that culture promoted by the followers of Salisbury and Bonar Law. New Conservatism turns out to have some old-fashioned characteristics. Many of the features of social disintegration and consequent economic failure were predicted again by Professor Hayek, a thinker much venerated by the New Conservatives, in 1944. He believed that the Left would transform British civilisation:

> There is one aspect of the change in moral values brought about by the advance of collectivism which at the present time provides special food for thought. It is that the virtues which are held less and less in esteem and which consequently become rarer are precisely those on which the British people justly prided themselves and in which they were generally recognised to excel. The virtues possessed by the British people, possessed in a higher degree than most other people...were independence and self-reliance, individual initiative and local responsibility, the successful reliance on voluntary activity, non-interference with one's neighbour and tolerance of the

different and queer, respect for custom and tradition, and a healthy
suspicion of power and authority. British strength, British character,
and British achievements are to a great extent the result of a
cultivation of the spontaneous. But almost all the traditions and
institutions in which British moral genius has found its most
characteristic expression, and which in turn have moulded the
national character and the whole moral climate of England, are those
which the progress of collectivism and its inherently centralistic
tendencies are progressively destroying.[14]
What would happen to the Tory culture of individualism, voluntaryism
and communitarianism ?

Mrs Thatcher has declared that the nation has not paid sufficient
attention to traditional values. The Prime Minister argues that this has led
to a sabotaging of economic performance. Mrs Thatcher herself invokes
the world that her Victorian and Edwardian predecessors defended. The
aspects of this civilisation are well elaborated and suggest continuities in
Tory thinking. Historians have entered the political fray to evaluate the
Prime Minister's vision of the past.[15] Mrs Thatcher's emphasis on the link
between culture and economic progress is worthy of especial note. The
Tory vision of progress seems to have undergone a resurrection:

> I was brought up by a Victorian grandmother. You were taught to
> work jolly hard, you were taught to improve yourself, you were
> taught self-reliance, you were taught to live within your income, you
> were taught that cleanliness was next to Godliness. You were taught
> self-respect, you were taught always to give a hand to your neigh-
> bour, you were taught tremendous pride in your country, you were
> taught to be a good member of your community. All of these things
> are Victorian values... There are some values which are eternal and
> in fact you found a tremendous improvement in conditions during
> Victorian times because people were brought up with a sense of
> duty. I was brought up with a very strong sense of duty. And part of
> the sense of duty was if you were getting on better, you turned
> yourself to help others; that as you did better yourself so you had a
> duty to your community to turn to help others. And so, as you got an
> increasing prosperity during Victorian times and as you got an
> immense national pride during Victorian times, so you had a duty
> voluntarily to help others. And many of the very good things, the im-
> provements that were made, were made voluntarily in those times,
> for example, people built hospitals, there were voluntary hospitals.
> Many of the church schools were built during that time. Many
> people say we simply must do better with the prisons, a better prison
> system, prison reform but it came from this tremendous sense of
> reliance and duty. You don't hear so much about those things these
> days, but they were good values and they led to tremendous
> improvements in the standard of living.[16]

Many commentators see in such views a 'rebirth of liberalism'[17] but it would be more accurate to say that a restatement of Toryism is underway. The stress on social duty betokens a implicit rejection of mere market motivations. An analysis of Great Britain's contemporary culture, and the origins of this culture, would contradict or confirm the Victorian and Edwardian idea that collectivism would produce desocialisation. If Mrs Thatcher and those of like mind are correct, there has taken place a fading of old Conservative ways. Somewhere along the historical line, it is implied, there has occurred the strange death of Tory England. And all this despite the Right's striking electoral success.

The contemporary Conservative strategy for economic and cultural reform is expressed in the return to the market. There are appropriate invocations to 'citizenship' and 'community' but overall it is assumed that economic success can be achieved by reforms in the economic sphere and that economic reform will lead to cultural reform. As in the years 1886–1914 there is no attempt at direct cultural change. This is despite an immensely gifted and articulate range of right-wing intellectuals. Perhaps never before has the Conservative Party been sustained by such a talented Tory intelligentsia. Let Mrs Thatcher enunciate the approach in sentences which involve a rejection of desocialisation:

> What's irritated me about the whole direction of politics in the last thirty years is that it's always been towards the collectivist society. People have forgotten about the personal society. And they say: do I count, do I matter? To which the answer is, Yes. And therefore, it isn't that I set out on economic policies; it's that I set out really to change the approach, and changing the economics is the means of changing that approach. If you change the approach you really are after the heart and the soul of the nation. Economics are the method; the object is to change the heart and soul.[18]

This is the key assumption of the Tory plan for the national civilisation. But is it well conceived? Lampedusa warned Conservatives that a historic process of compromise could lead to an imperceptible accquisition of many of the opponent's features. Are there not other cultural factors behind the decline of 'the personal society'?

To answer this question it is necessary to consider of what deeper forces British collectivism is, and was, a part. No discussion is complete without a consideration of such major modern movements as relativism, Freudianism, feminism, egalitarianism, societalism and physiologism, all of which seem to be concomitants of deChristianisation. Are they all part of a distinct matrix? Collectivism's emphasis on material welfare, and the modern Tory stress on prosperity, bring to mind Solzhenitsyn's interpretation of Western history:

> Once it was proclaimed and accepted that above man there is no supreme being, and that instead man is the crowning glory of the

universe and the measure of all things, then man's needs, desires –
and indeed his weaknesses – were taken to be the supreme impera-
tives of the universe. Consequently the only good in the world – the
only thing that needs to be done – is that which satisfies our feelings.
It was in Europe that this philosophy came to life several centuries
ago; at the time its materialistic excesses were explained away by
the previous excesses of Catholicism. But in the course of several
centuries it inexorably swamped the whole of the Western world...We
have become hopelessly enmeshed in our slavish worship of all that
is pleasant, all that is comfortable, all that is material.[19]

Such ideas have received support from important quarters.[20] Is it possible
that the advance of collectivism, the Thatcherite emphasis on the possibilities of the market, and the cultural state of desocialisation itself, are all
products of the rise of Materialism? This would place the Left–Right
conflict of 1886–1914 in a rather new light.

Notes

INTRODUCTION

1. *The Economist*, 7 April 1894, p. 417a.
2. *Ibid.*, p. 417b.
3. P.Johnson, *A History of the Modern World From 1917 to the 1980s* (1984), p. 729. I am much indebted to this work.
4. W H. Greenleaf, *The British Political Tradition, Vol. 1, The Rise of Collectivism* (1983), p. 33, table 1. Despite obvious disagreements, I am greatly indebted to Professor Greenleaf's pioneering study.
5. *Ibid.*, p. 34, table 2.
6. *Ibid.*, p. 36, table 3.
7. See A.H.Hanson and M.Walles, *Governing Britain: A Guidebook to Political Institutions* (Oxford, 1984), pp. 278–313.
8. *The Conservative Manifesto 1979* (1979), p. 5 (foreword by Margaret Thatcher).
9. T.Russel, *The Tory Party : Its Policies, Divisions and Future* (1978), p. 16.
10. Conservative Central Office files, file marked 'Thatcher 1983–1984', Conservative Party News Service, Mrs Thatcher to the Conservative Party Conference, 14 Oct. 1983, p. 14.
11. W.H.Greenleaf, *The British Political Tradition*, vol. 1, p. 42.
12. A.Bloom, *The Closing of the American Mind: How Higher Education has Failed Democracy and Impoverished the Souls of Today's Students* (1988), p. 104.
13. *The Sunday Times*, 7 Aug. 1988, p. B2a.
14. *The Times*, 15 Nov. 1907, p. 8c.
15. NUACLUO, *The Campaign Guide* (1914), p. 513. This study makes much use of these guides. Until 1914 they were 'prepared by a committee of the Central Council of the National Union of Conservative Associations for Scotland. Issued at the request of the Central Conservative Office, London, and of the Central Council of the Scottish National Union': *The Campaign Guide* (Edinburgh, 1900), p. iii.
16. F.Pym, *The Politics of Consent* (1984), p. 174.
17. C.E. Bellairs, *Conservative Social and Industrial Reform* (1977), foreword by Margaret Thatcher.
18. T.Russel, *The Tory Party*, p. 7.
19. B.Harrison, 'The Centrist Theme in Modern British Politics', in *Peaceable Kingdom: Stability and Change in Modern Britain* (Oxford, 1982), pp. 309–377.
20. W.H. Greenleaf, *The British Political Tradition, Vol. 2, The Ideological Heritage* (1983), p. 199.
21. *Ibid.*, p. 195.
22. W.H.Greenleaf, *The British Political Tradition*, vol. 1, p. 28.
23. M.Wiener, *English Culture and the Decline of the Industrial Spirit 1850–1980* (Cambridge, 1982), p. 126.
24. E.g., M.Cowling, *The Impact of Labour, 1920–1924* (Cambridge, 1971); A.B. Cooke and J.R. Vincent, *The Governing Passion: Cabinet Government and Party Politics in Britain 1885–1886* (Brighton, 1973).

CHAPTER ONE

1. Industrial Remuneration Conference, *The Report of the Proceedings and Papers Read...on the 28th, 29th, and 30th January 1885 (1885)*, A.J.Balfour, 'Land, Land Reformers, and the Nation', pp. 336–7.
2. *The Times*, 9 Sept. 1885, p. 6a.
3. N.Blewett, 'The Franchise in the United Kingdom, 1885–1918', *Past and Present*, 32 (1965), pp. 27–56.
4. R.Tanner, 'The Parliamentary Electoral System, the 'Fourth' Reform Act and the Rise of Labour in England and Wales', *Bulletin of the Institute of Historical Research*, vol. 61 (1983), pp. 205–19; R.Tanner, 'Political Realignment in England and Wales, c.1906–1922' (University of London PH.D. thesis, 1985), pp. 34–86, quotation p. 86. I am indebted to this thesis.
5. J.L.Garvin, *The Life of Joseph Chamberlain, Vol. 1 1836–1885 Chamberlain and Democracy* (1932), p. 563.
6. The phrase is here used by Lansdowne, John Sandars Papers, (hereafter JSP), Bodleian Library, MS Eng. hist. c. 758, fos. 5–7, Lansdowne to J. Sandars, 7 Jan. 1909.
7. See A.J. Lee, *The Origins of the Popular Press in England, 1855–1914* (1976).
8.A.M. Gollin, *The Observer and J.L.Garvin 1908–1914* (1960).
9. N. Blewett, *The Peers, the Parties, and the People: The General Elections of 1910* (1972), pp. 301–2.
10. G.K. Fry, *The Growth of Government: The Development of Ideas about the Role of the State and the Machinery and Functions of Government in Britain Since 1780* (1979), pp. 114–17; H. Parris, *Constitutional Bureaucracy: The Development of British Central Administration Since the Eighteenth Century* (1969), pp. 50–53.
11. V. Hicks Beach, *The Life of Sir Michael Hicks Beach*, vol.1 (1932), p. 331.
12. *The Times*, 8 Oct. 1885, p. 7d.
13. *The Times*, 27 Jan. 1911, p. 10b.
14. H. Parris, *Constitutional Bureaucracy*, p. 208.
15. *The Times*, 28 Feb.1889, p. 10a.
16. J.Prest, *Lord John Russel* (1972), p. 393.
17. M.Pinto-Duschinsky, *The Political Thought of Lord Salisbury 1854–1868* (1967), p. 107.
18. Lord Salisbury, 'The Budget and the Reform Bill', in P.Smith (ed.), *Lord Salisbury on Politics* (Cambridge, 1972), p. 126.
19. Lord Salisbury, 'Disintegration', in P.Smith, *op.cit.*, pp. 356–7.
20. G.M.Trevelyan, *A Shortened History of England* (1959), p. 529.
21. *The Times*, 6 Jan. 1885, p. 7d.
22. B.Dugdale, *Arthur James Balfour, First Earl of Balfour*, vol. 1 (1936), p. 207.
23. Arthur Steel-Maitland Papers, (hereafter SMP), Scottish Record Office, GD193/159/6/ 9–11, A.Steel-Maitland to A.Glazebrook, 24 Dec. 1913 (copy).
24. *The Nation*, 22 March 1913, p. 1013a.
25. Liberal Publication Department, (hereafter LPD), no. 1790, *Our Leader's Legacy* [n.d., 1899], p. 3.
26. *The Times*, 13 Oct. 1913, p. 13f.
27. F.W.S. Craig, *British General Election Manifestos 1900–1974* (1975), pp. 3–4, 9–10, 19–20, 24–5.
28. M. D. Pugh, *The Making of Modern British Politics 1867–1939* (Oxford, 1982) , p. 138, table 7.1.,'General Elections 1892–1910'.
29. See, e.g., R.K.Ensor, *England 1870–1914* (Oxford, 1936); H.Pelling, *Modern Britain, 1885–1955* (1969); R.Shannon, *The Crisis of Imperialism 1865–1915* (1976); R.Rhodes James, *The British Revolution: British Politics 1880–1939* (1978).
30. Lord Robert Cecil, First Viscount Cecil of Chelwood Papers, British Library, Add. Mss. 51075B, fos. 99–111, Lord R. Cecil to Col. Heaton Ellis, April 1922 (copy).
31. H.Macmillan, *The Past Masters: Politics and Politicians 1906–1939* (1975), p. 32.
32. *The Land Union Journal*, May 1914, p. 17b. It was called 'Brer Fox an' Brer Rabbit. The New Land Game'.

33. David Lloyd George, First Earl Dwyfor Papers (hereafter LGP), House of Lords Record Office, c/15/1/4, Land Values Group, 'Memorial', 18 May 1911.
34. See, e.g., The Liberal Land Committee, *Land and the Nation (1925), Towns and the Land (1925); Report of the Liberal Land Conference...February 17th, 18th, and 19th 1926* (1926).
35. A. Cooper, 'The Transformation of Agricultural Policy 1912–1936: A Study in Conservative Politics' (University of Oxford D.Phil. thesis, 1979), pp. 256–75.
36. D.Spring (ed.), *European Landed Elites in the Nineteenth Century* (Baltimore, 1977), p. 6.
37. The Land Union, *Objects and Policy* (Reading, 1913), p. 2, foreword by E.G.Pretyman.
38. For useful definitions of the land question see contents tables of The Land Enquiry Committee, *The Land: Vol.1 Rural* (1913), pp. v–xi; *The Land: Vol 2 Urban* (1914), pp. vii–xxi.
39. E.g., F.W.Maitland, J.A.R.Marriot, R.Prothero, G.Slater, R.H.Tawney, P.Vinogradoff.
40. F.W.S.Craig, *British General Election Manifestos 1900–1974*, pp. 3–4, 9–10, 19–20, 24–25.
41. J. Ramsden, *The Age of Balfour and Baldwin 1902–1940* (1978), p. x.
42. T.F. Lindsay and M. Harrington, *The Conservative Party 1918–1970* (1979), p. 1.
43. F. Pym, *The Politics of Consent* (1979), p. 172.
44. R. Scruton, *The Meaning of Conservatism* (1980), p. 11.
45. I.Berlin, 'Two Concepts of Liberty', in *Four Essays on Liberty* (Oxford, 1969), pp. 118–72.
46. NUCAS, *The Campaign Guide* (Edinburgh, 1909), p. 339.
47. Arthur Balfour, First Earl of Balfour Papers (hereafter ABP), British Library, Add. Mss. 49767, fos. 1–4, J. Sandars to A. Balfour, 2 Oct. 1910.
48. Lord Hugh Cecil, *Conservatism* (1912), p. 118.
49. G.K. Fry, *The Growth of Government*, p. 40.
50. A. J. Peacock, 'Land Reform 1880–1919: A Study of the Activities of the English Land Restoration Leagues and the Land Nationalisation Society' (University of Southampton M.A. thesis, 1961), pp. 15–17.
51. T. Hobbes, *Leviathan* (Fontana, 1962), p. 143.
52. R.B. O'Brien, *Thomas Drummond: Under Secretary in Ireland 1835–40, Life and Letters* (1889), p. 284.
53. See P. Joyce, *Work, Society and Politics: The Culture of the Factory in Later Victorian England* (Brighton, 1982); I.Bradley, *Enlightened Entrepreneurs* (1987).
54. See F. Prochaska, *Women and Philanthropy in Nineteenth-Century England* (Oxford, 1980), esp. pp. 222–30.
55. See P. H. J. H. Gosden, *Self-Help: Voluntary Associations in Nineteenth-Century Britain* (1973).
56. J. W. Mason, 'Thomas Mackay: The Anti-Socialist Philosophy of the Charity Organisation Society', in K. D. Brown (ed.), *Essays in Anti-Labour History: Responses to the Rise of Labour in Britain* (1974), pp. 290–316.
57. *The Times*, 8 Oct. 1885, p. 7e.
58. *The Times*, 31 Oct. 1895, p. 10b.
59. *The Times*, 27 Nov. 1889, p. 6e–f.
60. *Handy Notes on Current Politics*, 6, 62, 1 Feb. 1895, p. 29.
61. A.J. Balfour, *A Defence of Philosophic Doubt: Being an Essay on the Foundations of Belief* (1879); *The Foundations of Belief: Being Notes Introductory to the Study of Theology* (1895).
62. *The Times*, 15 Nov. 1907, p. 8c, b.
63. Viscount Cecil of Chelwood, *All the Way* (1949), p. 88.
64. Ernest Pollock, First Viscount Hanworth of Hanworth Papers, Bodleian Library, MS Eng. hist. d. 432, fos. 134–188, E. Pollock, 'The Fall of the Coalition Government Under Lloyd George in October 1922', [n.d., ?1926, typescript], p. 28.

65. J.M. Keynes, *Essays in Biography* (1961), p. 40.
66. National Union Records, Bodleian Library, annual conference of 1913, p. 61.
67. Earl Winterton, *Orders of the Day* (1953), p. 59.
68. *The Times*, 29 July 1912, p. 8a.
69. *The Times*, 22 May 1912, p. 10c.
70. NUCAS, *The Campaign Guide* (Edinburgh, 1909), p. 335.
71. *Ibid.*, p. 343.
72. *Ibid.*, p. 344.
73. M.D. Pugh, *The Tories and the People 1880–1935* (Oxford 1985), p. 168.
74. *Ibid.*, p. 28.
75. *Ibid.*, p. 71.
76. The Primrose League, leaflet no. 181, *A Few Words to Working Men and Women about the Primrose League* (1907).
77. There is a collection of Primrose League propaganda in the British Library, cat. no. 8138.g.
78. J. Robb, *The Primrose League 1883–1906* (New York, 1942), p. 49.
79. The Primrose League, *The Primrose League. How Ladies Can Help It* (1885).
80. J. Robb, *The Primrose League*, p. 87.
81. Earl Winterton, *Pre-War* (1932), p. 18.
82. A.S.T. Griffith-Boscawen, *Memories* (1925), p. 36.
83. Winterton, *Pre-War*, p. 4.
84. Samuel Hoare, First Viscount Templewood Papers, University of Cambridge Library, xx/1, S. Hoare, 'At Home and Abroad' [typescript memoirs, n.d., ?1950], p. 78.
85. JSP MS Eng. hist. c. 763, fos. 69–73, J. Sandars to Lansdowne, 7 April 1911 (copy).
86. S. Hoare, 'At Home and Abroad', p. 78.
87. Austen Chamberlain Papers, (hereafter ACP), University of Birmingham Library, AC8/5/18, J. Arkwright to A. Chamberlain, n.d., [Feb. 1910].
88. See p. 111.
89. JSP MS Eng. hist. c. 751, fos. 127–128, Lansdowne to J. Sandars, 26 Jan. n.y. [1906].
90. Fourth Marquess of Salisbury Papers, (hereafter MSP), in the possession of the Marquess of Salisbury, Hatfield House, Hertfordshire, S(4)60/131, Onslow to Salisbury, 27 May 1907.
91. R.T. McKenzie, *British Political Parties* (1964), p. 82.
92. NUCCA no. 228, *Speech by Sir Albert Kaye Rollit, LL.D., M.P., on Organisation and Social Reform...* (1889), p. 3.
93. *Ibid.*, p. 4.
94. Winterton, *Orders of the Day*, p. 59.
95. G.Phillips, *The Diehards: Aristocratic Society and Politics in Edwardian England* (Harvard, 1979), p. 27.
96. The evidential bases of this prosopography are discussed in Fforde, Oxford D.phil. thesis (1985), pp. 17–19. The landowner category includes heirs; the services are the colonial, diplomatic and Indian services; the overlap column gives a percentage figure of the category itself; MPs often belonged to more than two categories.
97. W.D.Rubinstein, 'Wealth, Elites and the Class Structure of Modern Britain', *Past and Present*, 76 (1977), pp. 99–126.
98. M.Fforde, 'The Conservative Party and Real Property in England, 1900–1914', pp. 38–40.
99. Winterton, *Orders of the Day*, p. 22.
100. Lord R.Cecil Papers, Add. Mss. 51160, fos. 51–56, anon., 'List of Unionist MPs, and Interests Represented 1911'.
101. W.S.Churchill, *Great Contemporaries* (1938), p. 71.
102. Andrew Bonar Law Papers, (hereafter BLP), House of Lords Record Office, 26/3/11, Willoughby de Broke to A.Bonar Law, 5 May 1912.
103. *The Times*, 28 Nov. 1889, p. 6d.
104. Alexis de Tocqueville, *Journeys to England and Ireland*, ed. J.P.Mayer (1957), p. 59.
105. Alexis de Tocqueville, *The Ancien Regime and the French Revolution* (Fontana, 1971), p. 122.

106. Anon. [F.Cornford], *Microcosmographia Academica: Being a Guide for the Young Academic Politician* (Cambridge, 1908), pp. 31–9.
107. J.S. Sandars, *Studies of Yesterday* (1928), p. 48.
108. P. Smith, *Disraelian Conservatism and Social Reform* (1967), esp. pp. 319–25.
109. R. Shannon, *The Crisis of Imperialism 1865–1915* (1976), pp. 101–41; M.Bentley, *Politics Without Democracy*, pp. 219–30.
110. A. Maurois, *Disraeli: A Picture of the Victorian Age* (1927), p. 316.
111. Giuseppe di Lampedusa, *The Leopard* (1960), p. 31.

CHAPTER TWO

1. V. Hicks Beach, *The Life of Sir Michael Hicks Beach, Earl St. Aldwyn*, vol.1 (1932), pp. 301–2.
2. C.H.D.Howard, 'Joseph Chamberlain and the "Unauthorized Programme"', *English Historical Review*, 65, 257 (1950), pp. 477–91.
3. E.g., P. Fraser, *Joseph Chamberlain: Radicalism and Empire, 1868–1914* (1966); J.L.Garvin and J.Amery, *The Life of Joseph Chamberlain*, vols. 1–6 (1932–1969); M. Balfour, *Britain and Joseph Chamberlain* (1985); R. Jay, *Joseph Chamberlain: A Political Study* (Oxford, 1981); D. Judd, *Radical Joe: A Life of Joseph Chamberlain* (1977); J.E Powell, *Joseph Chamberlain*, (1977).
4. *The Times*, 6 Jan. 1885, p. 7c.
5. *The Times*, 9 Sept. 1885, p. 6d.
6. *The Times*, 15 Jan. 1885, p. 7b.
7. *The Times*, 6 Aug. 1885, p. 6c.
8. D. A. Hamer, (ed.), *The Radical Programme* (Leicester, 1971), esp. Hamer's summary on pp. xv–xvi.
9. *Ibid.*, p. xxxix.
10. C.H.D. Howard (ed.), *J.Chamberlain, A Political Memoir, 1880–92* (1953), pp. 9–37, 53–75.
11. A. S. Wohl (ed.), *The Bitter Cry of Outcast London* (Leicester, 1970), pp. 53–78.
12. A. S. Wohl, 'The Bitter Cry of Outcast London', *International Review of Social History*, 13 (1968), pp. 189–245.
13. D. A. Reeder, 'The Politics of Urban Leaseholds in Late Victorian England', *International Review of Social History*, 6 (1961), pp. 413–30.
14. See C.A. Barker, *Henry George* (1955), pp. 341–416.
15. J. A. Hobson, 'The Influence of Henry George in England', *Fortnightly Review*, 1 Dec. 1897, p. 844.
16. Henry George, *Progress and Poverty* (1881), p. x.
17. The history of these pressure groups is described by A. J. Peacock, 'Land Reform 1880–1919: A Study of the Activities of the English Land Restoration Leagues and the Land Nationalisation Society' (University of Southampton M.A. thesis, 1961), and S. B. Ward, 'Land Reform in England 1880–1914' (University of Reading Ph.D. thesis, 1982). For a useful inside account see P.W. Raffan, *The Policy of the Land Values Group in the House of Commons* (1912), (pamphlet).
18. A. J. Peacock, 'Land Reform 1880-1919', pp. 152–78.
19. *Handy Notes on Current Politics*, 7, 79, 1 July 1896, p. 121.
20. A. J. Peacock, 'Land Reform 1880–1919', p. 86.
21. P.W. Raffan, *The Policy of the Land Values Group*, p. 17.
22. A. J. Peacock, 'Land Reform 1880–1919', pp. 29–38.
23. H. Pelling, *The Origins of the Labour Party 1880–1900* (Oxford, 1965), pp. 17–23.
24. See A. M. McBriar, *Fabian Socialism and English Politics 1884–1918* (Cambridge, 1962), pp. 1–28.
25. NLF, *Fourth Annual Report* (Oct. 1881), p. 6.
26. NLF, *Eighth Annual Report* (1885), p. 6.
27. *The Times*, 17 Jan., 1884, p. 10.
28. NLF, *Proceedings of the Annual Meeting of the Council of the National Liberal Federation* (1888), pp. 8–9.

29. NLF, *Tenth Annual Report* (1887), p. 9.
30. NLF, *Proceedings...of the Annual Meeting*(1889), p. 10.
31. D. A. Hamer, *Liberal Politics in the Age of Gladstone and Rosebery* (1972), p. 191.
32. NLF, *Proceedings...of the Annual Meeting* (1891), p. 8, (rearranged text).
33. NLF, *Proceedings...of the Annual Meeting* (1895), p. 7.
34. NLF, *Proceedings...of the Annual Meeting* (1899), p. 6.
35. NLF, *Proceedings...of the Annual Meeting* (1904), p. 5.
36. NLF, *Proceedings...of the Annual Meeting* (1905), p. 6.
37. NLF, *Proceedings...of the Annual Meeting* (1891), pp. 6–8.
38. LPD no. 1648, *The Land and the Budget* [n.d., 1894].
39. LPD no. 1639, *The Peers & the People* [n.d., 1894].
40. LPD no. 1733, *The Landlords' Government*. [n.d., 1896].
41. LPD no. 1823, *How I Became a Liberal* [n.d., 1899].
42. LPD, *Five Years of Tory Government 1895–1900* (1900), pp. 12–17.
43. *The Times*, 22 Dec. 1905, p. 7b–c.
44. A. K. Russell, *Liberal Landslide: The General Election of 1906* (Newton Abbot, 1973), p. 65.
45. P.F. Clarke, *Lancashire and the New Liberalism* (Cambridge, 1971), p. 393.
46. H. Pelling, *A History of British Trade Unionism* (1963), pp. 89–120, quotation p. 104.
47. See H. Pelling, *The Origins of the Labour Party*, pp. 99–124.
48. H. Pelling, *A Short History of the Labour Party* (1961), p. 4.
49. See H. Pelling, *The Origins of the Labour Party*, pp. 192–215.
50. F.W.S. Craig, *British General Election Manifestos 1900–1974*, p. 4.
51. *Ibid.*, pp. 9–10.
52. Association of Municipal Corporations Records, Public Record Office, 30/72/24, 'Twenty-Second Annual Meeting' (22 March 1895), pp. 5, 8.
53. AMC Records PRO 30/72/26, 'Annual Meeting...27th. February, 1897', p. 3.
54. AMC Records PRO 30/72/27, 'Annual Meeting...26th. day of March, 1898', p. 40.
55. A. J. Peacock, 'Land Reform 1880–1919', pp. 86–116.
56. NUCCA, *The Unionist Record, 1895–1905* [n.d., 1905], p. 200.
57. Industrial Freedom League, *Annual Meeting...20 July, 1904*, Lord Avebury, p. 2.
58. J. Morley, *The Life of William Ewart Gladstone*, vol. 3 (1903), p. 173.
59. D.A. Hamer, *Liberal Politics in the Age of Gladstone and Rosebery*, pp. 220–1.
60. J. Morley, *The Life of William Ewart Gladstone*, vol. 1 (1903), p. 348.
61. A.J. Balfour, *Chapters of Autobiography* (1930), p.76.
62. P. Stansky, *Ambitions and Strategies: The Struggle for the Leadership of the Liberal Party in the 1890s* (Oxford, 1964), p. 2.
63. 350 HC deb. 3 ser. 27 Feb. 1891, W.Gladstone, 1878.
64. D. C. Savage, 'The General Election of 1886 in Great Britain and Ireland' (University of London PH.D. thesis, 1958), p. 554.
65. J. Vincent, *Pollbooks: How Victorians Voted* (Cambridge, 1967), p. 47.
66. LPD no. 2345, *?Which Will You Be – Peers' Men or Free Men* (1910).
67. P. Stansky, *Ambitions and Strategies*, pp. 172, 180.
68. Lord Rosebery, *The Value of Good Manners. An Address by...the Earl of Rosebery...* (1913).
69. R. Rhodes James, *Rosebery* (1963), p. 343.
70. A. G. Gardiner, *The Life of Sir William Harcourt*, vol. 2 (1923), p. 284.
71. *The Times*, 11 Sept. 1909, p. 8b.
72. Viscount Chilston, *W. H. Smith* (1965), p. 295.
73. *Ibid.*, p. 296.
74. Lord Salisbury, 'The Budget and the Reform Bill', in P. Smith (ed.), *Lord Salisbury on Politics*, pp. 124–5.
75. BLP 33/4/28, A. Bonar Law to Gibbs, 3 April 1912 (copy).
76. NUCAS, *The Campaign Guide* (Edinburgh, 1895), pp. 114–124.
77. NUCCA, *The Unionist Record, 1895–1905* [n.d., 1905], pp. 171–207.
78. *The Times*, 20 Nov. 1895, p. 7c.
79. A.S.T. Griffith-Boscawen, *Fourteen Years in Parliament* (1907), p. 96.

Notes

179

80. V. Hicks Beach, *The Life of Sir Michael Hicks Beach*, vol. 2, p. 33.
81. PRO CAB 37/58/109, M. Hicks Beach [Financial Difficulties: appeal for economy in estimates], Oct. 1901, p. 4.
82. V. Hicks Beach, *The Life of Sir Michael Hicks Beach*, vol. 2, p. 152.
83. 78 HL deb. 4 ser. 30 Jan. 1900, the Queen's Speech, 4.
84. PRO CAB 37/64/15, C. Ritchie, 'Our Financial Position', 21 Feb. 1903.
85. PRO CAB 37/69/23, E. Hamilton, 'The Financial Outlook of 1904–1905', 11 Feb. 1904, p. 9.
86. JSP MS Eng. hist. c. 748, fos. 241–8, A. Chamberlain to Selborne, 12 Nov. 1904 (copy).
87. A. T. Peacock and J. Wiseman, *The Growth of Public Expenditure in the United Kingdom* (1967), p. 108.
88. K. Smellie, *A History of Local Government* (1968), esp. pp. 37–9, 55–6.
89. Local authorities and their finance : Parliamentay Papers 1901, XXIV (16), Royal Commission on Local Taxation, *Final Report (England and Wales)*, Cd 638, chs. I, II; PP 1914, XL (30), Departmental Committee on Local Taxation, *Final Report*, Cd 7315 (1914), pp. 6–99. Ratio of grants to rates: B. Mitchell and P. Deane, *Abstract of British Historical Statistics* (Cambridge, 1962), pp. 414–15. Rising rate demands: A. Offer, *Property and Politics 1870–1914: Landownership, Law, Ideology and Urban Development in England* (Cambridge, 1981), fig. 15.2, p. 226. Grants out of step with increasing local duties: Departmental Committee on Local Taxation, *Final Report*, pp. 15–18. Useful contemporary discussions of the local taxation question: E. Cannan, *The History of Local Rates in England in Relation to the Proper Distribution of the Burden of Taxation* (1912); J. C. Graham, *Taxation (Local and Imperial) and Local Government* (1914).
90. Conservative Central Office, *Campaign Notes* (1885), 'F'.
91. Parliamentary debates on the subject brought out the Conservative approach: e.g., 303 HC deb. 3 ser. 23 March 1886, 1643–1700; 184 HC deb. 4 ser. 18 Feb. 1908, 727–70; 1 HC deb. 5 ser. 25 Feb. 1909, 891–940.
92. PRO CAB 37/16/70, M. Hicks Beach, 'Local Taxation', 21 Dec. 1885, p. 1.
93. K. Smellie, *A History of Local Government*, p. 48, 53.
94. PP 1893–4, LXXVII (28), H.H.Fowler, *Report on Local Taxation* (1893), p. xlvi.
95. E.g., NUCCA, *The Unionist Record, 1895–1905*, p. 199.
96. PP 1901, XXIV (16), Royal Commission on Local Taxation, *Final Report (England and Wales)*, Cd 638, p. ii.
97. PP 1899, XXXV, (25), Royal Commission on Local Taxation, *Local Rates in England and Wales. Valuation and Collection*, Cd 9141 (1899), pp. 40–2.
98. Royal Commission on Local Taxation, *Final Report*, pp. 11-33.
99. 98 HC deb. 4 ser. 26 July 1901, A. Balfour, 242.
100. 59 & 60 Vict., 1896, 16, 'Agricultural Rates Act'.
101. AMC Records PRO 30/72/34, 'Annual Meeting of the Association, held in the Guildhall...28th day of May 1913', p. 112.
102. E.g., PRO CAB 37/49/21, M. Hicks Beach, 'Rating of Tithe Rent Charge', 14 March 1899; PRO CAB 37/48/84, Balfour of Burleigh, 'Memorandum', 28 Dec. 1898.
103. 62 & 63 Vict., 1899, 17, 'Tithe Rentcharge (Rates) Act'.
104. See Conservative Central Office, *Nine Years' Work: A Review of the Legislation and Administration of the Conservative and Unionist Government 1895–1904* (1904), pp. 74–80.
105. PRO CAB 37/58/109, M. Hicks Beach, [Financial Difficulties: Appeal for Economy in Estimates], Oct. 1901, p. 7.
106. PRO CAB 37/64/15, C. Ritchie, 'Our Financial Position', 21 Feb. 1903, p. 5.
107. PRO CAB 37/73/162, W. Long, 'Agricultural Rates – Tithe Rent-charge Rates – Valuation', 10 Dec. 1904, p. 2.
108. See, e.g., NUCAS, *The Campaign Guide* (Edinburgh, 1900), pp. 462–89; NUCAS, *The Campaign Guide* (Edinburgh, 1906), pp. 553–85.
109. PP 1884–5, XXX (17), Royal Commission on the Housing of the Working Classes, *First Report*, Cd 4402 (1884), p. 42.

110. *Ibid.*, 'Memorandum by the Marquess of Salisbury', p. 61.
111. PP 1892, XVIII (8), Select Committee on Town Holdings, *Report* (1892), p. lxi.
112. NUCAS, *The Campaign Guide* (Edinburgh, 1900), p. 478.
113. Royal Commission on Local Taxation, *Final Report* (1901), pp. 39–45.
114. *Ibid.*, Lord Balfour of Burleigh *et al.*, 'Separate Report on Urban Rating and Site Values', pp. 149–76.
115. AMC Records, PRO 30/72/34, 'Minutes of the Proceedings and Resolutions of the Meeting of the Council...4th day of February 1904...Appendix', p. 16.
116. 103 HC deb. 4 ser. 19 Feb. 1902, 546–8; 120 HC deb. 4 ser. 27 March 1903, 531–6; 131 HC deb. 4 ser. 11 March 1904, 911–16; 145 HC deb. 4 ser. 14 April 1905, 263–8.
117. AMC Records PRO 30/72/24, 'Twenty-Second Annual Meeting'...(22 March 1895), pp. 6–7.
118. NUCAS, *The Campaign Guide* (Edinburgh, 1906), pp. 851–2.
119. PP 1903, VII (3), Select Committee on Municipal Trading, *Report* (1903).
120. See A. M. McBriar, *Fabian Socialism and English Politics*, pp. 187–233.
121. P.Fraser, *Joseph Chamberlain: Radicalism and Empire, 1868–1914* (1966), pp.152–3.
122. See NUCAS, *The Campaign Guide* (Edinburgh, 1900), p. 342.
123. See K. Young, *Local Politics and the Rise of Party: The London Municipal Society and the Conservative Intervention in Local Elections 1894–1963* (Leicester, 1975), pp. 35–112.
124. See C. Cook, 'Labour and the Downfall of the Liberal Party, 1906–1914', in C. Cook and A. Sked (eds.), *Crisis and Controversy : Essays in Honour of A. J. P. Taylor* (1976), pp. 38–65.
125. *The Times*, 27 Nov. 1889, p. 6e–f.
126. *The Times*, 31 Oct. 1895, p. 10b.
127. C. Feinstein, *National Income, Expenditure and Output of the United Kingdom 1855–1965* (Cambridge, 1972), summary table 3, p. T10; D. H. Aldcroft and H. W. Richardson, *The British Economy 1870–1939* (1969), pp. 4–5.
128. NUCCA, *The Unionist Record, 1895–1900*, pp. 3–4.
129. E.g., PP 1897, XV (1), Royal Commission on Agricultural Depression, *Final Report*, Cd 8540 (1897); PP 1906, XCVI (32), Board of Agriculture, *Decline in the Agricultural Population of Great Britain, 1881–1906*, Cd 3273 (1906).
130. PP 1930–1, VIII (4), Select Committee on Procedure on Public Business, *Special Report* (1931), p. 338, qs 3448–51.
131. C. Turnor, *Land Problems and National Welfare* (1911), pp. 313–14.
132. See p. 143.
133. Fourth Earl of Onslow Papers, Guildford Muniment Room, Surrey (hereafter EOP), 173/17/56, Onslow, 'A Brief Epitome of Public work done 1874 to 1908 which may serve for an Obituary Notice' [n.d., ?1908] (unpaginated), p. 5
134. E.g., *Ibid.* p. 5; C. Turnor, *Land Problems*, p. 2.
135. Charles Bathurst, First Viscount Bledisloe Papers, in the possession of Lord Bledisloe, Lydney Park, Gloucestershire, H. Chaplin to C. Bathurst, 27 Jan. 1913.
136. CLA Records, C/2, anon., 'Some Reminiscences of Lord Bledisloe', n.d. .
137. A.H.H. Matthews, *Fifty Years of Agricultural Politics: Being the History of the Central Chamber of Agriculture 1865–1915* (1915), p. vii.
138. For official histories of the CCA see A.H.H. Matthews, *Fifty Years of Agricultural Politics* and W. A. Jeffcock, *Agricultural Politics 1915–1935* (Ipswich, 1937).
139. A.H.H. Matthews, *Fifty Years of Agricultural Politics*, pp. 340–4.
140. *Ibid.*, pp. 379–82.
141. ABP Add. Mss. 49690, fos. 70–2, Salisbury to A. Balfour, 31 Dec. 1892.
142. JSP MS Eng. hist. c. 748, fos. 229–32, Onslow to A. Balfour, 22 Oct. n.y. [1904].
143. Onslow, 'A Brief Epitome of Public work' p. 5; *Journal of the Proceedings of the Central Chamber of Agriculture*, 4 April 1905, pp. 82–3.
144. Onslow, 'A Brief Epitome of Public work', pp. 5–6.
145. EOP 173/9/24, J. Collings to Onslow, 30 July 1903.
146. ABP Add. Mss. 49859, fos. 251–2, A. Balfour to J. Collings, 7 May 1908 (copy).
147. Onslow, 'A Brief Epitome of Public work', p. 6.

148. Matthews, *Fifty Years of Agricultural Politics*, p. 73.
149. *The Mark Lane Express*, 20 March 1905, p. 363b.
150. EOP 173/15/48, Onslow to H. Pike Pease, Oct. 1905 (copy).
151. ABP Add. Mss. 49771, fos. 102–3, A. Acland Hood to J. Sandars, 29 Oct. n.y., [1905].
152. F. M. L. Thompson (ed.), *The Rise of Suburbia* (Leicester, 1982), esp. pp. 2–23.
153. R. Blake, *The Conservative Party from Peel to Thatcher* (1985), p. 157.
154. J. Cornford, 'The Transformation of Conservatism in the Late Nineteenth Century', *Victorian Studies*, 7 (1963), p. 52.
155. *The Times*, 19 Dec. 1900, p. 12a.
156. C.F.G. Masterman, *The Condition of England* (1909), pp. 80–1.
157. N. Blewett, *The Peers, the Parties and the People*, pp. 400–1.
158. D. Baines, *Migration in a Mature Economy: Emigration and Internal Migration in England and Wales, 1861–1900* (Cambridge, 1985), p. 45.
159. *Ibid.*, p. 59.
160. J.M. Mackenzie, *Propaganda and Empire: The Manipulation of Public Opinion* (Manchester, 1984), pp. 160–2.
161. *The Times*, 27 Nov. 1889, p. 6e.
162. B. Porter, *The Lion's Share: A Short History of British Imperialism 1850–1983* (1984), p. 199.
163. W. Greenleaf, *The British Political Tradition*, vol. 2, pp. 219–23, 223–31.
164. R.Rhodes James, *The British Revolution: British Politics 1880–1939*, p. 112.
165. Lord Rosebery, *Lord Randolph Churchill* (1906), p. 131.
166. A.S.T. Griffith-Boscawen, *Memories*, p. 33.
167. R. Rhodes James, *Lord Randolph Churchill* (1970); R. Foster, *Lord Randolph Churchill: A Political Life* (1981).
168. W.S. Churchill, *Lord Randolph Churchill* (1906), vol. 2, pp. 18–19.
169. *Ibid.*, pp. 11–12.
170. *The Times*, 4 Oct. 1886, p. 10c–d; *The Times*, 27 Oct. 1886, p. 6e–f.
171. W.S. Churchill, *Lord Randolph Churchill*, vol. 2, p. 223.
172. *Ibid.*, pp. 164-165.
173. L. J. Jennings, *Speeches of the Right Hon. Lord Randolph Churchill 1880–1888*, vol. 1 (1889), p. 139.
174. 286 HC deb. 3 ser. 19 March 1884, Lord R. Churchill, 246.
175. W. S. Churchill, *Lord Randolph Churchill*, vol. 2, p. 506.
176. J. Ramsden, *The Age of Balfour and Baldwin*, p. 187.
177. R. E. Quinault, 'Lord Randolph Churchill and Tory Democracy, 1880–1885', *Historical Journal*, 22, 1 (1979), p. 163.
178. W. S. Churchill, *Lord Randolph Churchill*, vol. 1, p. 535.
179. W. S. Blunt, *Gordon at Khartoum* (1911), p. 414.
180. J.Morley, *The Life of William Ewart Gladstone*, vol. 3, p. 173.
181. R. Robinson and J. Callagher, *Africa and the Victorians* (1961), pp. 395–402.
182. Countess of Warwick, *Life's Ebb and Flow* (1929), p. 144.
183. J. Chamberlain, 'Labourers' and Artisans' Dwellings', *Fortnightly Review*, 1 Dec. 1883, p. 762.
184. *The Times*, 15 Jan. 1885, p. 7a–b.
185. P. Fraser, *Joseph Chamberlain: Radicalism and Empire 1868–1914* (1966), p. 51.
186. ABP Add.Mss. 49690, fos. 55–64, A.Balfour to Salisbury, 24 July 1892 (copy).
187. J. Chamberlain, 'The Labour Question', *The Nineteenth Century*, Nov. 1892, pp. 677–710.
188. P. Marsh, *The Discipline of Popular Government: Lord Salisbury's Domestic Statecraft 1881-1902* (1978), pp. 235–237.
189. ABP Add. Mss. 49690, fos. 55–64, A. Balfour to Salisbury, 24 July 1892 (copy).
190. D. Judd, *Radical Joe: A Life of Joseph Chamberlain* (1977), pp. 178–180.
191. P. Fraser, *Joseph Chamberlain*, p. 152.
192. K. Young, *Arthur James Balfour : the Happy Life of the Politician, Prime Minister, Statesman and Philosopher 1848–1930* (1963), p. 167.

182   *Notes*

193. NUCCA no. 228, *Speech by Sir Albert Kaye Rollit*, LL.D, M.P., *on Organisation and Social Reform...* (1889), pp. 4, 3.
194. *Ibid.*, pp. 8, 10.
195. *Municipalism: An Address by Sir Albert Kaye Rollit...Annual Congress of the British Institute of Public Health, at Hull, August 9th, 1895* (1895), p. 10 (bound with AMC Records PRO 30/72/24).
196. AMC Records, PRO 30/72/27, 'The 25th Annual Meeting...26th day of March, 1898', p. 65.
197. A. J. Balfour, *Chapters of Autobiography* (1930), p. 135.
198. N. Solden, 'Laissez-Faire as Dogma: The Liberty and Property Defence League, 1882–1914', in K. D. Brown (ed.), *Essays in Anti-Labour History*, p. 212.
199. E. Bristow, 'The Liberty and Property Defence League and Individualism', *Historical Journal*, 18, 4 (1975), p. 763.
200. LPDL, *Overlegislation in 1884* (1884), p. 43.
201. N. Solden, 'Laissez-Faire as Dogma', p. 228.
202. LPDL, *Report of the Proceedings at the First Annual Dinner of the Liberty and Property Defence League...July 12th, 1888*, p. 30.
203. LPDL, *Second Annual Dinner, 1889, Report of Proceedings and Speeches*, p. 32.
204. LPDL, *Annual Report, 1892–1893* (1893), p. 21.
205. N. Solden, 'Laissez-Faire as Dogma', pp. 222 6.
206. E.Bristow, 'The Liberty and Property Defence League', p. 764.
207. N. Solden, 'Laissez-Faire as Dogma', p. 227.
208. LPDL, *Annual Report, 1893–1894* (1894), pp. 6–7.
209. A. Simon, 'Joseph Chamberlain and the Unauthorized Programme', (University of Oxford D.Phil. thesis, 1970), pp. 265–7.
210. W. Long, *Memories* (1923), pp. 83–4.
211. EOP 173/1(4), anon, 'History of the Onslow Family', vol. 4 (typescript history, n.d.), pp. 1015–29.
212. Earl of Onslow, *Landlords and Allotments: The History and Present condition of the Allotments System* (1886), p. vii.
213. W. S. Churchill, *Lord Randolph Churchill*, vol.2, p. 223.
214. PRO CAB 37/18/53, Salisbury, 'Allotments Bill Note of Objections', 6 Dec. 1886, p. 5.
215. Conservative Central Office, *Campaign Notes* (1885), 'T' and 'U'.
216. E.g., anon. , *Mr.Joseph Arch and the Agricultural Labourers* [n.d., 1886]; anon., *Is Mr.Joseph Arch a Friend to the Agricultural Labourers* [n.d., 1886].
217. PRO CAB 37/18/53, Salisbury, 'Allotments Bill Note of Objections', 6 Dec. 1886, p. 5.
218. E.g., NUCAS, *The Campaign Guide* (Edinburgh, 1895), pp. 72–7.
219. Conservative Central Office, *Campaign Notes* (1885), 'T-Peasant Proprietorship and Land Nationalisation'.
220. Industrial Remuneration Conference, *The Report of the Proceedings...28th, 29th, and 30th January, 1885* (1885), A. J. Balfour, 'Land, Land Reformers, and the Nation', p. 343.
221. S. Ward, 'Land Reform in England 1880–1914', (University of Reading Ph.D. thesis, 1976), p. 134–5.
222. J. Collings, *Land Reform, Occupying Ownership, Peasant Proprietary and Rural Education* (1906); J. Collings, *The Colonization of Rural Britain, a Complete Scheme for the Regeneration of British Rural Life* (1914).
223. For a sample of the league's propaganda, British Library cat. no. 8138.g.60.
224. PP 1905, IV (4), 52, 'Purchase of Land (England and Wales) Bill'.
225. PP 1890, XVII (8), Select Committee on Small Holdings, *Report* (1890), pp. x–xvi.
226. ABP Add. Mss. 49690, fos. 3–5, Salisbury to A. Balfour, 22 Jan. 1892.
227. The Land Enquiry Committee, *The Land: Vol. 1 Rural* (1913), p. 192.
228. 55 & 56 Vict., 1892, 31, 'Small Holdings Act'.
229. E.g., PP 1904 , IV (4), 65, 'Small Holdings Bill'.
230. EOP 173/15/8, Onslow to A. J. Balfour, 21 Feb. 1905 (copy).

231. *Ibid.*; PRO CAB 37/75/40, [Agricultural policy], printed version of this letter, 27 Feb. 1905.
232. LPD, *Five Years of Tory Government, 1895–1900* (1900), p. 54.
233. ABP Add. Mss. 49690, fos. 65–6, Salisbury to A. Balfour, 26 July 1892.
234. ABP Add. Mss. 49690, fos. 76–9, Salisbury to A. Balfour, 26 Dec. 1893.
235. *Handy Notes on Current Politics,* 5, 51, March 1894, p. 39.
236. History of the bill: NUCAS, *The Campaign Guide* (Edinburgh, 1895), pp. 407–11.
237. A.S.T. Griffith-Boscawen, *Fourteen Years in Parliament,* p. 124.
238. E.g., NUCAS, *The Campaign Guide* (Edinburgh, 1900), p. 391.
239. PP 1894, XXXV (20), Royal Commission on Labour, *Fifth and Final Report,* Cd 7421 (1894), pp. 97–113.
240. 59 & 60 Vict., 1896, 30, 'Conciliation Act'.
241. J. S. Sandars, *Studies of Yesterday* (1928), p. 59.
242. See Sir C. Petrie Bt., *Walter Long and His Times* (1936), p. 171; William Bridgeman, First Viscount Bridgeman of Leigh Diary, in the possession of Viscount Bridgeman, Minsterly, Shropshire, 10 Nov. 1911.
243. PRO CAB 37/74/17, W. Long, 'The Unemployed', Jan. 1905.
244. PRO CAB 37/74/31, W. Long, 'The Unemployed', 16 Feb. 1905.
245. W. Long, *Memories,* p. 139.
246. PRO CAB 37/75/44, Salisbury, 'The Unemployed. Mr. Long's Scheme', 1 March 1905, p. 4.
247. ABP Add. Mss. 49776, fos. 40–1, A. J. Balfour to W. Long, 23 Dec. 1904 (copy).
248. J. Vincent (ed.), *The Crawford Papers: The Journal of David Lindsay, Twenty-Seventh Earl of Crawford and Tenth Earl of Balcarres 1871–1940 during the Years 1892 to 1940.* (Manchester, 1984), p. 81.
249. NUACLUO, *The History of Housing Reform* [n.d., 1913], pp. 7–14.
250. AMC Records, PRO 30/72/30, 'Proceedings of the Annual Meeting...22nd of March 1901', p. 42.
251. AMC Records, PRO 30/72/30, 'Deputation Upon the Rt. Hon. W. H. Long...29th of November, 1901', pp. 211–14.
252. Royal Commission on Labour, *Fifth and Final Report* (1894), p. 111.
253. NUCCA, *The Unionist Record, 1895–1900,* pp. 30–2.
254. NUCCA, *The Case Against Radicalism 1909* (1909), p. 651.
255. PP1895, XIV (1), Royal Commission on the Aged Poor, *Report,* Cd 7684 (1895), pp. vii–lxxxvii.
256. PP 1898, XLV (33), Departmental Commmittee on Old Age Pensions, *Report,* Cd 8911 (1898), pp. 1–16.
257. PP 1899, VIII (1), Select Commmittee on the Aged Deserving Poor, *Report* (1899), pp. iii–xiii.
258. PP 1900, X (1), Departmental Committee on the Financial Aspects of the Proposals made by the Select Committee of the House of Commons of 1899 about the Aged Deserving Poor, *Report,* Cd 67 (1900), esp. pp. xlii–xlviii.
259. E.g., PRO CAB 37/51/95, J. Chamberlain, 'Aged Poor', Nov. 1899; PRO CAB 37/51/95, A. Balfour, 'Pensions and Poor Law Reform', 15 Nov. 1899, and see footnotes 260–2.
260. PRO CAB 37/49/12, W. Long, [Old Age Pension Scheme], 10 Feb. 1899, p. 1.
261. PRO CAB 37/51/89, M. Hicks Beach, 'Aged Poor', 18 Nov. 1899, pp. 6–7.
262. PRO CAB 37/61/60, W. Long, 'Aged Pensioners' Bill', 12 March 1902.
263. E.g., LPD, *Five Years of Tory Government 1895–1900* (1900), pp. 59–62.
264. E.g., Balfour: B. Gilbert, *The Evolution of National Insurance in Great Britain* (1966), p. 97; Bonar Law: *The Times,* 17 Dec. 1912, p. 8a; NUACLUO, *The Campaign Guide* (1914), p. 586.
265. See B. Gainer, *The Alien Invasion* (1972), esp. pp. 1–14.
266. PRO CAB 37/59/146, G. Balfour, 'Alien Immigration', Dec. 1901.
267. 5 Edw. VII, 1905, 13, 'Aliens Act'.
268. NUCAS, *Campaign Guide* (Edinburgh, 1906), pp. 271–4.
269. 63 & 64 Vict., 1900, 50, 'Agricultural Holdings Act'.
270. *The Times,* 31 Oct. 1895, p. 10b.

271. NUCAS no. 104, *Real Conservative Reform I. Legislation Affecting Land* [n.d., 1889]; no. 110, *Real Conservative Reform II. The Reform of the Labour Laws* [n.d., 1889]; no. 111, *Real Conservative Reform III. The Homes of the People* [n.d., 1889]; no. 112, *Real Conservative Reform IV. Aids to the Industry and Thrift of the People* [n.d., 1889]; no. 113, *Real Conservative Reform V. The Health of the People* [n.d., 1889]; no. 120, *Real Conservative Reform VI. Local Government – The English Act of 1888* [n.d., 1889]; no. 132, *Real Conservative Reform VII. Local Government – The Scotland Act of 1889* [n.d., 1889].

272. NUCAS, *The Campaign Guide* (Edinburgh, 1892), ch. 3, pp. 34–67; *The Campaign Guide* (Edinburgh, 1895), ch. 3, pp. 36–71; *The Campaign Guide* (Edinburgh, 1900), ch. 5, pp. 147–203; *The Campaign Guide* (Edinburgh, 1906), ch. 5, pp. 254–312.

273. *The Times*, 3 Feb. 1892, p. 6c.

274. For a useful survey of Unionist Irish policy: NUCCA, *The Unionist Record, 1895–1905*, pp. 5–13.

275. J.R. Fisher, 'The Farmers' Alliance: an Agricultural Protest Movement of the 1880s', *Agricultural History Review*, 26 (1978), pp. 15–25.

276. 286 HC deb. 3 ser. 19 March 1884, Lord R. Churchill, 244.

277. E.g., Conservative Central Office, *Campaign Notes* (1885), 'R-Leasehold Enfranchisement'; NUCAS, *The Campaign Guide* (Edinburgh, 1895), pp. 463–5.

278. PP 1889, XV (7), Select Committee on Town Holdings, *Report* (1889), pp. 39–40

279. W. S. Churchill, *Lord Randolph Churchill*, vol. 2, p. 15.

280. 62 & 63 Vict., 1899, 44, 'Small Dwellings Acquisition Act'.

281. 74 HL deb. 4 ser. 21 July 1899, Selborne, 1503.

282. The Land Enquiry Committee, *The Land: Vol. 2 Urban* (1914), p. 214.

283. W. S. Churchill, *Lord Randolph Churchill*, vol. 2, p. 224.

284. ABP Add. Mss. 49690, fos. 6–8, Salisbury to Mr. Maple, 14 March 1892 (copy).

285. P. Marsh, *The Discipline of Popular Government*, p. 236.

286. J. M. Mackenzie (ed.), *Imperialism and Popular Culture* (Manchester, 1985), esp. pp. 5–7.

287. R. Price, *An Imperial War and the British Working Class: Working-class Attitudes and Reactions to the Boer War 1899–1902* (1972) is the only substantial publication on the 1900 general election.

288. J.M. Mackenzie, *Propaganda and Empire*, pp. 148–158.

289. E.g., NUCCA, *The Unionist Record, 1895–1900*, pp. 77–87.

290. Compare the Unionist election addresses of 1906 and 1910: A. K. Russell, *The Liberal Landslide*, p. 83; N. Blewett, *The Peers, the Parties and the People*, pp. 317, 326.

291. B. Harrison, 'For Church, Queen and Family: The Girls' Friendly Society 1874–1920', *Past and Present*, 61, (1973), pp. 107–138.

292. Flora Thompson, *Lark Rise to Candleford* (Oxford, 1945), esp. pp. 208–9.

293. E.g., NUCAS, *The Campaign Guide* (Edinburgh, 1892), pp. 200–8; NUACLUO, *The Campaign Guide* (1914), pp. 59–90.

294. A.S.T. Griffith-Boscawen, *Fourteen Years in Parliament*, p. 41.

295. 62 & 63 Vict., 1899, 17, 'Tithe Rentcharge (Rates) Act'.

296. 54 & 55 Vict., 1891, 8, 'Tithe Act'.

297. *The Times*, 20 Nov. 1895, p. 7c.

298. For details of this complicated story see M. Cruickshank, *Church and State in English Education 1870 to the Present Day* (1963), pp. 61–99; J. E. B. Munson, 'The Unionist Coalition and Education, 1895–1902', *Historical Journal*, 20, 3 (1977), pp. 607–645.

299. A. G. Gardiner, *The Life of Sir William Harcourt*, vol. 2 (1923), pp. 299–300.

300. A.S.T. Griffith-Boscawen, *Fourteen Years in Parliament*, p. 55.

301. LPD no. 1653, *The Budget: What it is, and How it was Carried* [n.d., 1894].

302. NUCAS, *The Campaign Guide* (Edinburgh, 1892), pp. 281–3; NUCAS, *The Campaign Guide* (Edinburgh, 1895), pp. 520–34. See also, C.Weston, 'Salisbury and the Lords, 1868–1895', *Historical Journal*, 25, 1 (1982), pp. 103–29.

303. E.g., LPD, *Five Years of Tory Government* [n.d., 1900], pp. 146–54.

304. A point developed at greater length pp. 113-5.

CHAPTER THREE

1. E.g., W. Greenleaf, *The British Political Tradition*, vol. 2, pp. 233–44, 238–42;
J.Ridley, 'The Unionist Social Reform Committee, 1911–1914: Wets before the Deluge',
Historical Journal, 30, 2 (1987), pp. 391–413; A. Sykes, *Tariff Reform in British Politics
1903–1913* (Oxford, 1979), pp. 197, 285–7; M.Pugh, *The Making of Modern British
Politics 1867–1939*, p. 130.

2. E.g., A. M. Gollin, *Balfour's Burden: Arthur Balfour and Imperial Preference* (1965);
R. A. Rempel, *Unionists Divided: Arthur Balfour, Joseph Chamberlain and the Unionist
Free Traders* (Newton Abbot, 1972); B. Semmel, *Imperialism and Social Reform:
English Social and Imperial Thought 1895–1914* (1960); A. Sykes, *Tariff Reform in
British Politics*. The bibliography of this last can be consulted for articles. See also the bi-
ographies of Joseph Chamberlain by Amery and Garvin, Balfour, Fraser, Jay, and Judd
cited in note 3 of chapter 2.

3. J.Amery, *Joseph Chamberlain and the Tariff Reform Campaign, The Life of Joseph
Chamberlain Vol. 6, 1903–1968* (1969), p. 893.

4. ABP Add. Mss. 49736, fos. 21–32, A. Chamberlain to A. Balfour, 24 Oct. 1907.

5. *The Morning Post*, 12 Oct. 1908, p. 7e.

6. A. Chamberlain, *Politics From Inside* (1936), pp. 226–30.

7. *National Review*, 56 (1910), L. J. Maxse, 'Episodes of the Month', p. 368.

8. Lord Henry Cavendish Bentinck, *Tory Democracy* (1918), pp. 77–8.

9. ABP Add. Mss. 49736, fos. 21–32, A. Chamberlain to A. Balfour, 24 Oct. 1907.

10. SMP GD193/351/67, A. Steel-Maitland to W. Bridgeman, 3 Sept. 1909. SMP GD193/351
contains much material on the subject.

11. Viscount Milner, *The Nation and the Empire* (1913), p. 497.

12. *Ibid.*, pp. 214–15.

13. J. W. Mackail and G. Wyndham, *The Life and Letters of George Wyndham*, vol.2
[n.d., 1925], p. 540.

14. *Ibid.*, pp. 563–4.

15. J. Robb, *The Primrose League*, p. 83.

16. See B. H. Brown, *The Tariff Reform Movement in Great Britain 1881–1898* (Columbia, 1943).

17. National Union Records, Bodleian Library, annual conference of 1905 (unpaginated).

18. National Union Records, annual conference of 1907, p. 12; 1908, p. 15; 1909, p. 16;
1910, p. 26; 1911, p. 25; 1912, p. 20; 1913, p. 25.

19. ABP Add. Mss. 49765, fos. 11–16, J. Sandars to A. Balfour, 22 Jan. 1907.

20. NUCAS, *The Campaign Guide* (Edinburgh, 1909), pp. 202–3.

21. E.g., The Tariff Reform League, *Tariff Points and Tariff Pictures* (1905); TRL leaflets
in the British Library, cat. no. O8226.C.83.

22. E.g., The Tariff Reform League, *A Short Handbook for Speakers* (1905 edn., 1910
edn.); TRL, *The Tariff Reformers' Enquire Within* (1914). The TRL also published a
monthly *Notes on Tariff Reform* (British Library PP 3558.1c., 1904–1914), which gives a
detailed exposition of the tariff reform case.

23. ABP Add. Mss. 49737, fos. 40–2, R.Cecil to A.Balfour, 25 Jan. 1906.

24. A. Sykes, *Tariff Reform*, p. 294.

25. R. Jay, *Joseph Chamberlain: A Political Study* (Oxford, 1981), p. 332.

26. JSP MS Eng. hist. c. 737, fos. 137–8, A. Acland Hood, 'Corn Duty Repeal', n.d. [Nov.
1902].

27. JSP MS Eng. hist. c. 740, fos. 164–70, A. Acland Hood to A.Balfour, 12 Aug. 1903,
enclosing 'Fiscal Reform. Reports from the Constituencies'.

28. ABP Add. Mss. 49774, fos. 69–74, J. Chamberlain to A. Balfour, 24 Feb. 1905.

29. *The Times*, 16 April 1910, p. 10b. NUCCA no. 1278, *Tariff Reform and the Wheat Duty*
(1910).

30. *The Times*, 30 Nov. 1910, p. 9d.

31. *The Times*, 25 Jan. 1913, p. 10a.

32. ABP Add. Mss. 49690, fos. 65–6, Salisbury to A. Balfour, 26 July 1892.

33. J. Amery, *Joseph Chamberlain and the Tariff Reform Campaign, The Life of Joseph
Chamberlain Vol. 5, 1901–1903* (1969), p. 378.

34. ABP Add. Mss. 49736, fos. 12–15, A. Balfour to A. Chamberlain, 9 Feb. 1907 (copy).
35. J. Amery, *Joseph Chamberlain and the Tariff Reform Campaign*, vol. 6, p. 562.
36. R. Blake, *The Conservative Party from Peel to Thatcher*, p. 182.
37. W. H. Greenleaf, *The British Political Tradition*, vol. 2, pp. 233–4.
38. T. F. Lindsay and M. Harrington, *The Conservative Party 1918–1970*, p. 17.
39. J.Ridley, 'The Unionist Social Reform Committee, 1911–1914', p. 391.
40. SMP GD193/108/1/384, 'The First Dinner of the Unionist social Reform Committee', 28 Feb. 1911; GD193/108/1/361, 'Unionist Social Reform Committee', 1911.
41. M. Woods, 'Real Social Reform', *Our Flag*, June 1914, p. 86b.
42. The following contain much material on the activities of the USRC: SMP GD193/108/1, GD193/352. For a survey of activity see F. E. Smith, 'The Conservative Party and Social Reform', *The Conservative and Unionist*, May 1911, pp. 73–4.
43. J. Campbell, *F. E. Smith First Earl of Birkenhead* (1983), pp. 362–4.
44. SMP GD193/159/6/15-18, A. Steel-Maitland to A. Glazebrook, 26 Aug. 1913, (copy).
45. A. Chamberlain, *Politics From Inside*, p. 527.
46. SMP GD193/108/3/47-61, [A. Steel-Maitland], [Memorandum for Bonar Law], [1911].
47. E.g., SMP GD193/80/5/43-49, A. Steel-Maitland, 'Suggested Policy', n.d. [1912]; GD193/274/445, [A. Steel-Maitland], 'Memorandum on Land', n.d. [Feb. 1913]; GD193/274/245–253, A. Steel-Maitland, 'Cabinet Committees', 4 March 1912; GD193/119/5/139–43, A. Steel-Maitland, 'Memorandum on Land Question', n.d. [29 Oct. 1913]; BLP 39/4/40, A. Steel-Maitland, 'Memorandum for Mr. Bonar Law and Lord Lansdowne', 23 June 1914.
48. SMP GD193/152/1/175, A. Steel-Maitland to J. Sandars, 20 Jan. 1911 (copy); GD193/152/1/179, A. Steel-Maitland to J. Sandars, 28 Jan. 1911 (copy).
49. SMP GD193/152/1/176-177, J. Sandars to A. Steel-Maitland, 22 Jan. 1911.
50. SMP GD193/151/4/2 [A.Steel-Maitland], 'Memorandum', n.d. [Feb. 1913].
51. SMP GD193/151/2/55, G.Locker-Lampson to A.Steel-Maitland, 28 Jan. 1911.
52. SMP GD193/151/4/1 [A. Steel-Maitland] to Northcliffe, 7 Feb. 1911 (copy), enclosing GD193/151/4/2 [A.Steel-Maitland], 'Memorandum', n.d. [Feb. 1913] (quoted).
53. SMP GD193/108/1/326, circular to members for a meeting of 16 March 1911.
54. F. E. Smith, 'The Conservative Party and Social Reform', *The Conservative and Unionist*, May 1911, pp. 73–4; *The Times*, 3 July 1912, p. 7b; M.Woods, 'Real Social Reform', *Our Flag*, June 1914, p. 86.
55. W. A. S. Hewins, *Apologia of an Imperialist*, vol. 1 (1929), p. 304
56. Christopher Turnor Papers, Lincolnshire Archives Office, 4 Turnor 3/5, Malmesbury to C. Turnor, 18 Oct. 1913.
57. Willoughby de Broke Papers, House of Lords Record Office, WE/3/41, M. Woods to Willoughby de Broke, 16 Aug. n.y. [?1912].
58. SMP GD193/159/6/9–11, A. Steel-Maitland to A. Glazebrook, 24 Dec. 1913 (copy).
59. SMP GD193/159/6/15–18, A. Steel-Maitland to A. Glazebrook, 26 Aug. 1913 (copy).
60. SMP GD193/108/3/47–61, [A. Steel-Maitland], [Memorandum for Bonar Law], [1911], p. 13.
61. BLP 31/1/13, W. Ashley to A. Bonar Law, 7 Dec. 1913.
62. A.Offer, *Property and Politics 1870–1914*, p. 388.
63. Unionist Social Reform Committee, *Poor Law Reform: A Practical Programme* (1912).
64. Unionist Social Reform Committee, *Industrial Unrest: A Practical Solution* (1914).
65. Anon., (Unionist Social Reform Committee), *The Health of the People: A New National Policy* [n.d., 1918].
66. Unionist Social Reform Committee, *The Schools and Social Reform* (1914).
67. PP 1911, II (2), 385, 'Housing of the Working Classes Bill'; PP 1913, III (3), 4, 'Housing of the Working Classes Bill'; PP 1914, III (3), 4, 'Housing of the Working Classes Bill'.
68. A Group of Unionists, *A Unionist Agricultural Policy* (1913).
69. SMP GD193/274/244–253, A. Steel-Maitland, 'Cabinet Committees', 4 March 1912, p. 2.
70. SMP GD193/108/3/47–61, [A. Steel-Maitland], [Memorandum for Bonar Law], [1911], p. 13.

71. SMP GD193/152/1/175, A. Steel-Maitland to J. Sandars, 20 Jan. 1911 (copy).

CHAPTER FOUR

1. E.g., P. Adelman, *Victorian Radicalism: The Middle Class Experience 1830–1914* (1984); K. W. Aikin, *The Last Years of Liberal England, 1900–1914* (1972); P.F.Clarke, *Lancashire and the New Liberalism* (Cambridge, 1971); P. F. Clarke, *Liberals and Social Democrats* (Cambridge, 1979); H. V. Emy, *Liberals, Radicals and Social Politics 1892–1914* (Cambridge, 1973); M. Freeden, *The New Liberalism: An Ideology of Social Reform* (Oxford, 1978); B. B. Gilbert, *The Evolution of National Insurance in Great Britain* (1966); J. Harris, *Unemployment and Politics: A Study in English Social Policy 1886–1914* (Oxford, 1972); R. McKibbin, *The Evolution of the Labour Party 1910–1924* (Oxford, 1974); K.O. Morgan, *The Age of Lloyd George* (1971); A. Offer, *Property and Politics 1870–1914: Landownership, Law, Ideology and Urban Development in England* (Cambridge, 1981); H. Pelling, *A Short History of the Labour Party* (1961); P. Rowland, *The Last Liberal Governments*, vol. 1 (1968), vol. 2 (1972), etc.
2. R. M. Punnett, *Front Bench Opposition* (1973).
3. JSP MS Eng. hist. c. 752, fos. 89–92, W. Kenyon-Slaney to A. Balfour, 14 Oct. 1906.
4. S. Ward, 'Land Reform 1880–1914', pp. 461–4; P.W. Raffan, *The Policy of the Land Values Group*, p. 8.
5. S. Ward, 'Land Reform 1880–1914', p. 461.
6. ABP Add. Mss. 49736, fos. 21–32, A. Chamberlain to A. Balfour, 24 Oct. 1907.
7. MSP S(4)60/134, Onslow to Salisbury, 14 June 1907.
8. Central Land Association Records, Institute of Agricultural History, University of Reading, CLA AVII/5, 'Landholders' Central Association. Minute Book', Junior Carlton Club Meeting, 19 April 1907.
9. EOP 173/16/126, anon., [A. Turnor], 'The Land and the Social Problem', 23 March 1907.
10. CLA Records, AVII/I, 'Report of the Proceedings at the Inaugural Meeting of the Landholders' Central Association', 3 July 1907.
11. CLA Records, AX/2, subscriptions book, 1907–1911.
12. C. Bathurst Papers, W. Long to C. Bathurst, 14 July 1909.
13. The Central Land Association, *Its Objects and Present Programme* (1910).
14. MSP S(4)60/134, Onslow to Salisbury, 14 June 1907.
15. 4 HC deb. 5 ser. 28 April 1909, A.J.Tennant, 345.
16. LPD, *100 Points in Liberal Policy and of the Liberal Record* (1914), p. 1.
17. W. A. S. Hewins, *The Apologia of an Imperialist*, vol.1 (1929), p. 309.
18. W. W. Rostow, *The World Economy: History and Prospect* (1978), p. 60.
19. Details of the Liberal legislative programme are to be found in those works cited in note 1.
20. F. W. S. Craig, *British General Election Manifestos 1900–1974*, p. 20.
21. M.D.Pugh, *The Making of Modern British Politics 1867–1939*, p. 132.
22. See H. Pelling, *A History of British Trade Unionism* (1963), pp. 121-148.
23. K. Middlemas, *Politics in Industrial Society* (1979), pp. 51–67.
24. B. Dugdale, *Arthur James Balfour*, vol. 1, pp. 438–9.
25. SMP GD193/352/89–103, J. W. Hills, 'Industrial Unrest. Report of Committee Appointed by the Unionist Social Reform Committee', 11 July 1913, p. 1.
26. PP1952-3, IV (2), Select Committee on Delegated Legislation, *Report*, (1953), p. v.
27. E.g., The Land Enquiry Committee, *The Land: Vol. 1 Rural*, pp. 217-226.
28. *The Times*, 17 July 1909, p. 6c.
29. D. Spring, 'Land and Politics in Edwardian England', *Agricultural History*, 58 (1984), p. 32.
30. E.g., LPD no. 2262, *Tariff Reform Means Happier Dukes* (1909); no. 2263, *Hands Off! the Land* (1909); no. 2265, *The Noble Poachers* (1909).
31. B. Harrison, 'Finding Out How the Other Half Live: Social Research and British

Government since 1780', in *Peaceable Kingdom*, p. 18.
32. See P. Keating (ed.), *Into Unknown England 1866–1913: Selections from the Social Explorers* (Manchester,1976), esp. pp. 11–32.
33. A. Briggs, *Social Thought and Social Action: A Study of the Work of Seebohm Rowntree 1871–1954* (1961), p. 49.
34. E.g., S. Rowntree, *Land and Labour: Lessons from Belgium* (1911); *How the Labourer Lives* (1913); *The Labourer and the Land* (1914).
35. A.Briggs, *Social Thought and Social Action*, pp. 64-66.
36. N. Blewett, *The Peers, the Parties and the People*, pp. 317, 326.
37. LPD no. 2400, *The Liberal Party and Social Reform* (1911).
38. *The Times*, 31 July 1909, p. 9b, d.
39. J. Saville,'Trade Unions and Free Labour: the Background to the Taff Vale Decision', in M.W.Flinn and T.C.Smart (eds.), *Essays in Social History* (Oxford, 1974), pp. 251–76.
40. A.H.H. Matthews, *Fifty Years of Agricultural Politics*, p. 203.
41. A.S.T. Griffith-Boscawen, *Fourteen Years in Parliament*, p. 96.
42. The Land Union, *The New Land Taxes Land Union Guide* (1910), p. 1.
43. Sample of Land Union propaganda, British Library cat. no. 8139.ee.46. For a summary of the Land Union's activities see speech by Pretyman *The Land Union Journal*, May 1911, pp. 8–10.
44. E.g., The Land Union, *The New Land Taxes*.
45. LPD no. 2341, *The New Law-Breakers* (1910).
46. D. Spring, 'Land and Politics in Edwardian England', p. 32.
47. The Land Union, *The New Land Taxes*, p. 5.
48. For the fate of the land taxes and the land valuation see PP 1920, XIX (11), Select Committee on Land Values, *Report*, Cd. 556 (1920), 'Evidence given by Mr.Percy Thompson...', pp. 16–20.
49. 10 & 11 Geo.V, 1920, 18, 'Finance Act 1920', part VI.
50. ABP Add. Mss. 49729, fos. 228–30, A. Balfour to Lansdowne, 13 April 1906 (copy).
51. Onslow, 'A Brief Epitome of Public work', p. 6
52. EOP 173/19/9, 'Note of Proceedings', n.d. [1910]; Third Earl Carrington, Marquess of Lincolnshire diary (on microfilm), Bodleian Library, MS Film 1105, 11 Nov. 1906.
53. Onslow, 'A Brief Epitome of Public work', p. 6
54. EOP 173/17/8, Lansdowne to Onslow, 31 Jan. 1908.
55. J. Morgan, *The House of Lords and the Labour Government 1964–1970* (Oxford, 1975), pp. 122–5.
56. For a useful survey of events see SMP GD193/195/4, J. Seymour Lloyd, 'Parliament Bill (Unionist Committee) The House of Lords and Government Legislation, 1902–1909', April 1911 (printed, 19 pp.); Liberal complaints and further details, e.g., LPD no. 2273, *Is the House of Lords a Fair and Impartial Chamber?* (1909); LPD no. 2314, *The Black Record of the House of Landlords* (1909).
57. P. W. Raffan, *The Policy of the Land Values Group*, p. 9.
58. NUCAS, *The Campaign Guide* (Edinburgh, 1909), pp. 552, 555.
59. W. Bridgeman diary, p. 49.
60. B. Dugdale, *Arthur James Balfour*, vol. 2, p. 55.
61. ACP AC24/1/37, A. Chamberlain to D. Lloyd George, 7 April 1919 (copy).
62. A. Chamberlain, *Politics From Inside* (1936), p. 176.
63. *The Conservative and Unionist*, May 1909, p. 92a; G. Lane Fox diary, in the possession of G.Lane Fox, Bramham Park, West Yorkshire, 13 May 1909.
64. G. Lane Fox diary, 12 Aug. 1909.
65. B.K.Murray, *The People's Budget 1909/10: Lloyd George and Liberal Politics* (Oxford, 1980), p. 193.
66. W. Bridgeman diary, p. 49.
67. E.g., NUCAS, *The Campaign Guide* (Edinburgh, 1900), pp. 562–76.
68. SMP GD193/119/5/66-69, J. Hope to A. Steel-Maitland, 16 Jan. 1914.
69. NUCCA, *The Case Against Radicalism* (1909), pp. 332–3; Lord Newton, *Lansdowne: A Biography* (1929), pp. 360–4.
70. Newton, *Lansdowne*, pp. 384–415; the file SMP GD193/195 contains many reform

schemes; response of the Apaches EOP 173/19/9, 'Notes of Proceedings', n.d. [1910] and accompanying documents.

71. Newton, *Lansdowne*, pp. 416–431; L. S. Amery, *My Political Life: Vol. 1, England Before the Storm 1896–1914* (1953), p. 378.

72. B. Dugdale, *Arthur James Balfour*, vol. 2, pp. 69–70.

73. See, e.g, NUCAS, *The Campaign Guide* (Edinburgh, 1900), pp. 599–600.

74. B. Harrison, *Separate Spheres: The Opposition to Women's Suffrage in Britain* (1978), pp. 27–9.

75. E.g., NUCAS, *The Campaign Guide* (Edinburgh, 1892), p. 286.

76. NUACLUO, *The Campaign Guide* (1914), pp. 53–4.

77. E.g., NLF, *Proceedings...the Fourteenth Annual Meeting...1891*, p. 7.

78. E.g., NUCAS, *The Campaign Guide* (Edinburgh, 1892), p. 287.

79. E.g., NUCAS, *The Campaign Guide* (Edinburgh, 1906), pp. 628–9.

80. J.Vincent (ed.), *The Crawford Papers*, p. 82.

81. *Journal of the Proceedings of the Central Chamber of Agriculture*, 31 Oct. 1905, pp. 211–15; J. Vincent (ed.), *The Crawford Papers*, p. 82.

82. See, e.g., NUCAS, *The Campaign Guide* (Edinburgh, 1909), chs. 6, 9, 10, 14, 15, 16, 18, 19.

83. K.D. Brown, 'The Anti-Socialist Union, 1908-1949', in K. D. Brown (ed.), *Essays in Anti-Labour History*, pp. 234–61.

84. SMP GD193/108/3/47–61, [A. Steel-Maitland], [Memorandum for Bonar Law], [1911], p. 5.

85. E.g., British Library collection of leaflets cat. no. 8139.cc; ASU, *Socialism Exposed. By the Statistical Committee of the Anti-Socialist Union of Great Britain* (1914).

86. See, e.g., ASU, *Anti-Socialist Union Speakers' Handbook* (1911); E. E. Williams, *Socialism and the Family* (1910); J. Richardson, *The Creed of Socialism* (1910); M. D. O'Brien, *Socialism and Character* (1910).

87. K. D. Brown, 'The Anti-Socialist Union, 1908–1949', p. 244.

88. ABP Add. Mss. 49736, fos. 63–5, A. Chamberlain to A. Balfour, 29 Jan. 1910.

89. A. Chamberlain, *Politics From Inside*, p. 228.

90. JSP MS Eng. hist. c. 762, fos. 6–11, A. Acland Hood to J. Sandars, 6 Nov. 1910.

91. See NUCCA leaflets nos. 1218–1449 (1910), and NUCCA *Fighting Campaign Notes* (1910).

92. JSP MS Eng. hist. c. 762, fos. 6–11, A. Acland Hood to J. Sandars, 6 Nov. n.y. [1910].

93. ABP Add. Mss. 49767, fos. 19–22, J. Sandars to W. Short, 2 Nov. 1910, enclosing 'Repeal of Land Taxes Budget 1909–10' (quoted), described as 'Note sent to me by Sir A. Acland Hood'.

94. ACP AC8/6/19, E. Pretyman to A.Chamberlain, 26 Sept. 1910; AC8/6/30, E. Pretyman to A. Chamberlain, 5 Oct. 1910.

95. ABP Add. Mss. 49767, fos. 13–17, J. Sandars to W.Short, 24 Oct. 1910.

96. JSP MS Eng. hist. c. 762, fos. 6–11, A. Acland Hood to J. Sandars, 6 Nov. 1910.

97. E.g., ACP AC8/3/8, A. Balfour to A. Chamberlain, 24 Dec. 1909.

98. ACP AC8/6/26, A. Chamberlain to E. Pretyman, 30 Sept. 1910 (copy).

99. BLP 30/3/43, E. Pretyman to A. Bonar Law, 21 Oct. 1913.

100. AMP MS Milner dep. 40, fos. 91–4, Salisbury *et al.*, 'Report of the Committee Appointed to Consider the Land Policy of the Unionist Party', 12 Aug. 1913, p. 5.

101. *The Land Union Journal*, 1 Dec. 1912, pp. 25–6.

102. E.g., LPD, *100 Points in Liberal Policy and of the Liberal Record* (1914), p. 22.

103. E.g., NUACLUO, *The Campaign Guide* (1914), p. 16; NUCCA, no. 915, *Unionists and the Old Age Pensions Act* (1909).

104. SMP GD193/108/1 contains letters and memoranda relating to the 'Insurance Bill Amendment Committee'.

105. L. S. Amery, *My Political Life*, vol.1, pp. 373–5.

106. SMP GD193/80/5/43–9, A. Steel-Maitland, 'Suggested Policy', n.d. [1912], p. 3.

107. E.g., NUACLUO, *The Campaign Guide* (1914), pp. 379–504.

108. National Union Records, annual conference of 1913, p. 37.

109. *The Times*, 14 Nov. 1913, p. 10b.

110. SMP GD193/80/5/43-49, A. Steel-Maitland, 'Suggested Policy', n.d. [1912], p. 5.

111. See, e.g., NUCCA, no. 1557, *Labour Unrest* (1912); NUACLUO, no. 1611, *Unionists and Trade Unions* (1913); no. 1777, *Fair Wages for the Workers* (1914).

112. See, e.g, NUACLUO, *The Campaign Guide* (1914), pp. 513–604.

113. The Tariff Commission, *Report of the Agricultural Committee* (1906), paras. 370–2.

114. *The Morning Post*, 12 Oct. 1908, p. 7f.

115. Sir G. Parker, *The Land for the People* (1909).

116. [A. Turnor], 'The Land and the Social Problem', 23 March 1907, p. 1.

117. CLA Records, AVII/I, 'Report of Proceedings at the Inaugural Meeting...', p. 6.

118. The Central Land Association, *Its Objects and Present Programme* (1910), p. 9.

119. ABP Add. Mss. 49736, fos. 21–32, A. Chamberlain to A. Balfour, 24 Oct. 1907.

120. ABP Add. Mss. 49776, fos. 199–200, W. Long to A. Balfour, 8 April 1907.

121. ACP AC8/1/3, Onslow, 'Suggestions for an Agricultural Policy', n.d. [March 1909].

122. *The Times*, 7 Oct. 1908, p. 12c.

123. Sir H.Plunkett Papers, the Plunkett Foundation, Oxford, Plunkett diary, 8 March 1909.

124. Sir G. Parker, *The Land for the People* (1909), pp. 1–4.

125. *The Times*, 23 Sept. 1909, p. 7e.

126. NUCCA no. 878, *Back to the Land* (1909).

127. C.Bathurst Papers, J. Collings to C. Bathurst, 28 Jan. 1910.

128. *The Times*, 18 Nov. 1909, p. 9d.

129. ACP AC8/1/12, Onslow to A. Chamberlain, 30 Jan. 1910.

130. EOP 173/19/48, A. Chamberlain to Onslow, 4 Feb. 1910.

131. Lady Theresa Londonderry, Sixth Marchioness of Londonderry Papers, Durham Records Office, D/LO/C.666(91), W. Long to Lady Londonderry, 20 Aug. 1909.

132. Walter Long, First Viscount Long of Wraxall Papers, Wiltshire County Record Office, (hereafter WLP), 947/438, unaddressed, unsigned and undated letter [W. Long to J.Collings, Sept. 1910].

133. *The Conservative and Unionist*, Sept. 1910, p. 148b.

134. JSP MS Eng. hist. c. 760, fos. 188–9, Sir G. Parker to J. Sandars, 6 June 1910. Friction ACP AC4/1/505, A.Chamberlain to Mary Chamberlain, 17 March 1910

135. J. Collings and J. Green, *The Life of the Right Hon. Jesse Collings* (1920), p. 280. Also *The Times*, 15 April 1910, p. 10b.

136. *The Times*, 6 Oct. 1910, p. 7d–e.

137. ABP Add. Mss. 49860, fos. 275–7, A. Balfour to J. Collings, 16 Sept. 1910 (copy).

138. *The Times*, 6 Oct. 1910, p. 7d.

139. E.g., NUCCA no. 1472, *Unionist Policy* (1911), pp. 22–5; NUCCA no. 1520, *Fighting Notes* (1912), pp. 23–8; NUACLUO no. 1563, *The Unionist Land Policy* (1912).

140. SMP GD193/274/245–253, A. Steel-Maitland, 'Cabinet Committees', 4 March 1912, p. 2.

141. E.g., BLP 26/3/28, J. Collings to A. Bonar Law, 17 May 1912; H. Petty-Fitzmaurice, Fifth Marquess of Lansdowne Papers, in the possession of the Marquess of Lansdowne, Bowood Park, Wiltshire, file marked 'Land Policy: Small Holdings etc. 1907–1913', J. Collings to Lansdowne, 3 April 1911; E. Green to M. Dawkins, 18 April 1912; Lovat to Lansdowne, 23 Dec. 1912.

142. 34 HC deb. 5 ser. 23 Feb. 1912, 888–958; 11 HL deb. 5 ser. 7 March 1912, 336–88.

143. WLP 947/439, H. T[rustram] E[ve], 'Random Notes in June, 1912. Suggestions for the Unionist Party', n.d. [1912], p. 7.

144. *Ibid.*, p. 2.

145. Duke of Bedford, *A Great Agricultural Estate* (1897), pp. 4–5.

146. *Ibid.*, pp. 7–8.

147. Plunkett Papers, Bri.1, anon., [Sir H. Plunkett] to Brigstoke, 5 March 1909 (copy).

148. CLA Records, AVII/I, 'Report of the Proceedings at the Inaugural Meeting...', p. 7.

149. CLA Records, AVII/5, 'Landholders' Central Association. Minute Book', provisional committee meeting, 23 April 1907.

150. MSP S(4) 66/42, R. Yerburgh to Salisbury, 28 Sept. 1909; WLP 947/438, R. Yerburgh to Lloyd, 22 Oct. 1909 (copy, quoted).

151. wlp 947/438, W. Long to Derby, 19 Oct. 1909 (copy).

152. C. Turnor, *Land Problems and National Welfare* (1911), p. 4.

153. *The Times*, 23 Dec. 1913, p. 12b.

154. amp ms Milner dep. 159, fos. 154–5, anon. [C. Turnor], 'Proposals for a Landowners' Society', n.d. [Oct. 1913]

155. smp gd193/119/5/99, Lansdowne to A. Steel-Maitland, 31 Oct. 1913.

156. C. Turnor, *Land Problems and National Welfare*, p. 2.

157. For a full exposition of the new gospel see Lord Bledisloe, *The Proper Position of the Landowner in Relation to the Agicultural Industry* (Hull, 1922).

158. E.g., nucas, *The Campaign Guide* (Edinburgh, 1909), pp. 133–210; nuacluo, *The Campaign Guide* (1914), pp. 747–834.

159. E.g., nucas, *The Campaign Guide* (Edinburgh, 1909), pp. 59–81; nuacluo, *The Campaign Guide* (1914), pp. 25–58.

160. E.g., nucas, *The Campaign Guide* (Edinburgh, 1909), pp. 293–328; nuacluo, *The Campaign Guide* (1914), pp. 281–354.

161. E.g., nucas, *The Campaign Guide* (Edinburgh, 1909), pp. 329–33; nuacluo, *The Campaign Guide* (1914), pp. 59–90.

162. E.g., nucas, *The Campaign Guide* (Edinburgh, 1909), pp. 33–58; nuacluo, *The Campaign Guide* (1914), pp. 605–42.

163. E.g., nucca, *Fighting Notes for Speakers* (1909), pp. 81–97; nucca, *Fighting Campaign Notes* (1910), pp. 111–19.

164. E.g., nucas, *The Campaign Guide* (Edinburgh, 1909), pp. 445–57; nuacluo, *The Campaign Guide* (1914), pp. 192–210. For a general picture of the Conservative platform in 1910 see N. Blewett, *The Peers, the Parties and the People*, (1972), profiles of Tory election addresses, pp. 317, 326.

165. L. Davidoff, *The Best Circles: Society, Etiquette and the Season* (1973) attempts a history of high society.

166. E.g., Viscountess Barrrington, *Through Eighty Years* (1936), pp. 194, 227–8; Frances Horner, *Time Remembered* (1933), p. 162; Duke of Portland, *Men, Women and Things* (1937), pp. 1–3, 157; W. Churchill, *My Early Life* (1947), pp. 88–90.

167. A. Clarke (ed.), *'A Good Innings': The Private Papers of Viscount Lee of Fareham* (1974), p. 120.

168. blp 24/5/166, H. Chaplin to A. Bonar Law, 31 Dec. 1911, 'Lady Londonderry becomes very much disposed to do all she can to help.'

169. S. Salvidge, *Salvidge of Liverpool: Behind the Political Scene 1890–1928* (1934), pp. 97–9.

170. Earl Carrington diary, ms Film 1106, 24 June 1909.

171. Arthur Lee, First Viscount Lee of Fareham Papers, the Courtauld Institute, London, Box 1, A. Lee, 'A Good Innings', vol. 1 (privately published autobiography, 1936), p. 403.

172. S. Hoare Papers, S. Hoare, 'At Home and Abroad', p. 83.

173. See J. D. Fair, *British Interparty Conferences: A Study of the Procedure of Conciliation in British Politics, 1867–1921* (Oxford, 1980).

174. jsp ms Eng. hist. c. 760, fol. 210, A. Balfour, 'Memdm', June 1910 (copy).

175. J. Grigg, *Lloyd George: The People's Champion* (1978), pp. 366–7.

176. blp 30/2/26, A. Steel-Maitland to A.Bonar Law, 24 Sept. 1913.

177. *The Times*, 19 Jan. 1914, p. 10a.

178. J. D. Fair, *British Interparty Conferences*, pp. 103–19.

179. E.g., W. J. Reader, *Professional Men: The Rise of the Professional Classes in Nineteenth Century England* (1966); D. Duman, *The English and Colonial Bars in the Nineteenth Century* (1983); F. Engel, *From Clergyman to Don: The Rise of the Academic Profession in Nineteenth Century Oxford* (1983).

180. G.B.Shaw, *The Doctor's Dilemma* (Penguin, 1975), p. 115.

181. Anon., 'The Encroaching Bureaucracy', *Quarterly Review*, 221 (1914), p. 75.

182. See E.W. Cohen, *The Growth of the British Civil Service 1780–1939* (1941), pp. 104–70.

183. pp 1913, lxxviii, (38), Census of England and Wales, *Vol. X, Part I Occupations and*

Industries, Cd 7018 (1913), p. xxiii.
184. F.M.L. Thompson, *Chartered Surveyors: The Growth of a Profession* (1968), esp. pp. 128–201.
185. *Ibid.*, p. 320.
186. 58 HC deb. 5 ser. 17 Feb. 1914, E.Davies, 826.
187. D.H.Chapman, *The Chartered Auctioneers' and Estate Agents' Institute: A Short History* (1970), pp. 19–20.
188. Census of England and Wales, *Vol. X, Part I Occupations and Industries* (1913), p. xxxiii.
189. J. P. Coast, *The Land Agents' Society 1901–1939* [n.d., 1939], p. 29.
190. The Land Agents' Society Records, in the possession of the Royal Institution of Chartered Surveyors, minute book vol. 1, provisional council meeting, 9 Oct. 1901.
191. Earl Carrington diary, MS Film 1105, 3 July 1907.
192. Surveyors' Institution Records, in the possession of the Royal Institution of Chartered Surveyors, minute book of committees 1909–1913, parliamentary bills committee, 16 June 1909. The result was the Surveyors' Institution, *Further Memorandum of the Surveyors' Institution on the Budget Proposals for the Taxation of Land* (1909)
193. Lansdowne Papers, file marked 'Budget 1909–1910', *Memorandum of the Parliamentary Committee of the Land Agents' Society on the Proposals of the Finance Bill, 1909, Affecting Land* (1909); *Memorandum by the Council of the Surveyors' Institution on the Budget Proposals for the Taxation of Land* (1909); *Proposed Duties on Land Values. Statement by the Surveyors' Association* (1909); *Finance Bill 1909. Memorandum by the "1894" Club* (1909).
194. C. Bathurst Papers, W. Cornwallis-West to C. Bathurst, 31 May 1909.
195. WLP 947/451, 'Election of Leader of the Unionist Party in the House of Commons. Meeting of the Conservative and Unionist Party', (typescript report), n.d. [Nov. 1911], unpaginated (p. 5).
196. ACP AC8/1/11, Onslow to A. Chamberlain, 31 May 1909.
197. *The Times*, 14 July 1909, p. 9e.
198. *The Estates Gazette*, 20 Nov. 1909, pp. 833–4.
199. NUACLUO, *The Campaign Guide* (1914), pp. 519–20.
200. BLP 18/8/12, A.Bonar Law to A.Chamberlain, 1 Oct. 1910 (copy).
201. NUACLUO, *The Campaign Guide* (1914), pp. 522–6.
202. See Sykes, *Tariff Reform*, pp. 219–23.
203. See K.D.Brown, 'The Trade Union Tariff Reform Association 1904–1913', *Journal of British Studies*, 9, 2 (1970), pp. 141–53; Sykes, *Tariff Reform*, pp. 221–2.

CHAPTER FIVE

1. Lloyd George speeches: *The Times*, 23 Oct. 1913, pp. 9–10; 31 Oct. 1913, pp. 9–10; 10 Nov. 1913, p. 4; 1 Dec. 1913, p. 64; 5 Feb. 1914, p. 10. Internal summary of the Chancellor's speeches: LGP C/2/3/37, 'Summary of the Proposals Outlined by the Chancellor in his Speeches', n.d. [?June 1914]. PRO CAB 37/120/78, 'Land Policy. Declarations of Ministers', June 1914. LPD, *100 Points in Liberal Policy and of the Liberal Record* (1914), p. 86; LPD no. 2481, *The Nation's Treasure House. How it is to be Opened* (1913).
2. LGP C/15/2/2, 'Ministry of Land', 25 June 1914, p. 2.
3. PRO CAB 37/116/56, 'Some Members of the Cabinet' (p.1), 'Land', 21 Aug. 1913, p. 1.
4. BLP 30/3/50, Milner to A. Bonar Law, 24 Oct. 1913.
5. MSP S(4)73/172, Lansdowne to Salisbury, 8 Oct. 1913.
6. Finances: Mitchell and Deane, *Abstract*, pp. 414–15; local authority clamour: AMC PRO 30/72/44, 'Imperial and Local Taxation. Conference of Administrative Counties and County Boroughs held in the Council Chamber of the Guildhall...24th April, 1913', pp. 62–85; valuation: Departmental Committee on Local Taxation, *Report* (1914), pp. 81–99.
7. AMC Records, PRO 30/72/39, 'Annual Meeting of the Association...26th day of March 1909', p. 46.

8. 6 HC deb. 5 ser. 22 June 1909, D. Lloyd George, 1578.
9. AMC Records, PRO 30/72/39, 'Deputation to the Right Hon. David Lloyd-George M.P.... July 8th, 1909', p. 157.
10. E.g., AMC Records, PRO 30/72/44, 'Imperial and Local Taxation. Conference...', pp. 62 85.
11. United Committee for the Taxation of Land Values, *The Fifth Annual Report of the United Committee for the Taxation of Land Values 1911–1912* (1912), p. 6.
12. A. J. Peacock, 'Land Reform 1880–1914', pp. 240–1.
13. LGP C/15/1/4, Land Values Group, 'Memorial', 18 May 1911.
14. P.W. Raffan, *The Policy of the Land Values Group*, p. 18.
15. SI Records, Box 8, The Land Conference, *Memorandum on the Working of the Finance (1909–10) Act, 1910* (1913), 'Appendix', pp. 19–20, reproduces the memorial.
16. PP 1913, V (5), 175, 'Revenue Bill', clause 11.
17. 62 HC deb. 5 ser. 4 May 1914, D. Lloyd George, 60–85. See also LPD no. 2508, *The 1914 Budget Balance Sheet* (1914).
18. C. Kirby, 'The Attack on the English Game Laws in the Forties', *Journal of Modern History*, 4, 1 (1932), pp. 18–37.
19. A. Simon, 'Joseph Chamberlain and the Unauthorized Programme', (University of Oxford D.Phil. thesis, 1970), pp. 222–68.
20. S. Ward, 'Land Reform in England and Wales 1880–1914', pp. 292–337.
21. The CLHC's journal *The Homeland* is a valuable source.
22. For an account of the campaign by the secretary of the Central Land and Housing Council see LGP C/2/4/20, G. Wallace Carter to D. Lloyd George, 28 May 1914.
23. E.g., *Punch*, 1 Oct. 1913, p. 281; 29 Oct. 1913, p. 369; 17 Dec. 1913, p. 501.
24. A. S. King, 'Some Aspects of the History of the Liberal Party in Britain, 1906–1914', (University of Oxford D.Phil. thesis, 1962), pp. 325–6.
25. *Ibid.*, p. 325.
26. JSP MS Eng. hist. c. 765, fos. 175–6, A. Balfour to J. Sandars, 16 Dec. 1913.
27. BLP 27/1/48, St. Audries to A. Bonar Law, 21 Aug. n.y. [1912].
28. E.g., D. Graham and P. Clarke, *The New Enlightenment: The Rebirth of Liberalism* (1986), pp. 117–140.
29. *The Fifth Annual Report of the United Committee for the Taxation of Land Values 1911–1912* (1912), p. 6.
30. WLP 947/448/8, W. Long to Northumberland, 5 July n.y. [1911] (copy).
31. BLP 30/3/43, E. Pretyman to A. Bonar Law, 21 Oct. 1913.
32. Lord Dynevor, *My Reminiscences* (Carmarthen, 1937), pp. 69–70.
33. See J. Ramsden, *The Age of Balfour and Baldwin*, pp.79–80.
34. A. Griffith-Boscawen, *Memories*, p. 166.
35. BLP 30/1/5, E. Pretyman to A. Bonar Law, 3 Aug. 1913.
36. The Land Union, *The Lost Revenue Bill - And After* (1913), pp. 3–5; *Our Flag*, Sept. 1913, p. 144a.
37. NUACLUO, *The Campaign Guide* (1914), pp. 372–3.
38. *Annual Register* (1914), p. 129.
39. B.B. Gilbert, 'David Lloyd George: The Reform of British Landholding and the Budget of 1914', *Historical Journal*, 21, 1 (1978), p. 136.
40. B.K. Murray, 'Lloyd George and the Land: The Issue of Site Value Rating', in J. Benyon *et al.*, *Studies in Local History* (Cape Town, 1976), p. 47.
41. See 63 HC deb. 5 ser. 22 June 1914, H.Samuel, 1591–2, for a clear summary.
42. PRO CAB 37/120/77, H. Samuel, 'Rating Bill', 29 June 1914.
43. See Robert Sanders, First Baron Bayford of Stoke Trister Papers, Bodleian Library, (hereafter BP), dep. d. 752, Sanders diary, 13 Nov. 1913; SMP GD193/119/5/100–2, Lansdowne to A. Steel-Maitland, 30 Oct. 1913; BLP 31/2/3, J. Hope to A. Steel-Maitland, 1 Jan. 1914 (copy); 31/2/72, H. Chaplin to A. Bonar Law, 30 Jan. 1913.
44. LGP C/5/4/7, D. Lloyd George to P. Illingworth, 24 Oct. 1913 (copy).
45. BLP 39/4/40, A. Steel-Maitland, 'Memorandum for Mr. Bonar Law and Lord Lansdowne', 23 June 1914.
46. E.g., NUACLUO, *The Campaign Guide* (1914), pp. 59–90 (Welsh disestablishment);

pp. 281–354 (Ireland); pp. 175–210 (imperial and national defence); pp. 747–834 (tariff reform).

47. J. A. Cross, *Sir Samuel Hoare: A Political Biography* (1977), p. 30.
48. J. Ramsden, *The Age of Balfour and Baldwin*, pp. 80–2.
49. E.g., NUACLUO no. 1736, *New Landlords for Old* (1914).
50. NUACLUO, *The Campaign Guide* (1914), p. 24.
51. *Our Flag*, March 1914, p. 38a.
52. E.g., 62 HC deb. 5 ser. 6 May 1914, A.Chamberlain, 310; NUACLUO no. 1815, *The 'Official Incubus'* (1914); no. 1820, *The True Urban Land Policy* (1914), p. 11.
53. E.g., SMP GD193/163/21–2, E. V. Hiley, (clerk to Birmingham Town Council), to A. Steel-Maitland, 20 June 1914.
54. E.g., NUACLUO no. 1577, *The Single Tax and the Taxation of Land Values* (1912); NUACLUO, *The Campaign Guide* (1914), pp. 107–32.
55. Mitchell and Deane, *Abstract of British Historical Statistics*, p. 239.
56. E.g., NUACLUO no. 1575, *The Housing Problem* (1912); NUACLUO no. 1566, *Land and Housing* (1912).
57. R. B. Yardley, *Land Value Taxation and Rating* [n.d., 1930], p. 645.
58. NUACLUO no. 1633, *You Want a Cheap House?* (1913).
59. D. Spring, 'Land and Politics in Edwardian England', p. 29.
60. F. M. L. Thompson, *English Landed Society in the Nineteenth Century* (1963), pp. 322–4.
61. E.g., NUACLUO, *The Campaign Guide* (1914), pp. 226–9.
62. PP 1912–13, XLVII (38), Departmental Committee on Tenant Farmers and Sales of Estates, *Report*, Cd 6030 (1912), pp. 4–17.
63. 58 HC deb. 5 ser. 17 Feb. 1914, E. Fitzroy, 820.
64. 58 HC deb. 5 ser. 17 Feb. 1914, E. Royds, 802.
65. 58 HC deb. 5 ser. 17 Feb. 1914, 800.
66. E.g., NUACLUO, *The Campaign Guide* (1914), pp. 240–5; NUACLUO no. 1649, *Wages* (1914).
67. NUACLUO no. 1659, *A Chat About Rent Courts* (1914).
68. Anon., 'The Encroaching Bureaucracy', *Quarterly Review*, 221, (1914), p. 51.
69. *Ibid.*, p. 59.
70. *Ibid.*, p. 75.
71. J. Ramsden, *The Age of Balfour and Baldwin*, p. 67.
72. BLP 30/2/7, Lansdowne to A. Bonar Law, 4 Sept. 1913.
73. A. Chamberlain, *Politics From Inside*, p. 527.
74. *Ibid.*, p. 527.
75. W.A.S. Hewins, *The Apologia of an Imperialist*, vol.1 (1929), p. 303.
76. E.g., *The Times*, 27 Jan. 1912, p. 10d; *The Times*, 22 May 1912, p. 10c.
77. WLP 947/439, H. Trustram Eve to W. Long, 14 July 1912.
78. George Curzon, First Earl Curzon of Kedlestone Papers, India Office Library, Eur.F.112/93, A. Steel-Maitland to Curzon, 19 March 1913, enclosing, anon., untitled, undated, printed memorandum (43 pp.), [Milner], [Memorandum on Land], [March 1913]. Other copies: AMP MS Milner dep.159, fos.9–51; WLP 947/439.
79. C. Bathurst Papers, W. Long to C. Bathurst, 4 July 1912.
80. WLP 947/438, or BLP 27/1/17, anon., untitled and undated report, [B. Peto *et al.*], [Report on Land], [Aug. 1912].
81. See SMP GD193/80/3/2, Committee Investigating Questions Connected with Imperial and Local Taxation, 'Interim Report', 1 Aug. 1912; BLP 30/1/1, W. Hayes Fisher to A. Bonar Law, 1 Aug. 1913; MSP S(4)74/135–6, J. Hope to Salisbury, 7 April 1914.
82. WLP 947/441, W. Hayes Fisher to Lansdowne, 16 Dec. 1913 (copy).
83. AMP MS Milner dep.40, fos. 61–2, E. Talbot to Milner, 15 July 1913.
84. AMP MsMilner dep.40, fos. 91–4, Salisbury *et al.*, 'Report of the Committee Appointed to Consider the Land Policy of the Unionist Party', 12 Aug. 1913. Another copy in the Eve papers. For the minutes of the committee see CLA Records, AIII/2, 'Land Committee'.
85. BLP 31/3/33, Salisbury to A. Bonar Law, 18 Feb. 1914, enclosing anon., untitled and

undated report [Salisbury *et al.*], [Report on Rural Wages], [Feb. 1914]. Another copy SMP GD193/119/5/32–3.

86. *The Times*, 23 June 1913, p. 4a–d.

87. See AMP MS Milner dep. 39 and dep. 159 for extensive material.

88. E.g., *Our Flag*, July 1913, p. 111; NUACLUO no.1674, *Your own Land in Your own Country* (1913).

89. National Union Records, annual conference of 1913, p. 55.

90. NUACLUO no.1803, *Unionist Land Policy as Stated by the Marquess of Lansdowne* (1914).

91. See pp. 142, 144.

92. [Milner], [Memorandum on Land], [March 1913], pp. 1–2.

93. *Ibid.*, esp. pp. 2, 14–27.

94. AMP MS Milner dep. 159, fos. 52–66, L[ansdowne], 'Observations on Lord Milner's Memorandum (Agricultural Reform)', 13 April 1913, pp. 4–11.

95. Salisbury *et al.*, 'Report of the Committee Appointed to Consider the Land Policy of the Unionist Party', 12 Aug. 1913, pp. 6–8.

96. A Group of Unionists, *A Unionist Agricultural Policy* (1913), pp. 12–14, 21–6.

97. National Union Records, annual conference of 1912, p. 38.

98. E.g., NUACLUO no. 1715, *Notes on the Unionist Land Policy* (1913), pp. 9–11; NUACLUO no. 1803, *Unionist Land Policy as Stated by the Marquess of Lansdowne* (1914).

99. [B. Peto *et al.*], [Report on Land], [Aug. 1912], p. 5.

100. MSP S(4)74/27, A. Steel-Maitland to Salisbury, 11 Jan. 1914.

101. SI Records, minute book vol.6, council meeting, 15 April 1912.

102. SMP GD193/119/5/213-217, Joint Committee of the Provincial Divisions of South Wales and Glamorganshire, 'Scheme for a Leasehold Enfranchisement Bill', Feb. 1914.

103. NUACLUO, *The Campaign Guide* (1914), pp. 260–2.

104. WLP 947/441, H.Frank to A.Steel-Maitland, 25 May 1914 (copy).

105. E.g., AMP MS Milner dep. 39, fos. 144–54, G. Wyndham, 'Notes on Lord Milner's Memorandum on Land Policy', n.d. [March 1913], p. 2; MS Milner dep. 159, fos. 75–82, A. Steel-Maitland, 'Land Scheme', n.d. [March 1913], p. 4.

106. See AMP MS Milner dep. 39, fos. 155–6, H. Trustram Eve to Milner, 4 May 1914; MS Milner dep. 41, fos. 9–10, B. Tollemache to Milner, 17 Feb.1914; MS Milner dep. 349(1), fos. 43–4, B. Tollemache to Milner 14 Jan. 1914.

107. E.g., Salisbury *et al.*, 'Report of the Committee Appointed to Consider the Land Policy of the Unionist Party', 12 Aug. 1913, p. 6; L[ansdowne], 'Observations on Lord Milner's Memorandum (Agricultural Reform), p. 15.

108. E.g., ACP AC9/5/45, Lansdowne to A. Chamberlain, 18 April 1913.

109. Lord Robert Cecil Papers, Add. Mss. 51161, fos. 131–2, J. Collings to Lord R. Cecil, 18 April 1914.

110. *The Times*, 11 Oct. 1986, p. 4c, Mrs Thatcher to the party conference.

111. A. Chamberlain, *Politics From Inside*, p. 229. A copy of the proposal was sent to Balfour, ABP Add. Mss. 49736, fos. 69–82, 'P.S. to XVI', 9 March 1910.

112. A. Chamberlain, *Politics From Inside*, p. 229.

113. E.g., *The Times*, 18 Nov. 1909, p. 9d, A. J. Balfour; NUCCA no. 883, *Why the Budget is Bad for the Rates* (1909).

114. ACP AC8/5/13, Lansdowne to A. Chamberlain, 16 March 1910.

115. ACP AC8/6/35, E. Pretyman to A. Chamberlain, 28 Oct. 1910.

116. ACP AC8/6/36, E. Pretyman, 'Outline Proposals', 28 Oct. 1910.

117. Salisbury *et al.*, 'Report of the Committee', p. 5.

118. SMP GD193/80/3/2, Committee Investigating Questions Connected with Imperial and Local Taxation, 'Interim Report', 1 Aug. 1912.

119. SMP GD193/301/5, Unionist Central Office Circular, 12 Aug. 1912, introducing GD193/301/5, 'Imperial and Local Taxation', n.d. [Aug. 1912].

120.NUACLUO no. 1577, *The Single Tax and the Taxation of Land Values* (1912).

121. E.g., NUACLUO no. 1820, *The True Urban Land Policy* (1914), pp. 9-11; The Land Union, *The Finance Bill 1914, Part IV* (1914).

122. ACP AC 8/6/36, E. Pretyman, 'Outline Proposals', 28 Oct. 1910.
123. Mitchell and Deane, *Abstract of British Historical Statistics*, pp. 416–420.
124. ACP AC 8/6/36, E. Pretyman, 'Outline Proposals', 28 Oct. 1910.
125. 51 HC deb. 5 ser. 2 April 1913, A. Bonar Law, 515. NUACLUO no. 1650, *To Help Agriculture* (1913).
126. ACP AC 4/1/1002, A. Chamberlain to Mary Chamberlain, 30 April 1913.
127. 62 HC deb. 5 ser. 6 May 1914, A. Chamberlain, 305.
128. See, e.g., W. Hayes Fisher, 'Ratepayers and the Budget', *Our Flag*, June 1914, pp. 88–9;NUACLUO no. 1815, *The 'Official' Incubus* (1914); NUACLUO no. 1820, *The True Urban Land Policy* (1914), pp. 9–11; NUACLUO no. 1822, *The Liberals and Agricultural Rates* (1914).
129. SMP GD193/163/30, AMC, 'Supplementary Report of the Joint Committee. Imperial and Local Taxation', 25 June 1914; GD193/163/31, 'Addition to the Joint Committee's Report', n.d. [June 1914]. The AMC records for 1914 are not present in the PRO.
130. SMP GD193/163/21-22, E.V.Hiley to A.Steel-Maitland, 20 June 1914.
131. NUACLUO, *The Campaign Guide* (1914), pp. 377–8.
132. 21 HC deb. 5 ser. 13 Feb. 1911, 700–814; 34 HC deb. 5 ser. 16 Feb. 1912, 188–266; 50 HC deb. 5 ser. 11 March 1913, 81–152; 58 HC deb. 5 ser. 19 Feb. 1914, 1157–1270.
133. *The Land Union Journal*, Feb. 1914, p. 107a.
134. E.g., NUACLUO no. 1669, *The Housing Problem* (1913); NUACLUO no. 1685, *Healthy Homes for the People* (1913).
135. BLP 29/5/57, W.Long to A.Bonar Law, 28 June 1913.
136. MSP S(4)73/150, M.Woods to Salisbury, 3 Sept. 1913.
137. NUACLUO, *The History of Housing Reform* [n.d., 1913], p. 70.
138. WLP 947/441, W.Hayes Fisher to Lansdowne, 16 Dec. 1913 (copy).
139. SMP GD193/119/5/73-6, Lansdowne to W.Hayes Fisher, 16 Dec. 1913 (copy).
140. WLP 947/441, anon., untitled and undated memorandum, [W. Long], [Memorandum on Town Tenants], [Dec. 1913].
141. WLP 947/441, W. Hayes Fisher to Lansdowne, 16 Dec. 1913 (copy).
142. WLP 947/441, G.H. Touche to W. Long, 6 Jan. 1914.
143. *The Times*, 19 Jan. 1914, pp. 9e–10a.
144. NUACLUO no. 1736, *New Landlords for Old* (1914).
145. The Land Union, *The Town Tenants' League and its Bill* (1914), p. 3.
146. *The Land Union Journal*, Feb. 1914, p. 82b.
147. Inferred from SMP GD193/274/445-7, anon., [A.Steel-Maitland], 'Memorandum on Land', n.d. [Feb. 1913], p. 1; BLP 29/6/19, J. Baird to A. Bonar Law, 11 July 1913; AMP MS dep. 40 fos. 61–2, E. Talbot to Milner, 25 July 1913.
148. *The Times*, 5 Feb. 1913, p. 6b.
149. For lists of names see documents cited in notes 213 and 214.
150. LGP C/8/2/1, L.Scott to D.Lloyd George, 29 Sept. 1913; C/8/2/2, L.Scott to D.Lloyd George, 6 Oct. 1913.
151. BLP 29/6/19, J.Baird to A.Bonar Law, 11 July 1913. For a list of the committee's members see CLA Records, AIII/2, 'Land Committee'. The agreed report: Salisbury *et al.*, 'Report of the Committee Appointed to consider the Land Policy of the Unionist Party', 12 Aug. 1913.
152. PP 1913, LXVII (38), Census of England and Wales, *Vol. X. Part 1 Occupations and Industries*, Cd 7018, p. xlv.
153. S. Sturmey, 'Owner-Farming in England and Wales, 1900–1950', in W.E. Minchinton (ed.), *Essays in Agrarian History*, vol. 2 (1968), p. 287.
154. ABP Add. Mss. 49797, fos. 96–104, H.Chaplin, 'Reply to the Proposals for Omitting the Shilling Duty on Corn', Jan. 1910, p. 8.
155. *The Agricultural Annual and Mark Lane Express Almanac 1908* (1908), p. 66.
156. BLP 31/2/32, H.W.Palmer (NFU secretary) to A.Bonar Law, 12 Jan. 1914. The NFU's records are deposited in the Institute of Agricultural History, the University of Reading.
157. ABP Add. Mss. 49765, fos. 194–195, J.Sandars to A.Balfour, 16 Dec. 1908.
158. C.Turnor Papers, 4 Turnor 3/5, A.Steel-Maitland to C.Turnor, 25 Oct. 1913.
159. Plunkett Papers, Plunkett diary, 18 June 1907.

160. Leslie Renton Papers, House of Lords Record Office, Box 8, fol. 95, J.Passmore to L.Renton, 16 July 1908.
161. Lady Londonderry Papers, D/LO/C.666(238), W.Long to Lady Londonderry, 9 March 1913.
162. BLP 30/2/32, C.Turnor to A.Bonar Law, 28 Sept. 1913.
163. BLP 28/2/66, H.W.Palmer to A.Bonar Law, 16 Jan. 1913.
164. See B.Gilbert, 'Agriculture *versus* Bonar Law', *The English Review*, vol. 18, Aug./ Nov. 1914, pp. 91–99.
165. B.Gilbert, *Farmers and Tariff Reform* (1913); *What the Farmer Wants* (1914).
166. See R.J.Olney, *Lincolnshire Politics 1832–1885* (Oxford, 1973).
167. E.g., BLP 30/3/51, C. Campbell and G. Bellwood to A. Bonar Law, 24 Oct. 1913; 34/ 4/24, G. Bellwood to A. Bonar Law, 11 Nov. 1913.
168. B.Gilbert, 'Agriculture *versus* Bonar Law', p. 97. The Tory MP was Rowland Hunt, who ceaselessly pestered Bonar Law, e.g., BLP 31/2/8, R.Hunt to A.Bonar Law, 2 Jan. 1913; 32/1/91, R.Hunt to A.Bonar Law, 31 March 1914.
169. BLP 30/3/4, Lansdowne to A.Bonar Law, 4 Oct. 1913.
170. BP dep. d. 752, Sanders diary, 8 Feb. 1914.
171. BLP 30/3/62, A.Steel-Maitland to A.Bonar Law, 28 Oct. 1913.
172. *The Times*, 14 Nov. 1913, p. 10a.
173. E.g., NUACLUO no. 1671, *Farmers and Rates* (1913); NUACLUO no. 1739, *Fighting Notes* (1914), p. 99; NUACLUO no. 1803, *Unionist Land Policy as Stated by the Marquess of Lansdowne* (1914).
174. A.H.H.Matthews, *Fifty Years of Agricultural Politics*, pp. 203–7.
175. BLP 30/3/62, A.Steel-Maitland to A.Bonar Law, 28 Oct. 1913.
176. SMP GD193/119/5/121, R.Prothero to A.Steel-Maitland, 28 Oct. 1913.
177. BLP 30/3/62, A.Steel-Maitland to A.Bonar Law, 28 Oct. 1913.
178. BLP 30/3/68, Lansdowne to A.Bonar Law, 29 Oct. 1913.
179. E.g., NUACLUO, *The Campaign Guide* (1914), p. 250.
180. 59 HC deb. 5 ser. 6 March 1914, 763–820; 16 HL deb. 5 ser. 16 July 1914, 1219–27.
181. *Punch*, 22 Oct. 1913, p. 349.
182. *The Times*, 23 June 1913, p. 4c, Lansdowne at Matlock Bath.
183. *The Times*, 8 Nov. 1913, p. 6c.
184. SMP GD193/119/5/83-88, H.Trustram Eve, 'Wages', 2 Nov. 1913, p. 4.
185. C.Bathurst Papers, W.Long to C.Bathurst, 4 July 1912.
186. [B.Peto *et al.*], [Report on Land], [Aug. 1912], p. 7.
187. *Ibid.*, p. 6.
188. BLP 27/1/48, St.Audries to A.Bonar Law, 21 Aug. n.y. [1912].
189. BP dep. d. 752, Sanders diary, 13 Oct. 1912.
190. BLP 28/1/12, B.Peto to A.Bonar Law, 9 Dec. 1912.
191. [Milner], [Memorandum on Land], [March 1913], pp. 35–6.
192. *Ibid.*, pp. 38–43, 'Appendix. Note on Some Experiments in Profit Sharing'.
193. 52 HC deb. 5 ser. 7 May 1913, 2079.
194. MSP S(4)73/134–5, F.Mildmay to Salisbury, 8 Aug. 1913.
195. C.Bathurst Papers, W.Long to C.Bathurst, 24 April 1913.
196. BLP 30/3/77, W.Long to A.Bonar Law, 31 Oct. 1913.
197. C.Turnor Papers, 4 Turnor 3/2, P.Lloyd Graeme to C.Turnor, 16 June 1913; P.Lloyd Graeme to C.Turnor, 17 June n.y., [1913]; C.Bathurst Papers, Lansdowne to C.Bathurst, 17 June 1913.
198. *The Times*, 23 June 1913, p. 4d.
199. Salisbury *et al.*, 'Report of the Committee', p. 8.
200. BLP 30/1/31, A.Thynne to E.Talbot, 22 Aug. 1913 (copy).
201. BLP 30/1/31, E.Talbot to A.Bonar Law, 29 Aug. 1913.
202. BLP 30/2/7, Lansdowne to A.Bonar Law, 4 Sept. 1913.
203. BLP 30/2/33, E.Talbot to A.Bonar Law, 28 Sept. 1913.
204. BLP 30/2/17, Lansdowne to A.Bonar Law, 20 Sept. 1913.
205. SMP GD193/119/5/139–43, A.Steel-Maitland, 'Memorandum on Land Question', n.d. [29 Oct. 1913], quotation p. 1.

206. BP dep. d. 752, Sanders diary, 13 Nov. 1913.

207. SMP GD193/119/5/77, anonymous report, 6 Dec. 1913.

208. BLP 31/1/6, C.Bathurst to A.Bonar Law, 4 Dec. 1913.

209. ABP Add. Mss. 49863, fos. 44–5, E.Talbot to J.Sandars, 13 Dec. 1913.

210. See, e.g., BLP 31/1/29, Lansdowne to A.Bonar Law, 13 Dec. 1913; BP dep. d. 752, Sanders diary 13 Nov. 1913; SMP GD193/119/5/57–8, Lansdowne to A.Steel-Maitland, 20 Jan. 1914; MSP s(4)74/45–6, A.Steel-Maitland to Salisbury, 20 Jan. 1914; SMP GD193/119/5/54–6, A.Steel-Maitland to Lansdowne, 22 Jan. 1914 (copy).

211. A Group of Unionists, *A Unionist Agricultural Policy*, pp. 9-12.

212. G.Raine, *Lloyd George and the Land* (1914), pp. 85-91. SRG promotion: SMP GD 193/119/5/47, J.M.Fraser to A.Steel-Maitland, 6 Feb. 1914; GD193/119/5/51. A.B.P., 'Mr.G.Raine's Book 'Lloyd George and the Land'', 6 Feb. 1914.

213. 61 HC deb. 5 ser. 21 April 1914, 776; PP 1914, I (1), 196, 'Agricultural Employment Boards Bill'.

214. BLP 30/4/12, W.Astor *et al.* to A.Bonar Law, 8 Nov. 1913.

215. C.Turnor Papers, 4 Turnor 3/5, C.Turnor to H.Trustram Eve, 23 April 1914 (copy).

216. *The Times*, 14 Nov. 1913, p. 10b–c.

217. BLP 30/3/66, E.Pretyman to A.Bonar Law, 29 Oct. 1913.

218. *The Times*, 26 Nov. 1913, p. 5a.

219. E.g., BLP 30/4/60, J.Hills to A.Bonar Law, 29 Nov. 1913; C.Turnor Papers, 4 Turnor 3/5, C.Turnor to A.Steel-Maitland, 30 Nov. 1913 (copy).

220. SMP GD193/119/5/77, anonymous report, 6 Dec. 1913.

221. SMP GD193/119/5/106–10, G.Terrell, 'North West Wilts The Policy as to Agricultural Wages', 29 Oct. 1913.

222. AMP MS Milner dep. 40, fo. 168, A.Steel-Maitland to Milner, 29 Oct. 1913.

223. SMP GD193/119/5/49–0, Salisbury to A.Steel-Maitland, 10 Feb. 1914.

224. CLA Records, AII/3, excutive committee minutes, 10 Dec. 1913.

225. CLA Records, AVII/3, A.H.Smith, typescript circular, 19 Dec. 1913.

226. MSP s(4)73/215, A.H.Smith to Salisbury, 31 Dec. 1913.

227. WLP 947/439, C.Bathurst to W.Long, 2 Jan. 1914.

228. WLP 947/439, A.H.Smith to W.Long, 1 Jan. 1914; A.H.Smith to W.Long, 13 Jan. 1914; A.H.Smith to W.Long, 15 Jan. 1914.

229. E.g., NUACLUO no. 1649, *Wages* (1914); NUACLUO, *The Campaign Guide* (1914), pp. 240–5.

230. E.g., NUACLUO no. 1722, *A Practical Method of Raising Labourers' Wages* (1913); NUACLUO no. 1743, *How Unionists Raised Labourers' Wages and What Mr. Lloyd George Did* (1914).

231. SMP GD193/119/5/70, [A.Steel-Maitland] to St. Audries, 20 Dec. 1913 (copy).

232. SMP GD193/119/5/71–2, [St.Audries] to [A.Steel-Maitland], [Dec. 1913].

233. SMP GD193/119/5/63–5, Salisbury to A.Steel-Maitland, 13 Jan. 1914.

234. SMP GD193/119/5/149–59, unsigned and undated memorandum [Salisbury], [Wages], [2 Jan. 1914]; GD193/119/5/34-46, Salisbury, 'Memorandum on the Agricultural Labourers' Wages Question', 20 Jan. 1914.

235. BLP 31/3/33, W.Long to Salisbury, 8 Feb. 1914 (copy); SMP GD193/119/5/57–8, Lansdowne to A.Steel-Maitland, 20 Jan. 1914.

236. MSP s(4)74/45–6, A.Steel-Maitland to Salisbury, 20 Jan. 1914; SMP GD193/119/5/54-56, [A.Steel-Maitland] to Lansdowne, 22 Jan. 1914 (copy).

237. BLP 31/3/33, Salisbury to A.Bonar Law, 18 Feb. 1914, enclosing [Salisbury *et al.*], [Report on Rural Wages], [18 Feb. 1914].

238. SMP GD193/119/5/25-31, Salisbury, 'Note', 13 Feb. 1914.

239. MSP s(4)74/77, E.Pretyman to Salisbury, 15 Feb. 1914; MSP s(4)74/80, J.Hills to Salisbury, 17 Feb. 1914.

240. SMP GD193/119/5/1–2, [A.Steel-Maitland], 'Memorandum', 6 April 1914.

241. 15 HL deb. 5 ser. 21 April 1914, Salisbury, 942–55; 15 HL deb. 5 ser. 21 April 1914, Lansdowne, 976–89.

242. NUACLUO, *Gleanings and Memoranda*, vol. 42 (June 1914), pp. 543–4.

243. NUACLUO no. 1803, *Unionist Land Policy as Stated by the Marquess of Lansdowne* (1914)

244. NUACLUO no. 1813, *Unionists and the Agricultural Labourer* (1914).
245. W.A.S. Hewins, *The Apologia of an Imperialist*, vol.1, p. 307.
246. A. Webber, 'Government Policy and British Agriculture 1917–1939' (University of Kent PH.D. thesis, 1982), pp. 402–3.
247. E.g., Lloyd George's speeches: *The Times*, 13 Oct. 1913, p. 13a, d; 23 Oct. 1913, p. 10c; 23 Dec. 1913, p. 12a.
248. C. Turnor Papers, 4 Turnor 3/5, Malmesbury to C.Turnor, 18 Oct. 1913.
249. Willoughby de Broke, *The Passing Years* (1924), p. 167.
250. C.Morrison-Bell Papers, House of Lords Record Office, His.Col.193, C.Morrison-Bell, 'A Journey with Maps. A Back-Bencher's Story' (unpublished typescript memoir, n.d.), ch. 6, p. 14
251. Lord H.Cavendish Bentinck, *Tory Democracy* (1918), p. 135.
252. Willoughby de Broke, *Hunting the Fox* (1920), pp. 5–6.
253. M.Fforde, 'The Conservative Party and Real Property in England, 1900–1914', pp. 20–4.
254. C.Morrison-Bell, 'A Journey with Maps', ch. 9, p. 2.
255. *The Land Union Journal*, April 1914, pp. 157–9.
256. *Transactions of the Surveyors' Institution*, 41 (1908–9), 'The Opening Address by Howard Martin...November 9th. 1908', pp. 17–18.
257. BP dep. d. 752, Sanders diary, 13 Nov. 1913.
258. *The Times*, 30 Oct. 1913, p. 10c.
259. BLP 30/3/60, W.J.Marshall to A.Bonar Law, 27 Oct. 1913, enclosing 'Memorandum of Radical M.Ps & Shootings'
260. NUACLUO no. 1719, *Do Liberals Practice* [sic] *What They Preach?* (1913).
261. NUACLUO no. 1803, *Unionist Land Policy as Stated by the Marquess of Lansdowne* (1914).
262. A Group of Unionists, *A Unionist Agricultural Policy*, p. 4.
263. AMP MS Milner dep. 159, fos. 1–8, C.Turnor, 'Land and Labour and the Unionist Party', n.d. [1912], p. 8.
264. WLP 947/439, H.Trustram Eve to W.Long, 14 July 1912.
265. H.Trustram Eve, *Single Tax and Rating on Site Values* (1912); H.Trustram Eve, *Taxation and Rating on Site Values* (Bedford, 1912); H.Trustram Eve and E.Savill, *The Taxation of Land Values: The Case Against* (1913).
266. Land Agents' Society Records, minute book vol. 2, council meeting, 12 July 1912.
267. *The Times*, 10 Nov. 1913, p. 4c.
268. SMP GD193/119/5/3–7, H.Banks to A.Steel-Maitland, 7 May 1914.
269. Knight, Frank and Rutley, *The Land Question* (1913).
270. BLP 30/2/26, A.Steel-Maitland to Lansdowne, 24 Sept. 1913.
271. SI Records, minute book vol. 6, council meetings, 2 July 1913 and 29 July 1913.
272. LAS Records, minute book vol. 2, council meeting, 12 July 1912.
273. BLP 30/1/5, E.Pretyman to A.Bonar Law, 3 Aug. 1913.
274. SI Records, Box 8, The Land Conference, *Memorandum on the Working of the Finance (1909–10) Act, 1910* (14 July 1913).
275. Lansdowne Papers, file marked 'Political', folder marked 'Imperial and Local Taxation 1908–1914', Malcolm Fraser to Lansdowne, 16 March 1914, enclosing H.Trustram Eve, 'Imperial and Local Taxation', 16 March 1914.
276. E.g., *The Times*, 14 Nov. 1913, p. 10b, Bonar Law; *The Times*, 19 Nov. 1913, p. 12b, Lansdowne.
277. 58 HC deb. 5 ser. 17 Feb. 1914, D.Lloyd George, 837–8.
278. BLP 30/3/66, E.Pretyman to A.Bonar Law, 29 Oct. 1913.
279. The Central Land Association, *Official Circular*, March 1914, p. 3b.
280. H.Trustram Eve Papers, in the possession of J.R.Trustram Eve, London, A.Steel-Maitland to H.Trustram Eve, 19 Dec. 1913.
281. *The Times*, 10 Feb. 1914, p. 12b.
282. The Land Conference, *The Land Problem*, (1914).
283. MSP S(4)74/170–2, H.Trustram Eve to Salisbury, n.d. [Jan. 1914].
284. E.g., *The Times*, 20 Jan. 1914, p. 6c; *Our Flag*, Feb. 1914, pp. 18b–19a.

200   *Notes*

285. SMP GD193/119/5/117–20, 'Points in the Land Report', n.d..
286. SMP GD193/119/5/100–2, Lansdowne to A.Steel-Maitland, 30 Oct. 1913.
287. SMP GD193/119/5/59, C.H.Simpson to J.Boraston, 21 Jan. 1914.
288. LAS Records, minute book vol. 2, parliamentary committee meeting, 7 Nov. 1913.
289. LAS Records, minute book vol. 2, parliamentary committee meeting, 1 Oct. 1914.
290. Lord Ernle, *Whippingham to Westminster* (1938), p. 207.
291. The Central Land Association, *Earnings of Agricultural Labourers for Each County of England and Wales for the Year 1912-1913* (1913).
292. SI Records, Box 8, 'The Report of the Urban Land Enquiry Committee', Dec. 1914.
293. AMP MS Milner dep. 40, fos. 238–9, Clinton to Milner, 27 Dec. 1913.
294. AMP MS Milner dep. 40, fos. 240–1, 'The Land Conference. Resolutions'.
295. E.g., P.F.Clarke, 'The Electoral Position of the Liberal and Labour Parties 1910–1914', *English Historical Review*, 90 (1975), pp. 826-836; R. McKibbin, *The Evolution of the Labour Party 1910–1924* (Oxford, 1974); H.Pelling, 'Labour and the Downfall of Liberalism', in H. Pelling, *Popular Politics and Society in Late Victorian Britain* (1968), pp. 101–20; R.Douglas, 'Labour in Decline', in K.H.D. Brown (ed.), *Essays in Anti-Labour History*, pp. 105–25; K.O. Morgan,*The Age of Lloyd George* (1971); H.C.G.Matthew, R.I.McKibbin and J.A.Kay, 'The Franchise Factor in the Rise of the Labour Party', *English Historical Review*, 91 (1976), pp. 723–53. For a survey of the debate and more detailed references see R.Tanner, ' Political Realighment in England and Wales, c. 1906–1922', (University of London PH.D thesis, 1985), esp. pp. 12–27.
296. F.W.S.Craig, *British Parliamentary Election Results 1885-1918* (1974), pp. 226, 252, 273.
297. BLP 39/4/40, A.Steel-Maitland, 'Memorandum for Mr.Bonar Law and Lord Lansdowne', 23 June 1914.
298. LGP c/2/4/20, G.Wallace Carter to D.Lloyd George, 28 May 1914.
299. LGP c/2/4/22, W.Finnemore to D.Lloyd George, 29 May 1914; c/2/4/24, F.Burn to D.Lloyd George, 29 May 1914; c/2/4/28, J.Corrie to D.Lloyd George, 2 June 1914.
300. LGP c/2/4/27, W.W.Crook to D.Lloyd George, 31 May 1914; c/2/4/23, E.Perry to D.Lloyd George, 29 May 1914; c/2/4/26, H.Storey to D.Lloyd George, 29 May 1914.
301. LGP c/2/4/27, W. W.Crook to D.Lloyd George, 29 May 1914.
302. LGP c/2/4/30, B. S. Rowntree to D. Lloyd George, 19 June 1914 (reference to preparations for the autmun campaign).
303. LGP c/2/4/16, B.S.Rowntree to D.Lloyd George, 12 May 1914; c/2/4/20, G.Wallace Carter to D.Lloyd George, 29 May 1914, p. 5. Many of the regional reports cited above contain similar advice.
304. LGP c/2/4/20, G.Wallace Carter to D.Lloyd George, 29 May 1914, p. 3.
305. BLP 39/4/40, A.Steel-Maitland, 'Memorandum for Mr.Bonar Law and Lord Lansdowne', 23 June 1914.
306. E.g., LPD no. 2509, *The Budget of 1914 and the Ratepayer* (1914); no. 2515, *The Government and the Ratepayer* (1914).
307. LGP c/2/4/29, D.Lloyd George to Chairman, 'Meeting Liberal 12,000, Reform Club, Manchester' (copy of telegram), 12 June 1914.
308. J.Ramsden, *The Age of Balfour and Baldwin* , p. 85.
309. K.O.Morgan, *The Age of Lloyd George*, p. 51.
310. H.Pelling, 'The Working Class and the Origins of the Welfare State', in H.Pelling, *Popular Politics and Society in Late Victorian Britain* (1968), p. 13.

CONCLUSION: VICTORIAN VALUES

1. E.g., F.Pym, *The Politics of Consent* (1984) pp.174–5; W.Waldegrave, *Binding the Leviathan: Conservatism and the Future* (1978), pp. 47–9; I.Gilmour, *Inside Right: A Study of Conservatism* (1978), pp. 27–39.
2. J.M.Keynes, *Essays in Biography* (1961), p. 47.
3. SMP GD193/159/6/15–18, A.Steel-Maitland to A.Glazebrook, 26 Aug. 1913 (copy).
4. Compare Conservative Central Office, *Campaign Notes 1885* (1885), with NUACLUO, *The Campaign Guide* (1914).

5. SMP GD193/159/6/15–18, A.Steel-Maitland to A.Glazebrook, 26 Aug. 1913 (copy).
6. SMP GD193/80/5/50, illegible initials, 'Upon the Necessity, the Method and the Limits of Social Reform Considered as a Part of Unionist Policy', n.d. [second part of 1909], p. 32.
7. *Ibid.*, pp. 4–6 (rearranged text).
8. Viscount Simon, *Retrospect* (1952), p. 64.
9. C. Morrison-Bell, 'A Journey with Maps' (unpublished typescript memoir), ch. 10, p. 1.
10. For an account of the Mrs Thatcher's first government see M.Holmes, *The First Thatcher Government 1979–1983: Contemporary Conservatism and Economic Change* (1985).
11. *The Times*, 11 Oct. 1986, p. 4c.
12. R.Blake, *The Conservative Party from Peel to Thatcher*, pp. 322–3; M.Holmes, *The First Thatcher Government*, pp. 8–9.
13. I.Gilmour, *Inside Right*, p.109.
14. F.Hayek, *The Road to Serfdom* (1944), p. 159.
15. See, e.g., E.M.Sigsworth (ed.), *In Search of Victorian Values: Aspects of Nineteenth-Century Thought and Society* (Manchester, 1988).
16. Conservative Central Office, file marked 'Thatcher 1983–1984', Independent Radio News, 'Interview with the Prime Minister', 15 April 1983, pp. 7–8.
17. D.Graham and P.Clarke, *The New Enlightenment: The Rebirth of Liberalism* (1986).
18. M.Holmes, *The First Thatcher Government*, p. 209.
19. A.Solzhenitsyn, *Warning to the Western World* (1976), pp. 30, 45.
20. H.H. John Paul II, *Sollicitudo Rei Socialis* (Vatican City, 1988), esp. pp. 47–53.

Select Bibliography

If the amount of primary material on this period is mountainous, the quantity of secondary literature is deluvial. Consequently, and inevitably, this is a select bibliography. The secondary works listed below have either been cited in the text or are of strict utility.

1. PRIVATE PAPERS

Birmingham University Library
Papers of Austen Chamberlain,
Joseph Chamberlain,
Neville Chamberlain.

Bodleian Library, Oxford
Papers of C. Wynn-Carrington, 3rd Earl Carrington, 1st Marquess of Lincolnshire (on microfilm).
H.H. Asquith, First Earl of Oxford and Asquith,
A.S.T. Griffith-Boscawen,
H. Gwynne,
A. Milner, 1st Viscount Milner,
E. Pollock, 1st Viscount Hanworth of Hanworth,
J.S. Sandars,
R. Sanders, 1st Baron Bayford of Stoke Trister,
W. Palmer, 2nd Earl of Selborne,
R. Palmer, 3rd Earl of Selborne,
L. Worthington Evans,
the John Johnson Collection,
the Conservative Party records.

The Bothwick Institute, York
Papers of E. Wood, 1st Earl of Halifax.

British Library, London
Papers of A. J. Balfour, 1st Earl Balfour of Balfour,
Lord R. Cecil, 1st Viscount Cecil of Chelwood,
H. Giffard, 1st Earl Halsbury,
H. Gladstone, 1st Viscount Gladstone,
C. Ritchie.

Conservative Central Office
Party press files 1977–86.

Cambridge University Library
Papers of S. Baldwin, 1st Earl Baldwin of Bewdley,
S. Hoare, 1st Viscount Templewood.

Churchill College, Cambridge
Papers of H. Page Croft, 1st Baron Croft of Bournemouth.

Courtauld Institute, London
Papers of A. Lee, 1st Baron Lee of Fareham.

Durham County Record Office
Papers of Lady Theresa Londonderry, 6th Marchioness of Londonderry.

Hereford Record Office
Papers of J. Arkwright.

House of Lords Record Office
Papers of A. Bonar Law,
D. Blumenfeld,
A. Goulding, 1st Baron Wargrave,
D. Lloyd George, 1st Earl of Dwyfor,
C. Morrison-Bell,
L. Renton,
R. Verney, 19th Baron Willoughby de Broke.

India Office Library
Papers of George Curzon, 1st Earl Curzon of Kedlestone.

Institute of Agricultural History, University of Reading
Records of the Central Land Association,
the National Farmers' Union,
the National Union of Agricultural Workers.

Guildford Muniment Room
Papers of W. Onslow, 4th Earl of Onslow.

Lincolnshire Archives Office
Papers of C. Turnor.

The Plunkett Foundation, Oxford
Papers of Sir Horace Plunkett.

Public Record Office
Records of the Association of Municipal Corporations,
the Cabinet (1885–1914).

Reading University Library
Papers of W. Astor, 2nd Viscount Astor.

Royal Institution of Chartered Surveyors, London
Records of the Auctioneers' and Estate Agents' Institute of the United Kingdom,
the Land Agents' Society,
the Surveyors' Institution.

The Scottish Record Office, Edinburgh
Papers of A. Steel-Maitland.

Wiltshire County Record Office
Papers of W. Long, 1st Viscount Long of Wraxall.

Privately held
Papers of C. Bathurst, 1st Viscount Bledisloe, in the possession of Viscount Bledisloe, Lydney Park, Gloucestershire;
W. Bridgeman, 1st Viscount Bridgeman of Leigh, in the possession of Viscount Bridgeman, Minsterly, Shropshire;
G. Lane Fox, in the possession of G. Lane Fox, Bramham Park, W. Yorkshire;
H. Petty-Fitzmaurice, 5th Marquess of Lansdowne, in the possession of the Marquess of Lansdowne, Bowood Park, Wiltshire;
J. Gascoyne-Cecil, 4th Marquess of Salisbury, in the possession of the Marquess of Salisbury, Hatfield House, Hertfordshire;
H. Trustram Eve, in the possession of J.R.Trustram Eve, London.

2. THESES

A.Cooper, 'The Transformation of Agricultural Policy 1912–1936: A Study in Conservative Politics' (University of Oxford D.Phil. thesis, 1979).

D. Englander, 'Landlord and Tenant in Urban Britain: The Politics of Housing Reform, 1838–1924' (University of Warwick Ph.D. thesis, 1979).

M.Fforde, 'The Conservative Party and Real Property in England, 1900–1914' (University of Oxford D.Phil. thesis, 1985).

J.R.Fisher, 'Public Opinion and Agriculture 1875–1900' (University of Hull Ph.D thesis, 1973).

R.B.Jones, 'The Conservative Party, 1906–1910' (University of Oxford B.Litt. thesis, 1960).

A.S.King, 'Some Aspects of the History of the Liberal Party in Britain, 1906–1914' (University of Oxford D.Phil. thesis, 1962).

M.Madden, 'The National Union of Agricultural Workers 1906–1956' (University of Oxford B.Litt. thesis, 1957).

J.M.McEwen, 'Conservative and Unionist MPS 1914–1939 (University of London Ph. D. thesis, 1959).

A.Offer, 'Property and Politics: A Study of Landed and Urban Property in England between the 1880s and the Great War' (University of Oxford D.Phil. thesis, 1978).

A.J.Peacock, 'Land Reform 1880–1919: A Study of the Activities of the English Land Restoration Leagues and the Land Nationalisation Society' (University of Southampton M.A. thesis, 1961).

J.A.Ramsden, 'The Organisation of the Conservative and Unionist Party in Britain, 1910–1930' (University of Oxford D.Phil. thesis, 1974).

J.Ridley, 'Leadership and Management in the Conservative Party in Parliament, 1906–1914' (University of Oxford D.Phil. thesis, 1985)

W.D.Rubinstein, 'Men of Property: the Wealthy in Britain 1809–1939' (John Hopkins University Ph. D. thesis, 1975).

D.C.Savage, 'The General Election of 1886 in Great Britain and Ireland' (University of London Ph. D. thesis, 1958).

A.Simon, 'Joseph Chamberlain and the Unauthorized Programme' (University of Oxford D.Phil. thesis, 1970).

R.Tanner, 'Political Realignment in England and Wales, c. 1906–1922' (University of London Ph. D. thesis, 1985).

S.B.Ward, 'Land Reform in England 1880–1914' (University of Reading Ph. D. thesis, 1976).

A.Webber, 'Government Policy and British Agriculture 1917–1939' (University of Kent Ph. D. thesis, 1982).

P.R.Wilding, 'Government and Housing: A Study in the Development of Social Policy 1906–1939' (University of Manchester Ph. D. thesis, 1970).

W.I.Wilks, 'Jesse Collings and the 'Back to the Land' Movement' (University of Birmingham M.A. thesis, 1964).

3. PARLIAMENTARY PAPERS

i. Bills and Acts 1886–1914

ii. House of commons and House of Lords Debates, 1880–1914, third, fourth and fifth series

iii. Reports, in chronological order

Royal Commission on the Housing of the Working Classes, *First Report* (1884), Cd 4402.

Select Committee on Town Holdings, *Report* (1889).

Select Committee on Small Holdings, *Report* (1890).

Select Committee on Town Holdings, *Report* (1892).

H.H.Fowler, *Report on Local Taxation* (1893).
Royal Commission on Labour, *Fifth and Final Report* (1894), Cd 7421.
Royal Commission on the Aged Poor, *Report* (1895), Cd 7684.
Royal Commission on Agricultural Depression, *Second Report* (1896), Cd. 7981; *Final Report* (1897), Cd 8540.
Departmental Committee on Old Age Pensions, *Report* (1898), Cd 1891.
Select Committee on the Aged Deserving Poor, *Report* (1899).
Royal Commission on Local Taxation, *Local Rates in England and Wales. Valuation and Collection* (1899), Cd 9141.
Departmental Committee on the Financial Aspects of the Proposals Made by the Select Committee of House of Commons of 1899 about the Aged Deserving Poor, *Report* (1900), Cd 67.
Royal Commission on Local Taxation, *Final Report (England and Wales)* (1901), Cd 638.
Select Committee on Municipal Trading, *Report* (1903).
Board of Agriculture, *Decline in the Agricultural Population of Great Britain 1881-1906* (1906), Cd 3273.
Select Committee on the Land Values Taxation etc. (Scotland) Bill, *Report* (1906).
Departmental Committee on Small Holdings, *Report* (1906) Cd 3277.
Census of England and Wales, *Vol.X, Occupations and Industries* (1913).
Departmental Committee on Local Taxation, *Final Report* (1914), Cd 7315.
Select Committee on Land Values, *Report* (1920), Cd 556.
Select Committee on Procedure on Public Business, *Special Report* (1931).
Select Committee on Delegated Legislation, *Report* (1953).

4. NEWSPAPERS AND JOURNALS

Agricultural Gazette
Annual Register
The Conservative
The Conservative and Unionist
Co-operation in Agriculture
The Economist
The English Review
The Estates Gazette
Handy Notes on Current Politics
The Homeland
Journal of the Proceedings of the Central Chamber of Agriculture
The Land Agents' Journal
The Land Union Journal
The Liberal Magazine
The Mark Lane Express
The Morning Post
The Municipal Journal
The Nineteenth Century
The Nation
The National Review
Notes on Tariff Reform
Our Flag
Punch
The Quarterly Review
Rural World
The Times
The Tory

5. PUBLISHED DIARIES, MEMOIRS AND BIOGRAPHIES

R.Adelson, *Mark Sykes: Portrait of an Amateur* (1975).

B.M.Allen, *Sir Robert Morant* (1936).
L.S.Amery, *My Political Life: Volume 1 England before the Storm 1896–1914* (1953).
M.K.Ashby, *Joseph Ashby of Tysoe 1859–1919: A Study of English Social Life* (Cambridge, 1961).
Lord Askwith, *Lord James of Hereford* (1930).
A.J.Balfour, *Chapters of Autobiography* (1930).
F.Balfour, *A Memoir of Lord Balfour of Burleigh* (1925).
M.Balfour, *Britain and Joseph Chamberlain* (1985).
C.A.Barker, *Henry George* (New York, 1955).
Viscountess Barrington, *Through Eighty Years* (1936).
C.Battersea, *Reminiscences* (1930).
Earl of Birkenhead, *F.E. : The Life of F.E.Smith, First Earl of Birkenhead* (1960).
Earl of Birkenhead, *The Life of Lord Halifax* (1966).
R.Blake, *The Unknown Prime Minister: The Life and Times of Andrew Bonar Law 1858–1923* (1955).
R.Blake, *Disraeli* (1966).
A.Briggs, *Social Thought and Social Action: A Study of the Work of Seebohm Rowntree 1871–1954* (1961).
A.Brookfield, *Annals of a Chequered Life* (1930).
J.Campbell, *F.E.Smith, First Earl of Birkenhead* (1983).
G.Cecil, *Life of Robert Marquis of Salisbury*, vols. 1–2 (1921); vols. 3–4 (1931).
Viscount Cecil of Chelwood, *All the Way* (1949).
A.Chamberlain, *Politics From Inside: An Epistolary Chronicle 1906–1914* (1936).
J.Chamberlain, *A Political Memoir, 1880–92* ed. C.H.D.Howard (1953).
F.A.Channing, *Memories of Midland Politics 1885–1910* (1918).
Viscount Chilston, *Chief Whip: The Political Life and Times of Aretas Akers-Douglas, Viscount Chilston* (1961).
Viscount Chilston, *W.H.Smith* (1965).
R.S.Churchill, *Lord Derby: King of Lancashire* (1959).
W.S.Churchill, *Lord Randolph Churchill*, vols. 1, 2 (1906).
W.S.Churchill, *Great Contemporaries* (1938) .
W.S.Churchill, *My Early Life* (1947).
A.Clarke, *'A Good Innings': The Private Papers of Viscount Lee of Fareham* (1974).
Sir E.Clarke, *The Story of my Life* (1918).
J.Collings and J. Green, *The Life of the Right Hon. Jesse Collings* (1920).
Marquess of Crewe, *Lord Rosebery*, vols. 1, 2 (1931).
Lord Croft, *My Life of Strife* (1949).
J.A.Cross, *Sir Samuel Hoare: A Political Biography* (1977).
E.David (ed.), *Inside Asquith's Cabinet: From the Diaries of Charles Hobhouse* (1977).
M.Digby, *Horace Plunkett* (Oxford, 1949).
B.Dugdale, *Arthur James Balfour, First Earl of Balfour*, vols. 1, 2 (1936).
Lord Dynevor, *My Reminiscences* (Carmarthen, 1937).
A.R.D.Elliot, *The Life of G.J.Goschen, First Viscount Goschen 1831–1907*, vols. 1, 2 (1911).
Lord Ernle,*Whippingham to Westminster* (1938).
R.Foster, *Lord Randolph Churchill: A Political Life* (1981).
A.W.Fox, *The Earl of Halsbury, Lord High Chancellor (1823–1921)* (1921).
P.Fraser, *Joseph Chamberlain: Radicalism and Empire 1868–1914* (1966).
A.G.Gardiner, *The Life of Sir William Harcourt*, vol. 2 (1923).
J.L.Garvin and J.Amery, *The Life of Joseph Chamberlain*, vols. 1–6 (1932–1969).
Viscount Gladstone, *After Thirty Years* (1929).
A.M.Gollin, *The Observer and J.L.Garvin 1908–1914* (1960).
A.M.Gollin, *Proconsul in Politics: A Study of Lord Milner in Opposition and in Power* (1964).
Viscount Grey of Fallodon, *Twenty Five Years 1892–1916* (1925).
A.S.T.Griffith-Boscawen, *Fourteen Years in Parliament* (1907).
A.S.T.Griffith-Boscawen, *Memories* (1925).

J.Grigg, *Lloyd George: The People's Champion* (1978).

Earl of Halifax, *Fullness of Days* (1957).

Lord G.Hamilton, *Parliamentary Reminiscences and Reflections 1886–1906*, vol.1 (1916), vol.2 (1922).

H.Haward, *The London County Council from Within: Forty Years' Official Recollections* (1932).

W.A.S.Hewins, *Apologia of an Imperialist*, vol.1,(1929).

V.Hicks Beach, *The Life of Sir Michael Hicks Beach, Earl St. Aldwyn*, vols. 1, 2 (1932).

B.Holland, *The Life of Spencer Compton, Duke of Devonshire*, vols. 1, 2 (1913).

J.F.Hope, *A History of the 1900 Parliament* (1908).

Frances Horner, *Time Remembered* (1933).

R.Jay, *Joseph Chamberlain: A Political Study* (Oxford, 1981).

D.Judd, *Radical Joe: A Life of Joseph Chamberlain* (1977).

S.Koss, *Asquith* (1964).

The Marchioness of Londonderry, *Henry Chaplin: A Memoir* (1926).

S.Leslie, *Sir Mark Sykes: His Life and Letters* (1923).

W.Long, *Memories* (1923).

J.W.Mackail and G.Wyndham, *The Life and Letters of George Wyndham*, vols. 1, 2 (n.d., 1925).

T.Mackay (ed.), *The Reminiscences of Albert Pell* (1908).

H.Macmillan, *The Past Masters: Politics and Politicians 1906–1939* (1975).

P.Magnus, *Gladstone: A Biography* (1963).

D.Marquand, *Ramsay Macdonald* (1977).

A.Maurois, *Disraeli: A Picture of the Victorian Age* (1927.)

K.Middlemas and A.J.L.Barnes, *Baldwin: A Biography* (1969).

Lord Midleton, *Records and Reactions 1856–1939* (1939).

K.O.Morgan, *Keir Hardie Radical and Socialist* (1975).

J.Morley, *The Life of William Ewart Gladstone*, vols. 1-3 (1903).

Lord Newton, *Retrospection* (1941).

Lord Newton, *Lansdowne: A Biography* (1929).

R.B.O'Brien, *Thomas Drummond: Under Secretary in Ireland 1835–40, Life and Letters* (1889).

Lord Percy of Newcastle, *Some Memories* (1958).

Sir C.Petrie, *Walter Long and His Times* (1936).

Sir C.Petrie, *The Life and Letters of the Rt. Hon. Sir Austen Chamberlain* (1940).

Duke of Portland, *Men, Women and Things* (1937).

J.E.Powell, *Joseph Chamberlain* (1977).

J.Prest, *Lord John Russel* (1972).

J.Ramsden, *Real Old Tory Politics: The Political Diaries of Sir Robert Sanders, Lord Bayford 1910–1935*(1984).

R.Rhodes James, *Rosebery* (1963).

Lord Rosebery, *Lord Randolph Churchill* (1906).

S.Salvidge, *Salvidge of Liverpool: Behind the Political Scene 1890–1928* (1934).

Viscount Samuel, *Memoirs* (1945).

J.S.Sandars, *Studies of Yesterday* (1928).

Viscount Simon, *Retrospect* (1952).

J.A.Spender and C.Asquith, *The Life of Herbert Henry Asquith, Lord Oxford and Asquith*, vols. 1, 2 (1932).

J.T.Spinner, *George Joachim Goschen: The Transformation of a Victorian Liberal* (Cambridge, 1973).

A.J.P.Taylor, *Beaverbrook* (1972).

R.Taylor, *Lord Salisbury* (1973).

J.R. Vincent (ed.), *The Crawford Papers: The Journal of David Lindsay,Twenty-Seventh Earl of Crawford and Tenth Earl of Balcarres 1871–1940 during the Years 1892–1940* (Manchester, 1984).

Willoughby de Broke, *Hunting the Fox* (1920).

Willoughby de Broke, *The Passing Years* (1924).

T.W.Wilson, (ed.), *The Political Diaries of C.P.Scott 1911–1928* (1970).
Earl Winterton, *Pre-War* (1932).
Earl Winterton, *Orders of the Day* (1953).
Earl Winterton, *Fifty Tumultuous Years* (1955).
Countess of Warwick, *Joseph Arch: The Story of his Life, Told by Himself* (1898).
Countess of Warwick, *Life's Ebb and Flow* (1929).
K.Young, *Arthur James Balfour* (1973).
Marquess of Zetland, *Lord Cromer* (1932).

6. WORKS OF HISTORICAL INTEREST

i. Organisations and Institutions

The Agricultural Annual and Mark Lane Express Almanac 1908 (1908).
Anti-Socialist Union, *Anti-Socialist Union Speakers' Handbook* (1911).
ASU, *Socialism Exposed By the Statistical Committee of the Anti-Socialist Union of Great Britain* (1914).
ASU, collection of leaflets and pamphlets British Library cat. no. 8139.cc.
Central Land Association, *Annual Reports*, 1908–14.
CLA, *Official Circular*.
CLA, *Earnings of Agricultural Labourers for Each County of England and Wales for the Year 1912–1913* (1913).
Conservative Central Office, *Nine Years' Work. A Review of the Legislation and Administration of the Conservative and Unionist Government 1895–1904* (1904).
CCO, *The Conservative Manifesto 1979* (1979).
CCO, *The Conservative Manifesto 1983* (1983).
CCO, *Our First Eight Years* (1987).
CCO, *The Next Moves Forward* (1987).
Hart's Army List.
Industrial Freedom League, *Annual Reports* 1902–5.
Industrial Remuneration Conference, *The Report of the Proceedings and Papers Read... January 1885* (1885).
The Land Conference, *The Land Problem* (1913).
The Land Enquiry Committee, *The Land: Vol.1 Rural* (1913); *The Land: Vol. 2 Urban* (1914).
The Law List.
The Liberal Land Committee, *Land and the Nation* (1925); *Towns and the Land* (1925).
The Land Union, *The New Land Taxes Land Union Guide* (1910).
LU, *The Land Union's Reasons for Repeal of the New Land Taxes and Land Valuation* (1910).
LU, *Objects and Policy* (Reading, 1913).
LU, *The Lost Revenue Bill - And After* (1913).
LU, *The Finance Bill 1914, Part IV* (1914).
LU, *The Town Tenants' League and its Bill* (1914).
Liberal Publication Department, *Five Years of Tory Government, 1895–1900* (1900).
LPD, leaflets and pamphlets, 1890–1914.
LPD, *The House of Lords* (1910).
LPD, *100 Points in Liberal Policy and of the Liberal Record* (edns. of 1909, 1912, 1913, 1914).
Liberal Unionist Association, *Memoranda*, 1893–1912.
Liberal and Property Defence League, *Annual Reports* and *Annual Meetings*, 1888–1906.
LPDL, *Overlegislation in 1884* (1884).
LPDL, *The Dangers of Municipal Trading* (1899).
National Liberal Federation, *Annual Reports* and *Proceedings of Annual Meetings*, 1881–1914.
National Unionist Association of Conservative and Liberal Unionist Organisations, *The Campaign Guide* (1914).
NUACLUO, *The Constitutional Yearbook*, 1912–14.

NUACLUO, *Gleanings and Memoranda*, 1912–14.

NUACLUO, *The History of Housing Reform* [n.d., 1913].

National Union of Conservative Associations for Scotland, *The Campaign Guide* (Edinburgh, edns. of 1892, 1894, 1895, 1900, 1906, 1910).

National Union of Conservative and Constitutional Associations, *The Case Against Radicalism* (1909).

NUCCA, *The Constitutional Yearbook*, 1884–1911.

NUCCA, *The Unionist Record 1895–1900* [n.d., 1900].

NUCCA, *The Unionist Record, 1895–1905* [n.d., 1905].

NUCCA, *Fighting Notes for Speakers* (1909).

NUCCA, *Fighting Campaign Notes* (1910).

The Pall Mall Gazette's Illustrated Guide to the House of Commons (edns. of 1900, 1906 and 1910).

The Primrose League,*The Primrose League. How Ladies Can Help It* (1885).

The Primrose League, collection of leaflets and pamphlets, British Library cat. no. 8138.g.

The Surveyors' Institution, *Further Memorandum of the Surveyors' Institution on the Budget Proposals for the Taxation of Land* (1909).

SI, *Professional Notes*.

SI, *Transactions of the Surveyors' Institution*.

The Tariff Commission, *Report of the Agricultural Committee* (1906).

The Tariff Reform League, *A Short Handbook for Speakers* (edns. of 1905 and 1910).

TRL, *Tariff Points and Tariff Pictures* (1905).

TRL, *The Tariff Reformers' Enquire Within* (1914).

TRL, collection of leaflets and pamphlets, British Library cat. no. 08226.C.83.

United Committee for the Taxation of Land Values, *Annual Reports*, 1908–1913.

The Unionist Social Reform Committee, *Poor Law Reform :A Practical Programme* (1912).

USRC, *Industrial Unrest: A Practical Solution* (1914).

USRC, *The Schools and Social Reform* (1914).

Anon., [USRC], *The Health of the People: A New National Policy* [n.d., 1918].

A Group of Unionists [USRC], *A Unionist Agricultural Policy* (1913).

ii. Individuals

C.R.W. Adeane and E.Savill, *The Land Retort: A Study of the Land Question with an Answer to the Report of the Secret Enquiry Committee* (1914).

E.A.Alderson, *Pink and Scarlet, or Hunting as a School for Soldiering* (1913).

Anon., 'The Encroaching Bureaucracy', *Quarterly Review*, 221 (1914), pp. 51–75.

A.J.Balfour, *A Defence of Philosophic Doubt: Being an Essay on the Foundations of Belief* (1879).

A.J.Balfour, *The Foundations of Belief: Being Notes Introductory to the Study of Theology* (1895).

J.Bateman, *The Great Landowners of Great Britain and Ireland* (1883).

C.Bathurst, *To Avoid National Starvation* (1912).

Duke of Bedford, *A Great Agricultural Estate* (1897).

C.E.Bellairs, *Conservative Social and Industrial Reform* (1977).

Lord Henry Cavendish Bentinck, *Tory Democracy* (1918).

W.Beveridge, *Unemployment: A Problem of Industry* (1909).

W.S.Blunt, *Gordon at Khartoum* (1911).

C.Booth, *Life and Labour of the People in London* (1902).

W.Booth, *In Darkest England and the Way Out* (1890).

H.T.Broadhurst and R.T.Reid, *Leasehold Enfranchisement* (1886).

Lord Bledisloe, *The Proper Position of the Landowner in Relation to the Agricultural Industry* (Hull, 1922).

E.Cannan, *The History of Local Rates in England in Relation to the Proper Distribution of the Burden of Taxation* (1912).

Lord Hugh Cecil, *Conservatism* (1912).

J.Chamberlain, 'Labourers' and Artisans' Dwellings', *Fortnightly Review*, 1 Dec. 1883, pp. 761–76.

J.Chamberlain, 'The Labour Question', *The Nineteenth Century*, Nov. 1892, pp. 677–710.

H.Chaplin and W.A.S.Hewins, *The Budget and Agriculture* (1914).

J.Collings, *Land Reform, Occupying Ownership, Peasant Proprietary and Rural Education* (1906).

J.Collings, *The Colonization of Rural Britain, a Complete Scheme for the Regeneration of British Rural Life* (1914).

H.Trustram Eve, *Single Tax and Rating on Site Values* (1912).

H.Trustram Eve, *Taxation and Rating on Site Values* (Bedford, 1912).

H.Trustram Eve and E.Savill, *The Taxation of Land Values: The Case Against* (1913).

Lord Eversley, *Commons, Forests and Footpaths* (1910).

A.W.Fox, *The Rating of Land Values* (1908).

H.George, *Progress and Poverty* (1881).

B.Gilbert, *Farmers and Tariff Reform* (1913).

B.Gilbert, 'Agricultural *versus* Bonar Law', *The English Review*, Vol. 18, Aug./Nov. 1914, pp. 91–8.

B.Gilbert, *What the Farmer Wants* (1914).

I.Gilmour, *Inside Right: A Study of Conservatism* (1978).

G.Goschen, *Laissez-Faire and Government Intervention. An Address...* (1883).

D.Graham and P.Clarke, *The New Enlightenment: The Rebirth of Liberalism* (1986).

J.C.G.Graham, *Taxation (Local and Imperial) and Local Government* (1914).

G.Grossmith and W.Grossmith, *The Diary of a Nobody* (1892).

A.D.Hall, *A Pilgrimage of British Farming* (1913).

F.Hayek, *The Road to Serfdom* (1944).

T.Hobbes, *Leviathan* (Fontana, 1962).

L.T.Hobhouse, *Liberalism* [n.d., 1911].

J.A.Hobson, 'The Influence of Henry George in England', *Fortnightly Review*, 1 Dec. 1897, pp. 835–44.

L.J.Jennings, *Speeches of the Right Hon. Lord Randolph Churchill 1880–1888*, vol. 1 (1889).

H.H.John Paul II, *Sollicitudo Re Socialis* (Vatican, 1988).

Sir K.Joseph, *Why Britain Needs a Social Market Economy* (1975).

Knight, Frank and Rutley, *The Land Question* (1913).

Earl of Malmesbury, (ed.), *The New Order* (1908).

C.F.G.Masterman, *The Condition of England* (1909).

A.H.H.Matthews, *Fifty Years of Agricultural Politics: Being the History of the Central Chamber of Agriculture, 1865–1915.* (1915).

Viscount Milner, *The Nation and the Empire* (1913).

Earl of Onslow, *Landlords and Allotments: The History and Present Condition of the Allotments System* (1886).

Sir G.Parker, *The Land for the People* (1909).

Sir H.Plunkett, *Noblesse Oblige* (1908).

R.Prothero, *English Farming Past and Present* (1912).

F.Pym, *The Politics of Consent* (1984).

P.W.Raffan, *The Policy of the Land Values Group in the House of Commons* (1912).

G.Raine, *Lloyd George and the Land* (1914).

H.Rider Haggard, *Rural England* (1906).

Lord Rosebery, *The Value of Good Manners. An Address...* (1913).

S.Rowntree, *Poverty: A Study of Town Life* (1902).

S.Rowntree, *Land and Labour: Lessons from Belgium* (1911).

S.Rowntree, *How the Labourer Lives* (1913).

S.Rowntree, *The Labourer and the Land* (1914).

H.Samuel, *Liberalism: Its Principles and Proposals* (1902).

R.Scruton, *The Meaning of Conservatism* (1980).

G.B.Shaw, *The Doctor's Dilemma* (Penguin, 1975).

F.E.Smith, *Unionist Policies and Other Essays* (1913).
A.Solzhenitsyn, *Warning to the Western World* (1976).
F.Thompson, *Lark Rise to Candleford* (Oxford, 1945).
A. de Tocqueville, *Journeys to England and Ireland*, ed. J.P.Mayer (1957).
A. de Tocqueville, *The Ancien Regime and the French Revolution* (Fontana 1971).
B.Tollemache, *The Occupying Ownership of Land* (1913).
C.Turnor, *Land Problems and National Welfare* (1911).
W.Waldegrave, *Binding the Leviathan : Conservatism and the Future* (1978).
A.R.Wallace, *Land Nationalisation. Its Necessity and its Aims* (1882).
R.B.Yardley, *Land Value Taxation and Rating* [n.d., 1930].

7. WORKS OF HISTORIOGRAPHICAL INTEREST

M.Abramovitz and V.F.Eliasberg, *The Growth of Public Employment in Great Britain* (Princetown, 1957).
P.Adelman, *Victorian Radicalism: The Middle Class Experience 1830–1914* (1984).
K.W.Aikin, *The Last Years of Liberal England, 1900–1914.* (1972).
M.Albrow, *Bureaucracy* (1970).
D.H.Aldcroft and H.W.Richardson, *The British Economy 1870–1939* (1969).
W.Ashworth, *The Genesis of Modern British Town Planning* (1954).
D.Baines, *Migration in a Mature Economy: Emigration and Internal Migration in England and Wales, 1861–1900* (Cambridge, 1985).
M.Barker, *Gladstone and Radicalism: The Reconstruction of Liberal Policy 1885–1894* (Brighton, 1975).
I.Berlin, *Four Essays on Liberty* (Oxford, 1969).
R.Blake, *The Conservative Party from Peel to Thatcher* (1985).
N.Blewett, 'The Franchise in the United Kingdom, 1885–1918', *Past and Present*, 32 (1965), pp. 27–56.
N.Blewett, *The Peers, the Parties and the People: The General Elections of 1910* (1972).
A.Bloom, *The Closing of the American Mind: How Higher Education has Failed Democracy and Impoverished the Souls of Today's Students* (1988).
I.Bradley, *Enlightened Entrepreneurs* (1987).
E.Bristow, 'The Liberty and Property Defence League and Individualism', *Historical Journal*, 18 (1975), pp. 761–89.
B.H.Brown, *The Tariff Reform Movement in Great Britain 1881–1898* (Columbia, 1943).
K.D.Brown, 'The Trade Union Tariff Reform Association 1904–1913', *Journal of British Studies*, 9, 2 (1970), pp. 141–53.
K.D.Brown, *Labour and Unemployment 1900–1914* (1971).
K.D.Brown (ed.), *Essays in Anti-Labour History: Responses to the Rise of Labour in Britain* (1974).
M.Bruce, *The Coming of the Welfare State* (1961).
D.Cannadine, *Lords and Landlords: The Aristocracy and the Towns 1774–1967* (Leicester, 1980).
D.H.Chapman, *The Chartered Auctioneers' and Estate Agents' Institute: A Short History* (1970).
P.F.Clarke, *Lancashire and the New Liberalism* (Cambridge, 1971).
P.F.Clarke, *Liberals and Social Democrats* (Cambridge, 1979).
P.F.Clarke, 'The Electoral Position of the Liberal and Labour Parties 1910–1914', *English Historical Review*, 90 (1975), pp. 826–36.
P.F.Clarke, 'The Progressive Movement in England', *Transactions of the Royal Historical Society*, 5 ser. 24 (1974), pp. 159–81.
H.A.Clegg, A.Fox and A.F.Thompson, *A History of British Trade Unionism Since 1889*, Vol. 1, *1889–1910* (Oxford, 1964).
J.P.Coast, *The Land Agents' Society 1901–1939* [n.d., 1939].
E.W.Cohen, *The Growth of the British Civil Service 1780–1939* (1941).
D.Collins, 'The Introduction of Old Age Pensions into Great Britain', *Historical Journal*, 8 (1965), pp. 246–59.

C.Cook, 'Labour and the Downfall of the Liberal Party 1906–1914', in C.Cook and A.Sked(eds.), *Crisis and Controversy: Essays in Honour of A.J.P.Taylor* (1976), pp. 38–65.

A.B.Cooke and J.R.Vincent, *The Governing Passion: Cabinet Government and Party Politics in Britain 1885–1886* (Brighton, 1973).

J.Cornford, 'The Transformation of Conservatism in the Late Nineteenth Century' *Victorian Studies*, 7, (1963), pp. 35-66.

J.Cornford, 'The Parliamentary Foundations of the Hotel Cecil', in J.Robson (ed.), *Ideas and Institutions of Victorian Britain* (1967), pp.268–311.

M.Cowling, *The Impact of Labour, 1920–1924* (Cambridge, 1971).

M.Cowling, *Religion and Public Doctrine in Modern England*, vol. 1 (Cambridge, 1980); vol. 2, *Assaults* (Cambridge, 1985).

F.W.S.Craig, *British Parliamentary Election Results 1885–1918* (1974).

F.W.S.Craig, *British General Election Manifestos 1900–1974* (1975).

M.Cruickshank, *Church and State in English Education 1870 to the Present Day* (1963).

L.Davidoff, *The Best Circles: Society, Etiquette and the Season* (1973).

R.Douglas, 'Labour in Decline' in K.H.D.Brown (ed.), *Essays in Anti-Labour History*, pp. 105–25.

R.Douglas, *Land, People and Politics: A History of the Land Question in the United Kingdom 1878–1952* (1976).

D.Duman, *The English and Colonial Bars in the Nineteenth Century* (1983).

D.J.Dutton, 'The Unionist Party and Social Policy 1906–1914', *Historical Journal*, 24 (1981), pp. 871–84.

H.V.Emy, 'The Land Campaign: Lloyd George as Social Reformer', in A.J.P.Taylor, (ed.), *Lloyd George: Twelve Essays* (1971), pp. 35–68.

H.V.Emy, *Liberals, Radicals and Social Politics 1892–1914* (Cambridge, 1973).

F.Engel, *From Clergyman to Don: The Rise of the Academic Profession in Nineteenth Century Oxford* (1983).

D.Englander, *Landlord and Tenant in Urban Britain 1838–1918*,(Oxford, 1983).

R.K.Ensor, *England 1870–1914* (Oxford, 1936).

J.D.Fair, *British Interparty Conferences: A Study of the Procedure of Conciliation in British Politics 1867–1921* (Oxford, 1980).

C.H.Feinstein, *National Income, Expenditure and Output of the United Kingdom 1855–1965* (Cambridge, 1972).

J.R.Fisher, 'The Farmers' Alliance: An Agricultural Protest Movement of the 1880s', *Agricultural History Review*, 26 (1978), pp. 15–25.

P.Fraser, *The Evolution of the British Welfare State* (1973).

M.Freeden, *The New Liberalism: An Ideology of Social Reform* (Oxford, 1978).

G.K.Fry, *The Growth of Government: The Development of Ideas about the Role of the State and the Machinery and Function of Government in Britain since 1780* (1979).

B.Gainer, *The Alien Invasion* (1972).

E.Gauldie, *Cruel Habitations: A History of Working-Class Housing 1780–1918* (1974).

B.Gilbert, *The Evolution of National Insurance in Great Britain* (1966).

B.B.Gilbert, 'David Lloyd George: Land, the Budget and Social Reform, *American Historical Review*, 81 (1976), pp. 1058-1066.

B.B.Gilbert, 'David Lloyd George: The Reform of British Landholding and the Budget of 1914', *Historical Journal* 21, (1978), pp. 117–41.

A.M.Gollin, *Balfour's Burden: Arthur Balfour and Imperial Preferencee* (1965).

P.Goodhart, *The 1922: The Story of the Conservative Backbenchers' Parliamentary Committee* (1973).

P.H.J.Gosden, *Self-Help: Voluntary Associations in Nineteenth-Century Britain* (1973).

E.H.Green, 'Radical Conservatism: The Electoral Genesis of Tariff Reform', *Historical Journal*, 28 (1985), pp. 667–92.

W.H.Greenleaf, *The British Political Tradition*, vol. 1 (1983), vol.2, (1983), vol. 3 (1987).

D.A.Hamer (ed.), *The Radical Programme* (Leicester, 1971).

D.A.Hamer, *Liberal Politics in the Age of Gladstone and Rosebery* (1972).

A.H.Hanson and M.Walles, *Governing Britain: A Guidebook to Political Institutions* (1984).

J.Harris, *Unemployment and Politics: A Study in English Social Policy 1886–1914* (Oxford, 1972).

B.Harrison, 'For Church, Queen and Family: The Girls' Friendly Society 1874–1920', *Past and Present*, 61 (1973), pp. 107–38.

B.Harrison, *Separate Spheres: The Opposition to Women's Suffrage in Britain* (1978).

B.Harrison, *Peaceable Kingdom: Stability and Change in Modern Britain* (Oxford, 1982).

J.R.Hay, *The Origins of the Liberal Welfare Reforms* (1975).

U.K.Hicks, *British Public Finances: Their Structure and Development 1880–1952* (1954).

M.Holmes, *The First Thatcher Government 1979–1983: Contemporary Conservatism and Economic Change* (1985).

C.H.D.Howard, 'Joseph Chamberlain and the "Unauthorized Programme"', *English Historical Review*, 65, 257 (1950), pp. 477–91.

W.A.Jeffcock, *Agricultural Politics 1915–1935* (Ipswich, 1937).

P.Jenkins, *Mr.Balfour's Poodle* (1954).

P.Johnson, *A History of the Modern World From 1917 to the 1980s* (1984).

P.Joyce, *Work, Society and Politics: The Culture of the Factory in Later Victorian England* (Brighton 1982).

P.Keating, (ed.), *Into Unknown England 1866–1913: Selections from the Social Explorers* (Manchester, 1976).

J.M.Keynes, *Essays in Biography* (1961).

C.Kirby, 'The Attack on the English Game Laws in the Forties', *Journal of Modern History*, 4, 1 (1932), pp. 18–37.

G. di Lampedusa, *The Leopard* (1960).

A.J.Lee, *The Origins of the Popular Press in England, 1855–1914*, (1976).

T.F.Lindsay and M.Harrington, *The Conservative Party 1918–1970* (1979).

J.M.Mackenzie, *Propaganda and Empire: The Manipulation of Public Opinion* (Manchester, 1984).

J.M.Mackenzie (ed.), *Imperialism and Popular Culture* (Manchester, 1985).

B.Mallet, *British Budgets 1887–88 to 1912–13* (1913).

B.Mallet and C.O.George, *British Budgets 1913–14 to 1920–21* (1929).

P.Marsh, *The Discipline of Popular Government: Lord Salisbury's Domestic Statecraft 1881–1902* (1978).

J.W.Mason, 'Thomas Mackay The Anti-Socialist Philosophy of the Charity Organisation Society', in K.D.Brown (ed.), *Essays in Anti-Labour History* (1974), pp. 290–310.

H.C.G.Matthew, *The Liberal Imperialists: The Ideals and Politics of a Post-Gladstonian Elite* (Oxford, 1973).

H.C.G.Matthew, R.I.McKibbin and J.A.Kay, 'The Franchise Factor in the Rise of the Labour Party', *English Historical Review*, 91 (1976), pp. 723–53.

A.M.McBriar, *Fabian Socialism and English Politics 1884–1918* (Cambridge, 1962).

R.T.McKenzie, *British Political Parties* (1964).

R.I.McKibbin, *The Evolution of the Labour Party 1910–1924* (Oxford, 1974).

K.Middlemas, *Politics in Industrial Society* (1979).

B.R.Mitchell and P.Deane, *Abstract of British Historical Statistics* (Cambidge, 1962).

J.Morgan, *The House of Lords and the Labour Government 1964–1970* (Oxford, 1975).

K.O.Morgan, *The Age of Lloyd George* (1971).

A.J.A. Morris (ed.), *Edwardian Radicalism 1900–1914* (1974).

J.E.B.Munson, 'The Unionist Coalition and Education, 1895–1902', *Historical Journal*, 20 (1977), pp. 607–45.

B.K.Murray, 'Lloyd George and the Land: The Issue of Site Value Rating', in J.Benyon *et al., Studies in Local History* (Cape Town, 1976), pp.37–47.

B.K.Murray, *The People's Budget 1909/10: Lloyd George and Liberal Politics* (Oxford, 1980).

A.Offer, *Property and Politics 1870–1914: Landownership, Law, Ideology and Urban Devlopment in England* (Cambridge, 1981).

R.J.Olney, *Lincolnshire Politics 1832–1885* (Oxford, 1973).

The Oxford Paperback Dictionary (Oxford, 1983).

H.Parris, *Constitutional Bureaucracy: The Development of British Central Administration Since the Eighteenth Century* (1969).

A.T.Peacock and J.V.Wiseman, *The Growth of Public Expenditure in the United Kingdom* (1967).

H.Pelling, *A Short History of the Labour Party* (1961).

H.Pelling, *A History of British Trade Unionism* (1963).

H.Pelling, *The Origins of the Labour Party 1880–1900* (Oxford, 1965).

H.Pelling, *A Social Geography of British Elections 1885–1910*, (1967).

H.Pelling, *Popular Politics and Society in Late Victorian Britain* (1968).

H.Pelling, *Modern Britain, 1885–1955* (1969)

G.Phillips, *The Diehards: Aristocratic Society and Politics in Edwardian England* (Harvard, 1979).

M.Pinto-Duschinsky, *The Political Thought of Lord Salisbury 1854–1868* (1967).

B.Porter, *The Lion's Share: A Short History of British Imperialism 1850–1983* (1984).

R.Price, *An Imperial War and the British Working Class: Working-class Attitudes and Reactions to the Boer War 1899–1902.* (1972).

F.Prochaska, *Women and Philanthropy in Nineteenth-Century England* (Oxford, 1980).

M.D.Pugh, *Electoral Reform in War and Peace 1906–1918* (1978).

M.D.Pugh, *The Making of Modern British Politics 1867–1939* (Oxford, 1982).

M.D.Pugh, *The Tories and the People 1880–1935* (1985).

R.M.Punnet, *Front Bench Opposition* (1973).

R.Quinault, 'Lord Randolph Churchill and Tory Democracy 1880–1885', *Historical Journal*, 22 (1979), pp. 141–65.

J.Ramsden, *The Age of Balfour and Baldwin 1902–1940* (1978).

J.A.Ramsden, *The Making of Conservative Party Policy* (1980).

W.J.Reader, *Professional Men: The Rise of the Professional Classes in Nineteenth Century England* (1966).

D.A.Reeder, 'The Politics of Urban Leaseholds in Late Victorian England', *International Review of Social History*, 6 (1961), pp. 413–30.

R.A.Rempel, *Unionists Divided: Arthur Balfour, Joseph Chamberlain and the Unionist Free Traders* (Newton Abbot, 1972).

R.Rhodes James, *The British Revolution: British Politics 1880–1939* (1978).

J.Ridley. 'The Unionist Social Reform Committee, 1911–1914: Wets Before the Deluge', *Historical Journal*, 30 (1987), pp. 391–413.

J.Robb, *The Primrose League 1883–1906* (New York, 1942).

D.Roberts, *Victorian Origins of the British Welfare State* (New Haven, 1960).

R.Robinson and J.Callagher, *Africa and the Victorians* (1961).

M.E.Rose, *The Relief of Poverty 1834–1914* (1972).

W.W.Rostow, *The World Economy: History and Prospects* (1978).

P.Rowland, *The Last Liberal Governments*, vol. 1 (1968), vol.2 (1972).

W.D.Rubinstein, 'Wealth, Elites and the Class Structure of Modern Britain', *Past and Present*, 76 (1977), pp. 99–126.

A.K.Russel, *The Liberal Landslide: The General Election of 1906* (Newton Abbot, 1973).

T.Russel, *The Tory Party: Its Policies, Divisions and Future* (1978).

J. Saville, 'Trade Unions and Free Labour: The Background to the Taff Vale Decision', in M. W. Flinn and T. C. Smout (eds.), *Essays in Social History* (Oxford, 1974), pp. 251–76.

B.Semmel, *Imperialism and Social Reform: English Social and Imperial Thought 1895–1914* (1960).

R.Shannon, *The Crisis of Imperialism 1865–1915* (1976).

E.M.Sigsworth (ed.), *In Search of Victorian Values: Aspects of Nineteenth-Century Thought and Society* (Manchester, 1988).

K.Smellie, *A History of Local Government* (1968).

P.Smith (ed.), *Lord Salisbury on Politics* (Cambridge, 1972).

P.Smith, *Disraelian Conservatism and Social Reform* (1967).

N.Solden, 'Laissez-Faire as Dogma: The Liberty and Property Defence League, 1882–1914', in K.D.Brown (ed.), *Essays in Anti-Labour History*, pp. 208–33.

D.Spring (ed.), *European Landed Elites in the Nineteenth Century* (Baltimore, 1977).

D.Spring, 'Land and Politics in Edwardian England', *Agricultural History*, 58 (1984), pp. 17–42.

P.Stansky, *Ambitions and Strategies: The Struggle for the Leadership of the Liberal Party in the 1890s* (Oxford, 1964).

S.Sturmey, 'Owner-Farming in England and Wales, 1900–1950', in W.E.Minchinton (ed.), *Essays in Agrarian History*, vol. 2 (1968), pp. 281–306.

A.Sykes, *Tariff Reform in British Politics 1903–1913* (Oxford, 1979).

R. Tanner, 'The Parliamentary Electoral System, the 'Fourth' Reform Act and the Rise of Labour in England and Wales', *Bulletin of the Institute of Historical Research*, Vol. 61 (1983), pp. 205-19.

A.J.Taylor (ed.), *Laissez-Faire and State Intervention in Nineteenth Century Britain* (1975).

P.Thane (ed.), *The Origins of British Social Policy* (1978).

F.M.L.Thompson, *English Landed Society in the Nineteenth Century* (1963).

F.M.L.Thompson, 'Land and Politics in England in the Nineteenth Century', *Transactions of the Royal Historical Society*, 5 ser. 15 (1965), pp. 23–44.

F.M.L.Thompson, *Chartered Surveyors: The Growth of a Profession* (1968).

F.M.L.Thompson (ed.), *The Rise of Suburbia* (Leicester, 1982).

P.R.Thompson, *Socialists, Liberals and Labour: The Struggle for London 1885–1914* (1967).

G.M.Trevelyan, *A Shortened History of England* (1959).

J.R.Vincent, *Pollbooks: How Victorians Voted* (Cambridge, 1967).

J.R.Vincent, *The Formation of the British Liberal Party 1857–68* (1972).

C.Weston, 'Salisbury and the Lords, 1868–1895', *Historical Journal*, 25 (1982), pp. 103–29.

M.Wiener, *English Culture and the Decline of the Industrial Spirit 1850–1980* (Cambridge, 1982).

P.Wilding, 'Towards Exchequer Subsidies for Housing 1906–1914', *Social and Economic Administration* (1972), pp. 3–18.

R.Williams, *The Long Revolution* (1965).

T.Wilson, *The Downfall of the British Liberal Party 1914–1935* (1966).

A.S.Wohl (ed.), *The Bitter Cry of Outcast London* (Leicester, 1970).

A.S.Wohl, 'The Bitter Cry of Outcast London', *International Review of Social History*, 13 (1968), pp. 189–245.

K.Young, *Local Politics and the Rise of Party: The London Municipal Society and the Conservative Intervention in Local Elections 1894–1963* (Leicester, 1975).

Index

tariff reform, 14, 88-90, 105, 114, 117,
    121, 146, 161
Tariff Reform League (TRF), 88, 91, 94,
    125
Thatcher, M., 1, 5, 139, 168, 170-1
Thatcherism, 1-3, 10, 43, 168-72
Thompson, Flora, 85
Thompson, F.M.L., 123
three acres and a cow, 14, 76
Thynne, A., Lord, 147
tithes, 59, 86
Tocqueville, Count A. de, 5, 39
Tollemache, B., 137, 139
Tory democracy, 69-70, 75, 90, 91
Tory Reform Group, 73
town planning, 72, 92
town tenants, town tenancy, 83, 122, 126-
    7, 128, 137, 142, 144, 156, 164
the Trade, 35
trade unions, trade unionism, 6, 12-13, 15-
    6, 23, 51, 72, 74, 106, 124-5
    Conservative policy towards, 124-5,
        145, 148
    legal cases and, 110, 124-5
Trade Union Tariff Reform Association,
    125
Turnor, A., 104, 117
Turnor, C., 120, 143-4, 148, 152

unauthorised programmes, 44-6, 71, 90-1
United Committee for the Taxation of
    Land Values, 103-4, 111, 129, 131,
    138

Unionist Social Reform Committee
    (USRC), 73, 88, 96-101, 116, 136-7,
    138, 141-3, 148, 161

Victoria League, 84
Vincent, J., 53
voluntaryism, 27-9, 41-3, 76, 79-80, 116,
    145, 146-7, 148, 149-50, 162
wages question, 19, 54, 62, 89, 90, 100,
    105, 127-8, 134, 136, 137, 142,
    145-51, 157, 158, 162
Walden, B., 5
Wallace, A.R., 48
Webbs, 61, 108, 155
Weiner, M., 6, 152-3
Welsh disestablishment, 49, 85-6, 126,
    133
Wemyss, Earl, 74-6, 110
Westcott, Bishop., 30
whips, 29, 35
Whiteley, G., 50, 74
Williams, R., 8
Willoughby de Broke, Baron, 38, 151
Winchelsea, Earl, 65
Winterton, Earl, 33, 63
Wood, Sir C., 16
Wood, E, Viscount Halifax, 101
Woods, M., 99, 142
Worthington-Evans, L., 116
Wyndham, G., 92

Yerburgh, R.A., 119-20